Polling at a Crossroads

Survey research is in a state of crisis. People have become less willing to respond to polls and recent misses in critical elections have undermined the field's credibility. Pollsters have developed many tools for dealing with the new environment, an increasing number of which rely on risky opt-in samples. Virtually all of these tools require that respondents in each demographic category are a representative sample of all people in each demographic category, something that is unlikely to be reliably true. *Polling at a Crossroads* moves beyond such limitations, providing tools that work even when survey respondents are unrepresentative in complex ways. The book provides case studies that show how to avoid underestimating Trump support and how conventional polls exaggerate partisan differences. This book helps us think in clear and sometimes counterintuitive ways and points toward simple, low-cost changes that can better address contemporary polling challenges.

Michael A. Bailey is the Walsh Professor in the Department of Government and McCourt School of Public Policy at Georgetown University where he directs the Data Science for Public Policy program. His research has been published in top academic journals. He is the author of *Real Econometrics* (2020) and *The Constrained Court* (2011).

Methodological Tools in the Social Sciences

Series Editors
Paul M. Kellstedt, Associate Professor of Political Science, Texas A&M University
Guy D. Whitten, Professor of Political Science and Director of the European Union Center at Texas A&M University

The Methodological Tools in the Social Sciences series is comprised of accessible, stand-alone treatments of methodological topics encountered by social science researchers. The focus is on practical instruction for applying methods, for getting the methods right. The authors are leading researchers able to provide extensive examples of applications of the methods covered in each book. The books in the series strike a balance between the theory underlying and the implementation of the methods. They are accessible and discursive, and make technical code and data available to aid in replication and extension of the results, as well as enabling scholars to apply these methods to their own substantive problems. They also provide accessible advice on how to present results obtained from using the relevant methods.

Other Books in the Series
Eric Neumayer and Thomas Plümper, *Robustness Tests for Quantitative Research*
Nils B. Weidmann, *Data Management for Social Scientists: From Files to Databases*
William Roberts Clark and Matt Golder *Interaction Models: Specification and Interpretation*

Polling at a Crossroads
Rethinking Modern Survey Research

MICHAEL A. BAILEY
Georgetown University

Shaftesbury Road, Cambridge CB2 8EA, United Kingdom

One Liberty Plaza, 20th Floor, New York, NY 10006, USA

477 Williamstown Road, Port Melbourne, VIC 3207, Australia

314–321, 3rd Floor, Plot 3, Splendor Forum, Jasola District Centre, New Delhi – 110025, India

103 Penang Road, #05–06/07, Visioncrest Commercial, Singapore 238467

Cambridge University Press is part of Cambridge University Press & Assessment, a department of the University of Cambridge.

We share the University's mission to contribute to society through the pursuit of education, learning and research at the highest international levels of excellence.

www.cambridge.org
Information on this title: www.cambridge.org/9781108482790

DOI: 10.1017/9781108697798

© Michael A. Bailey 2024

This publication is in copyright. Subject to statutory exception and to the provisions of relevant collective licensing agreements, no reproduction of any part may take place without the written permission of Cambridge University Press & Assessment.

First published 2024

A catalogue record for this publication is available from the British Library

Library of Congress Cataloging-in-Publication Data
Names: Bailey, Michael A., 1969– author.
Title: Polling at a crossroads : rethinking modern survey research / Michael A. Bailey, Georgetown University, Washington, DC.
Description: Cambridge, United Kingdom ; New York, NY : Cambridge University Press, 2024. | Includes bibliographical references and index.
Identifiers: LCCN 2023037461 | ISBN 9781108482790 (hardback) | ISBN 9781108697798 (ebook)
Subjects: LCSH: Public opinion polls. | Social surveys – Methodology.
Classification: LCC HM1236 .B35 2024 | DDC 303.3/8–dc23/eng/20230816
LC record available at https://lccn.loc.gov/2023037461

ISBN 978-1-108-48279-0 Hardback
ISBN 978-1-108-71093-0 Paperback

Cambridge University Press & Assessment has no responsibility for the persistence or accuracy of URLs for external or third-party internet websites referred to in this publication and does not guarantee that any content on such websites is, or will remain, accurate or appropriate.

Dedicated to my father, Don Bailey: For his high response rate and even higher enthusiasm

Contents

List of Figures		*page* xi
List of Tables		xv
Preface		xvii
Acknowledgments		xix

PART I POLLING IN CONTEXT

1	Modern Polling: Challenges and Opportunities	3
	1.1 *We Need Good Polls*	6
	1.2 *Why Polling Is Difficult*	8
	1.3 *The Limits of Conventional Practice*	12
	1.4 *The Road Ahead: A Preview*	14
	1.5 *The Plan of the Book*	18
	1.6 *Who Should Read This Book*	20
	1.7 *Conclusion*	21
2	The Story of Polling in $2\frac{1}{2}$ Fiascos	23
	2.1 *Mass Polling*	24
	2.2 *Quota Sampling*	28
	2.3 *Random Sampling*	33
	2.4 *Conclusion*	46
3	Weighting: An Appreciation and Critique	47
	3.1 *The Big Picture*	48
	3.2 *Cell-Weighting*	51
	3.3 *Raking*	61
	3.4 *Variable Selection*	67
	3.5 *Weighting and Precision*	73
	3.6 *Conclusion*	76
4	The Wild West of Contemporary Polling	77
	4.1 *Probability-Based Samples*	78
	4.2 *Nonprobability-Based Samples*	85

viii   *Contents*

4.3	*Which Is More Accurate? Probability versus Nonprobability Samples*	92
4.4	*Conclusion*	97

PART II A FRAMEWORK FOR MODERN POLLING

5	Nonignorable Nonresponse	101
5.1	*Nonignorable Nonresponse: A Pervasive Concern*	102
5.2	*Nonignorable Nonresponse: Intuition*	107
5.3	*A General Model of Nonresponse*	112
5.4	*Heterogeneity in ρ*	119
5.5	*Conclusion*	120

6	Contemporary Polling and Nonignorable Nonresponse	123
6.1	*Effective Sample Size*	124
6.2	*The Power of Random Contact*	127
6.3	*Sources of Error at Different Stages of Survey Process*	131
6.4	*Conclusion*	133

PART III FIGHTING NONIGNORABLE NONRESPONSE

7	Bounding Damage from Nonignorable Nonresponse	137
7.1	*Bounds*	138
7.2	*Robustness Diagnostics*	140
7.3	*Conclusion*	142

8	Selection Models for Nonignorable Nonresponse	144
8.1	*A General Selection Model*	145
8.2	*Identifying Nonignorable Nonresponse: Intuition*	148
8.3	*The Heckman Model*	151
8.4	*Contrasting Weighting Models and Selection Models*	155
8.5	*Limitations of the Heckman Model*	160
8.6	*Conclusion*	164

9	Next-Generation Selection Models	165
9.1	*Copulas*	167
9.2	*Control Functions*	172
9.3	*Weights for Nonignorable Nonresponse*	174
9.4	*Models for Partially Observed Response Instruments*	178
9.5	*Conclusion*	181

10	Randomized Response Instruments	183
10.1	*Functional Form Is Not Enough*	184
10.2	*The Problem with Observational Instruments*	188
10.3	*Randomized Response Instruments*	191
10.4	*Nonparametric Tests for Nonignorability*	193
10.5	*Partially Observed Nonrespondent Data*	195
10.6	*Conclusion*	196

Contents ix

11 Putting It Together 198
  11.1 *Simulating Nonignorable Nonresponse* 199
  11.2 *Diagnosing Nonignorable Nonresponse* 203
  11.3 *Decision Tree for Selection Models* 205
  11.4 *Risks in Selection Models* 207
  11.5 *Conclusion* 210

PART IV APPLICATIONS

12 Nonignorable Nonresponse in Political Surveys 213
  12.1 *Designing a Survey with a Response Instrument* 214
  12.2 *Turnout* 218
  12.3 *Trump Approval* 221
  12.4 *Attitudes about Race* 225
  12.5 *Policy Preferences* 227
  12.6 *Conclusion* 232

13 Nonignorable Nonresponse in Public Health 235
  13.1 *Population-Level Health as a Nonresponse Problem* 236
  13.2 *First-Stage Instruments for Randomized Testing with*
    Nonresponse 240
  13.3 *Adjusting Prevalence for Testing Rates* 244
  13.4 *Conclusion* 250

14 Conclusion 252

References 253
Index 267

Figures

1.1	Support for Biden and feeling thermometer difference between Biden and Trump	*page* 16
1.2	Relationship between response rates and quiz performance for two types of nonresponse	18
2.1	Distribution of the sample average of $\overline{Y}$ for a small number of samples, each of size 2,000	35
2.2	Distribution of the sample average of $\overline{Y}$ for large number of samples, each of size 2,000	36
2.3	Distribution of individual observations in population	37
2.4	The distribution of the sample average of $\overline{Y}$ changes as the sample size changes	38
2.5	Margin of error for various sample sizes	40
2.6	Nonresponse rates in political surveys	42
3.1	Hypothetical population and survey sample for which weighting works	52
3.2	Hypothetical population and survey sample for which weighting does not work	54
3.3	Hypothetical population and survey sample for which weighting makes things worse	55
4.1	Response rates for major academic polls	81
4.2	Relative representation in Pew 2016 probability sample poll	83
4.3	Changes in polling types from 2016 to 2020 for national US presidential polls	86
4.4	Relative representation in YouGov 2004 nonprobability sample poll	89
5.1	Selection into the NBA	107
5.2	Height and performance in the NBA among those who made it and did not	108
5.3	Selection into a political survey	110
5.4	Education and trust among survey respondents and nonrespondents	110

5.5	Survey responses, weighted	111
5.6	Hypothetical distributions of response propensities and Y in a population	113
5.7	Error in mean from sample of 1,000 as a function of data quality and population	116
5.8	Sample of 20 from large (panel a) and small (panel b) populations	117
6.1	Two sampling distributions with the same mean-squared error	125
6.2	Effective sample sizes for sample of 1,000 as a function of population size and data quality	126
6.3	Random contact for large population: Contact (left) and response (right)	128
6.4	Error as a function of nonresponse and data quality	130
8.1	Two distributions of Y and response propensity	147
8.2	Statistical identification problem for survey that shows 55 percent support for the president	149
8.3	Traces of nonignorable nonresponse in observable data	150
8.4	Contour maps for two examples of bivariate normal error terms	152
8.5	Effect of increasing Y_i for a low probability observation in Heckman model	158
8.6	Bias across models as a function of correlation of error in selection and outcome equations	160
9.1	Examples of copula distributions	168
9.2	HIV prevalence from Marra et al. (2019)	171
9.3	Various estimates of population support	176
9.4	Extrapolations to nonrespondents	179
10.1	Simulation results	186
10.2	Comparing error when Z affects Y for direct pathway and non-normal errors (numbers indicate root mean-squared error; darker shades indicate higher error)	190
11.1	Comparing error for conventional weights and Heckman models for direct pathway	200
11.2	Comparing error for conventional weights and Heckman models for indirect pathway	201
11.3	Comparing error for conventional weights and Heckman models for direct pathway and non-normal errors	203
11.4	False positive rates (rejection rates of null hypothesis that error is ignorable when error is ignorable; should be 5 percent)	204
11.5	Decision tree for selection models	206
12.1	Survey design with randomized response instrument	216
12.2	Opt-in question	216
12.3	Estimated proportion who will say they are absolutely or very certain to turn out, by response group. Lines indicate 95 percent confidence intervals	219

List of Figures xiii

12.4	Estimated proportion who say they will certainly vote, by method. Lines indicate 95 percent confidence intervals	221
12.5	Trump approval, estimated ρ by data source	222
12.6	Predicted Trump approval by method and group	224
12.7	Racial conservatism: Estimated ρ and predicted mean, by group and model	226
12.8	Support for action on global warming: Estimated ρ and predicted mean by group and model	228
12.9	Support for tax cuts: Estimated ρ and predicted mean by group and model	229
12.10	Support for tariffs: Estimated ρ and predicted mean by group and model	230
12.11	Differences by party in feeling thermometer ratings between those who chose political questions and those who did not, 2019 survey. Lines indicate 95 percent confidence intervals	231
12.12	Differences among all respondents in answers to political questions between those who chose political questions and those who did not, 2019 survey, by response group. Lines indicate 95 percent confidence intervals	232
13.1	Relationship between prevalence and test results for various levels of ρ	238
13.2	Relationship between prevalence and test results for various levels of ρ and testing rates	239
13.3	Results for three states in the simulation study	242
13.4	Testing rates and positivity	245
13.5	Prevalence as a function of ρ for Arizona	246
13.6	Testing rates and positivity with equivalence lines	247
13.7	Cases, adjusted cases, and deaths by state, part 1	248
13.8	Cases, adjusted cases, and deaths by state, part 2	249
13.9	Cases, adjusted cases, and deaths by state, part 3	249

Tables

3.1	Examples of different types of nonresponse	*page* 50
3.2	Selected groups underrepresented in at least one sample	58
3.3	Selected groups overrepresented in at least one sample	59
3.4	Distributions in Lucid sample and population	63
3.5	Distributions after first round of raking	64
3.6	Distributions after second round of raking	65
3.7	Raking weights after two steps for Lucid sample	66
3.8	Group proportions in population and raking-weighted Lucid sample	67
7.1	Population bounds for multiple response-rate scenarios	139
8.1	Marginal effects of Y_i on $\hat{\beta}_0$ in different approaches	156
12.1	Heckman selection model of turnout	220
13.1	Characteristics of states in simulation	242
13.2	Summary of approaches to nonresponse	244

Preface

I started down the road of writing this book almost 10 years ago when Dan Hopkins, Todd Rogers, and I discovered something odd. We were analyzing a 2008 voter persuasion campaign that sent canvassers with pro-Barack Obama messages to 56,000 randomly selected households. After the canvassers did their work, project organizers conducted a phone survey to assess if the canvassing worked.

Canvassers had a surprising and unintended effect: The people they talked to were much less likely to answer the phone survey. This pattern was especially strong when the canvassers visited people who did not usually vote (Bailey, Hopkins, and Rogers 2016).

How were we going to assess whether the door-to-door canvassing worked when the survey was missing a set of people who seemed to have reacted especially poorly to the campaign visits? If we followed standard practice, we would have let those who answered the survey speak for those who did not by weighting our data. That didn't seem right for our purposes because the people who didn't respond to the poll seemed different in important ways.

Our pollster colleagues invariably recognized our predicament. Yes, they granted, weighting only works if the people who respond to polls have, on average, the same opinions as those who do not respond once we control for demographics. But there really is no alternative, they said. Even sophisticated alternatives to weighting made the same assumption.

I was unnerved by how strong – and potentially wrong – this assumption was. It didn't seem like a promising foundation for serious social science. This episode continued to trouble me as I watched the survey field struggle with the ongoing implosion of response rates and the challenges of polling in the Trump era.

This book tells the story of the journey that followed. You will see that the path goes through the history of polling and huge amounts of academic and professional research. But I like also to think of it as a bit of a fairy tale that goes something like this.

Once upon a time, there was a village of pollsters who wanted to learn about many people from the answers of a few. They had trouble, though, because a terrible beast – the beast of nonresponse – distorted the answers of the few, sometimes ridiculously so. The villagers fought the beast by making the few less few. They gathered piles of answers that stretched to the sky. Surely, they thought, this huge sample will tame the beast. The beast, however, was strong. He contorted the answers in this big sample far from the truth. The villagers' large sample polls were discredited beyond repair.

In the middle of the twentieth century, a band of heroic pollsters discovered "The Random Sampler," a weapon that could parry every attack the beast could muster. No longer fearing the beast, the pollsters prospered.

Time passed and the glory faded, however. The supply of respondents dried up, weakening the Random Sampler almost beyond recognition. The older pollsters now cover their Random Samplers with elaborate and weighty armor that defends against only the most rudimentary of the beast's attacks. Some pollsters try to ignore the beast; others believe he is invincible.

On most days, the pollsters are fine. Every so often, though, the nonresponse beast claims a victim. In 2020, it was Wisconsin. In 2016, it had been Michigan, Pennsylvania, and Wisconsin. The polling city mourns the losses with searing postmortems, but little changes. Everyone knows in their heart that the village is no longer safe. Some of the great polling heroes – including the dashing Gallup – hardly dare venture into political polling, lest they get too close to the beast. Many young pollsters have left the village, not even pretending to pack their Random Samplers.

The premise of this book is that the village needs a new generation of fighters. We must confront the beast. There is a path that leads to the cave of the nonresponse beast. We need to take it. It may be scary, but surely the polling city will not be safe until polling works even when nonrespondents differ from respondents after controlling for demographics.

Xiao-Li Meng in the Harvard Statistics Department is on this path, rallying support around the idea that we must build a new polling paradigm that fights all the attacks the nonresponse beast is capable of, not just the ones that weighting addresses. Meng's coauthors and others in survey methodology, political science, epidemiology, and economics are joining the fight.

Moving down this path requires new intuition, new theory, and new kinds of data. There are, however, reasons to be hopeful. We know a lot about how to design weapons to fight the beast. With the right data, we can force all the nonresponse beast's attacks into the open, vastly improving the chances we can vanquish them. Importantly, these tactics work where traditional weighted armor fails.

This is where this book comes in. The goal is to explain how we got here and how we can push the fight forward.

Alas, the story can only be told with the tools of modern survey research, so we must leave behind our polling fairy tale. The turn toward social science notwithstanding, I hope that what follows proves a useful addition to the epic of polling, one that helps us to shed assumptions that have comforted us in the past and to confront challenges facing the future of polling.

Acknowledgments

I have been blessed by having many smart, experienced, open-minded, and kind colleagues in the academy and the profession.

Paul Kellstedt and Guy Whitten are model editors: Supportive, inquisitive, and effective. They organized an incredibly helpful conference at Georgetown University to discuss a draft of the manuscript. Josh Clinton and Leonie Huddy were discussants at that conference and provided excellent feedback. Their comments improved this manuscript immensely. Xiao-Li Meng has been a major inspiration. I came upon his work somewhat fortuitously mid-stream; I will never forget feeling profoundly connected to his elegant and accessible summary of polling challenges. Xiao-Li has provided careful and highly consequential feedback that affected how I think and what appears in this book. Working with Dan Hopkins catalyzed much of my early thinking on this project. I am indebted to his keen intellect and generosity. Jon Ladd is an ideal colleague at Georgetown, deeply knowledgeable about survey research and always willing to gently direct me away from that which I cannot support. Ken Goldstein has been a good friend and my favorite quote machine on the topic of nonresponse. Andrew Mercer is a sage in the field, and I always learned from my conversations with him. Erin Hartman does such great work pushing boundaries at the intersection of real-world polling and cutting-edge social science; I've learned much from her work and conversations. Doug Rivers has been a giant in the field since he was my advisor in graduate school and I continue to stand in awe of his incisive intellect – and, honestly, in fear of his quick wit. Bob Groves is another giant in the field, and I've been privileged to have him as a colleague and Provost at Georgetown.

Josh Pasek, Drew Linzer, Sunshine Hillygus, Natalie Jackson, Michael Peress, Devin Caughey, Adam Berinsky, Gary Jacobson, and Jeff Gill have guided me through the vast polling literature with grace. Amnon Cavari and Guy Freedman (2018, 2023) are doing great work on nonresponse and partisan polarization.

Some of the most impressive conversations I have had have been with a new generation of polling talent, including Valerie Bradley, Meg Schwenzfeier, Shiro Kuriwaki, Jonathan Robinson, and Johannes Fischer. They give me confidence that the future of polling is in good hands.

xx *Acknowledgments*

Georgetown has been a wonderful place to work on this project. Tony Arend and Maria Cancian have capably led my two institutional homes, the Department of Government and the McCourt School of Public Policy. I am grateful for their support and friendship. Frank Vella has done pathbreaking work on sample selection, and I've enjoyed learning from him. Hans Noel, Michele Swers, Jamil Scott, Bill Gormley, Nadia Brown, Doug Reed, Kent Weaver, Clyde Wilcox, Mark Rom, and Mark Richardson have created a strong cohort of Americanists at Georgetown, and I value their feedback and collegiality. Michael Stoto is an impressive scholar who has real impact on public health and was a great resource for thinking about polling outside of politics. I got feedback on an early version and have long valued the intellectual energy and high standards of the political economy group at Georgetown: Erik Voeten, Dennis Quinn, Nita Rudra, Jen Tobin, George Shambaugh, James Habyarimana, Marc Busch, Kate McNamara, Nada Eissa, Rod Ludema, Jim Vreeland, Jenny Guardado, Steve Weymouth, and Marko Klasnja.

I presented a version of this book in a half-day workshop at the American Association of Public Opinion Research Conference in 2022, and the book is better for the chance to engage with expert pollsters from many backgrounds. I finished this book in a sabbatical at the mediaLab at Sciences Po in Paris. Such a wonderful place! Jean-Philippe Cointet, Pedro Ramaciotti Morales, Dominique Cardon, and Kevin Arceneaux were supportive and insightful. I was lucky to present to students there and was energized by their engagement with the topic.

My wife Mari and children Jack, Ken, and Emi have heard more about this book than perhaps anyone. They probably think that it is normal to talk about sampling statistics at the dinner table. May they never learn otherwise.

PART I

POLLING IN CONTEXT

1

Modern Polling

Challenges and Opportunities

Polling has had a rough ride recently. In 2016, pundits confidently predicted Hillary Clinton would be elected president, bolstered by survey evidence suggesting she led nationally and in the critical swing states needed to win the Electoral College. Donald Trump's victory shocked the world and many blamed polls for misleading them. In 2020, Donald Trump didn't win, but he came much closer than polls suggested. Almost every poll showed Joe Biden leading nationally and in crucial swing states – often by healthy margins. Biden did, in fact, prevail in the popular vote and most swing states, but not easily. Had 40,000 more voters in three states voted for Donald Trump, Trump would have shocked the world again. The shortcomings of the 2020 polls were particularly unnerving because pollsters tried to learn from the mistakes of 2016, only to produce the least accurate polls in 40 years (Clinton et al. 2021).

Problematic polling is not uniquely American. In October 2022, polls suggested that former President Luiz Inacio Lula da Silva led right-wing populist President Jair Bolsonaro by 14 percentage points in the first round of Brazil's presidential election. On election day, Bolsonaro lost by only 5 percentage points. Populists also outperformed polls in the 2016 Brexit vote in the United Kingdom. The polls showed the pro-Europe "remain" and populist "leave" sides to be very close, with the remain side generally ahead. On election day, the leave side won by 4 percentage points (Hanretty 2016).

Polling misfires like these have soured many people on the field. "If 2016 didn't prove it, 2020 certainly did: The polling industry is in crisis" (Roberts 2020). An editorial in the *Wall Street Journal* didn't mince words: "It's all garbage ... we now have convincing evidence that polling fails to measure accurately that which it seeks to measure, and pollsters have no idea why" (Stemberg 2020). For Republican pollster Frank Luntz, "the political polling profession is done" (Concha 2020). Perhaps polls need to go the way of phone books, video stores, and manual transmission cars. Parts of the public wouldn't miss them: Polls show (ironically) that a majority of Americans – and a super majority of conservatives – do not believe polls (Sheffield 2018).

4   *Part I: Polling in Context*

Polling experts tend to be more sanguine. They note that polls remain generally accurate, across time and countries (Jennings and Wlezien 2018; Morris 2022a; Silver 2021a). Polls performed especially well in the 2018 and 2022 congressional elections (Silver 2018; Morris 2022b). These experts worry less about bad predictions and more about the decline of random sampling.

Random sampling theory has traditionally anchored survey work, justifying how characteristics of relatively small groups of people will converge to the characteristics of a population as long as the small group is a random sample of the large one. But random sampling is for all intents and purposes dead. A truly random sample requires that people are randomly contacted and that they *all* respond. In 2018, the response rate for the *New York Times*/Sienna College polls was less than 2 percent. The raw numbers are staggering: They made 301,921 calls to get 5,612 responses. In some districts, only 1 percent responded; in Michigan's 8th congressional district, the pollsters made 40,230 calls to get 447 responses. They had particular difficulty reaching young people who responded only 0.5 percent of the time.[1]

Response rates have continued to deteriorate since 2018 (Cohn 2022a). They are now so low that pollsters doubt the future of traditional polling efforts: "If you were employed as one of our interviewers at a call center, you would have to dial numbers for two hours to get a single completed interview ... this is getting pretty close to 'death of telephone polling' numbers" (Cohn 2022a).

Many pollsters no longer even attempt random sampling. Typically, these nonprobability pollsters harvest contact information from internet ads and then use complex algorithms to decide whom to contact and how to weight their samples. Much of the energy in contemporary polling is devoted to refining these nonprobability methods. While nonprobability polls are often accurate, they require stronger assumptions than random sampling.

Polling has therefore reached a critical moment. Polls have failed us in high-profile elections and, at best, have a weak basis in the random sampling theory that historically justified polling. The goal of this book is to help us understand this moment and plot a course for where to go next.

To understand this moment, I interpret the history and current practices of polling in terms of two sources of polling bias. One arises when survey samples differ from the population with respect to demographic and other easily measurable characteristics. The other source of bias arises when survey samples differ from the population with respect to less easily measurable characteristics, such as social trust or even the concept being measured in the polls. This second source of bias is particularly tricky because it confounds the standard tools of contemporary survey analysis. For example, if the ideological or psychological attributes that attract some people to Trump also lower

---

[1] These response rates may be lower than for other polls because they called more people who were unlikely to answer (Cohn 2018).

their propensity to respond to polls, demographic adjustments will not offset artificially low support for Trump among survey respondents.

Traditionally, random sampling saved us from both sources of bias because as a random sample gets larger, *all* characteristics of the sample – observed or not – converge to the distribution of characteristics in the population. Now that random samples have become rare – and possibly extinct (due to nonresponse and increasing use of nonprobability samples) – we need a new framework that explains error in the nonrandom samples that modern polls produce. I focus in this book on Meng's (2019) framework because it elegantly characterizes polling error in all surveys, randomly sampled or not. Meng's paradigm doesn't contradict random sampling theory; random sampling is a special case and continues to be an attractive ideal. But Meng's more general framework helps us focus on *all* the ways that modern surveys can go wrong.

Some implications of Meng's framework are familiar. Error in polls is inversely proportional to sample size, just as in random sampling. Some implications are less familiar. Bias of the second type – bias that arises when respondent's willingness to respond depends on the variable being measured by the survey – creates errors that are directly proportional to the size of population being measured. For survey researchers trained in random sampling, linking sampling error to population size (as opposed to sample size) verges on heretical. And yet this result is easy to explain in Meng's framework.

Connecting sampling error to population size means that small amounts of nonresponse bias can metastasize into large error in nonrandom samples, making it imperative that we do everything we can to prevent or adjust for all sources of bias. Conventional methods handle one, but not both, sources, creating a dangerous blind spot. This book will show that handling both sources of error requires new methods and new types of data. In explaining how and why these new approaches work, this book maps out next steps to help us design surveys to address the full range of survey bias in a post-random sampling world.

The book is based on three premises. First, polls are important. We simply cannot understand politics, society, and the economy without them. Social scientists and survey methodologists need to do whatever they can to get them right. Second, getting polls right is not easy, however. Extrapolating from the responses of the increasingly rare and potentially atypical people who respond to modern polls is daunting, making polling vastly more difficult than when random sampling was viable. Therefore, we need to think deeply about all the ways that polls can go wrong in this new environment, not just the ways that are easy to fix. Third, to say that getting polling right is difficult is not to say that it is impossible. While some may believe that polls will never be able to correct for biases caused by unmeasured factors, this book shows that new theories, data, and methods can substantially improve our ability to account for this kind of bias as well.

6   *Part I: Polling in Context*

This chapter sets the stage for the book. Section 1.1 emphasizes how important accurate polling is for policymakers, researchers, and citizens. Section 1.2 identifies two fundamental sources of bias in nonrandom samples. Section 1.3 explains how current approaches to polling address only one of these sources. Section 1.4 previews the tools presented in this book that enable us to address both challenges. Section 1.5 provides an overview of the chapters of the book, and Section 1.6 describes whom this book is for.

1.1 WE NEED GOOD POLLS

Polls are essential to a well-functioning modern society. They provide an important window into the beliefs, desires, and realities of everyone in society. In a world without polls, we could still learn about these things with in-depth qualitative research (e.g., Cramer 2016), but it is really hard to keep such information steadily flowing in a way that is comparable, generalizable, and free from subjectivity.

Polls are especially useful to burst epistemic bubbles. An old chestnut in polling circles tells of a New York socialite who, after Richard Nixon's landslide win in 1972, stated that she didn't understand how Nixon could have won because she did not know anyone who voted for Nixon. The story turns out to be apocryphal, but circulates because it is very funny – and a little true. We all are tempted to think that everyone sees the world as we do. Polls make that harder because they measure the views of people who may experience the world dramatically differently.

Some believe that flaws in modern polling corrode their ability to inform political leaders about public preferences. Matt Yglesias (2022) worries about survey samples dominated by high-intensity voters, writing

the answers-polls electorate is to the left of the votes-in-elections electorate, so Democrats keep getting a skewed read of the landscape and mis-calibrating their own races. The actual country is simply less-educated, lower in social trust and openness to experience, and more right-wing than the country that shows up in surveys. Democrats can win those voters; they just need to realize the practical necessity of doing it.

A similar dynamic may occur for Republicans, especially Republican politicians in gerrymandered districts that are so strongly Republican that they worry more about primary challenges than general election races.

Polling's loss of credibility played out in interesting ways in the 2022 US congressional campaign. Preelection polls from traditional probability-based pollsters tended to show good results for Democrats. Nonprobability polling tended to favor Republicans. Having been burned in 2016 and 2020, many in the media assumed the Republican-leaning polls were more accurate. Their articles anticipated a bad night for Democrats: "Democrats' midterm hopes fade: 'We peaked a little early'" (*Politico*) or "Top Democrats Question Their Party's Strategy as Midterm Worries Grow" (*New York Times*) or even "Red Tsunami Watch" (*Axios*).

Modern Polling: Challenges and Opportunities

Some Republican insiders were particularly confident, in part because they believed that Republican support was strong among nonrespondents. Benjamin Wallace-Wells (2022) summarized what he was hearing from his Republican sources:[2]

[T]he polls were likely under representing certain segments of the electorate. In recent years, more educated voters, especially white women, have moved to the Democrats, and less educated ones, of all races and especially men, toward the Republicans. When it comes to polling, these shifts have created an imbalance, in which one of the most visible groups in politics, and one especially energized by the *Dobbs* decision, had shifted toward Democrats, and one of the least visible had shifted toward Republicans. "The fastest-moving portion of the electorate is Hispanic men, and the second-fastest-moving portion of the electorate is Black men," the Republican consultant told me. You want to get them on the phone? "Good f—ing luck."

Issue polling may be even harder, because unlike campaign polling, the true "answer" about public preferences is seldom revealed. Surveys during the Covid pandemic showed support for masking in response to Covid. What if people opposed to masking were less likely to respond? Polling often shows Republicans support tax cuts. What if the Republicans who respond to polls are more likely to support party initiatives than those who do not respond? After the police killing of George Floyd in 2020, surveys suggested that attitudes of white people shifted on race. Was this real movement? Or was it simply new patterns in nonresponse? The implications for understanding how society was responding to a crisis in race relations are profound (Graham 2020).[3]

Polling problems may even undermine democracy. Some Republicans feel that polls are another elite institution biased against them. James Baker, the former US Secretary of State and manager of five Republican presidential campaigns, took to the pages of the *Wall Street Journal* immediately after the 2020 election to argue that

It would be funny if it weren't a sad reality that American democracy is being undermined by bad polling.... Polls that repeatedly favor one side create false expectations that adversely influence the actions of both sides. The favored side becomes overconfident and suffers when the results on Election Day don't meet expectations. And the

---

[2] The article was aptly, but not presciently, titled "Why Republican Insiders Think the G.O.P. Is Poised for a Blowout: The Consensus among Pollsters and Consultants Is This Tuesday's Election Will Be a 'Bloodbath' for the Democratic Party."

[3] Some researchers defend issue polling because the conventional polls match larger federal polls on many demographic and lifestyle benchmarks (Kennedy, Mercer, Hatley, and Lau 2022). Finding one set of polls matches another is informative but does not definitely show that issue polling is accurate. Even in this analysis, the conventional poll differed substantially from federal polling benchmarks in several respects. Respondents to the conventional poll were 21 percentage points more likely to say they had a retirement account, 11 percentage points more likely to say they voted, and 8 percentage points less likely to say they received food stamps.

8   *Part I: Polling in Context*

disfavored side is disadvantaged in both fundraising and voter turnout by the appearance that the outcome is foreordained. ... It's little wonder that many Americans — especially Republicans — voice complaints when newspapers and networks misinform them on the state of an election. ... Being branded "rank propagandists," as one knowledgeable observer recently called pollsters, cannot be good for business. (Baker 2020)

Former President Trump was not above trying to take advantage of the state of affairs, claiming without evidence that his wild claims about the 2020 election had widespread support from the American public. "He might be wrong, but without reliable polls, who's to say otherwise?" (Graham 2020).[4]

1.2 WHY POLLING IS DIFFICULT

The problem of modern polling is not a problem with random sampling. Random sampling is a powerful tool for ascertaining the views of many from the responses of a few. It works because random samples will look more and more like the population from which they were drawn with regard to *all* features – measured or not – as the size of sample increases. But a sample is only random in this way if *everyone* who is randomly contacted responds. This has never literally been the norm, but the polling world has generally been comfortable using samples in which most people respond to approximate random sampling, especially when they reweight survey samples to match known population demographics.

The problem of modern polling is a *lack* of random sampling. Today's abysmally low response rates make it impossible to pretend that samples are random. The *New York Times* contacts a random group of people, but when only one or two in 100 respond, they hear from a nonrandom subset that is unlikely to constitute a random sample.[5] The people who responded differ from the target population if for no other reason than they chose to do something that most people do not do: Respond to a poll. Survey respondents are in a select group of the top 1 percent of people most willing to respond to a poll. For comparison, the top 1 percent of US households earn more than $700,000 per year (Mishel and Kandra 2020). The tallest 1 percent of American men are over 6 foot 4 inches tall. The tallest 1 percent of women are over 5 foot 10 inches tall.

---

[4] Trump's belief in polls is as Trumpian as one might guess. At a 2018 campaign rally, he stated "I believe in polls — only the ones that have us up. ... Other than that, they're the fake news polls" (Sheffield 2018).

[5] It's even hard these days to identify a target population from which to sample. In the past, most households had a landline phone linked to a specific geographic locale. Now people have complicated mixes of cell and landline phones, many of which are untethered to any geographic region, meaning that there is neither a white pages-type directory of people living in a region nor a guarantee that a randomly dialed cell phone will be answered by someone living where we think they live.

Modern Polling: Challenges and Opportunities

If we're going to extrapolate from the nonrandom people who answer surveys to the general population, we will need to adjust for their distinctive character. To do this, pollsters identify two ways that respondents and nonrespondents can differ. The first is with respect to variables that we can observe, often variables such as gender, age, race, income, and education. Such differences are common. In US surveys, respondents are often older, whiter, richer, and more educated than the population at large. This type of nonresponse is concerning, but relatively easy to fix. Suppose there are too few young people in a survey sample. Perhaps we observed 100 young people even though Census data indicated that a random sample should have yielded a sample with 200 young people. We can simply double count the responses of the young people we have, and our adjusted sample will have the correct proportion of young people.[6] The trick here is filling in for young people who didn't respond with the answers of the young people who did.

In academic parlance, nonresponse associated with observed characteristics such as age and education is called "ignorable nonresponse." The reason this nonresponse is called ignorable is that by adjusting the data with weighting (or a related technique), we render this kind of nonresponse harmless and, hence, ignorable.

We use this terminology because it is standard in the literature. It's not great, though. One might think, reasonably enough, that ignorable nonresponse can be ignored. That's not true. Pollsters do not ignore ignorable nonresponse. They diligently weight their way around it. The label is intended to capture the idea that *if* we do something (like weighting), *then* we can ignore it. A better description of ignorable nonresponse is "conditionally independent nonresponse," because ignorable nonresponse is independent of survey opinions once variables observed in the sample and population are accounted for. This means that while young people may have different views than old people, the young people who responded have on average the same views as the young people who did not and the old people who responded have on average the same views as the old people who did not.

The second way that nonrespondents can differ from respondents is more subtle. Nonrespondents may differ with regard to some characteristic related to the quantity we are trying to measure. For example, suppose that we are trying to measure political views such as ideology and that respondents are more liberal than nonrespondents, perhaps because liberals may be more willing to trust pollsters. Obviously, this creates problems because our sample will be too liberal. And we cannot use weights because we don't know how many people are liberal in the whole population – that's what we were trying to measure with the survey!

---

[6] Weighting is second nature for experienced pollsters. For people new to the idea, it can seem like cheating. I explain weighting in detail in Chapter 3.

10 *Part I: Polling in Context*

In academic terms, this is called "nonignorable" nonresponse because even after adjusting our sample data based on observable characteristics, this nonresponse will cause bias and hence cannot be ignored. At its root, nonignorable nonresponse arises when people's willingness to respond is related to their opinions even after accounting for demographics. This can happen in two ways. First, a factor might explain both response propensity and the variable being measured in the survey. Many suspect, for example, that socially trusting people are more willing to respond to polls and are more likely to be liberal. Second, the outcome variable itself could affect response propensity. This can happen if someone is more likely to respond to a customer satisfaction survey after having a bad experience.

I also use this label because it is standard in the literature on polling, but I do so grudgingly. Nonignorable nonresponse is not so much a label as an instruction. Do. Not. Ignore. The point is that we should not ignore this kind of nonresponse because it will bias our estimates even if we weight our data. If you prefer using a more informative label for nonignorable nonresponse, consider "outcome-related nonresponse," which more directly indicates that nonignorable nonresponse occurs when the survey outcome relates to nonresponse.[7]

There are many contexts in which nonignorable nonresponse is a legitimate concern. In political polling, for example, nonresponse appears nonignorable for questions about intention to vote (Lohr 1999, 256). This is not surprising because habitual voters tend to be more interested in politics and more willing to engage in the rituals of citizenship, ranging from talking to pollsters to turning out to vote. Voters are more likely to respond to polls even when we account for demographics, meaning that we cannot weight our way back to a representative sample because in every possible demographic group we'll expect to see higher turnout among respondents than among the population at large.

The following are examples in a wide range of contexts.

- In survey research, the opinions or characteristics being measured may directly influence people's willingness to respond, especially on sensitive topics. Whether a person owns a gun may directly affect whether they respond to a poll about gun ownership (Urbatsch 2018). Such dynamics may occur on surveys about race, sexuality, sexual harassment (Cantor et al. 2020), and other controversial topics.

---

[7] Some researchers use a different, but related, set of terms in which data produced by an ignorable nonresponse process is also characterized as "missing at random" (see, e.g., Lohr 1999, 265). A strong form of ignorable nonresponse occurs when data are "missing completely at random." In this case, there is no covariate that explains the missingness. This occurs, for example, when we have 100 percent response rates from a randomly selected sample of the population. When data are missing at random (in this technical sense), nonresponse is random once we have accounted for observed characteristics such as age, race, and gender.

Modern Polling: Challenges and Opportunities 11

- Marketing researchers interested in online reviews face likely nonignorable nonresponse because such feedback skews strongly positive (Schoenmueller, Netzer, and Stahl 2020). There is also considerable evidence that respondents to nonprobability internet surveys are more active on the internet, more likely to be early adopters, less traditional and more environmentally concerned than the population at large, attributes that seldom are included in weights but could affect opinions about products (Gittelman et al. 2015).
- In economics, researchers worry that the least and most well-off are the most reluctant to reveal their income on surveys (Bollinger and Hirsch 2013).
- In communication studies, extrapolating from any social media data to a population is extremely challenging. Not only may social media users be younger, wealthier, and more technically skilled (Hargittai 2020), their willingness to use social media may reflect distinctive personality traits and worldviews.
- In public health, the propensity of people to respond may be related to the behaviors and outcomes being surveyed. A health study in the United Kingdom tracked down nonrespondents and found that they were 59 percent more likely to be in poor health than respondents (Peytchev 2013, 94). Nonignorable nonresponse is a concern on vaccination surveys because people who get vaccinated may be more likely to respond, as we see later.

Ironically, most survey work ignores nonignorable nonresponse. Virtually every survey analysis in both applied and academic settings uses only weighting or another tool that counters only ignorable nonresponse. Part of this puzzling state of affairs is explained by the evolution of modern survey research that was built on random sampling foundations. When using random sampling, pollsters did not have to worry about the types of nonresponse because random sampling countered both ignorable and nonignorable nonresponse. As response rates declined, pollsters retained the random sampling justification – producing margins of error based on random sampling, for example – and used weights to tweak their nonrandom samples to make them look like they were actually random samples. Not having moved to more general theory most pollsters have not felt an urgency to move beyond weights and similar tools that address only ignorable nonresponse.

Another reason pollsters ignore nonignorable nonresponse is that many believe that nothing can be done. One reason for this belief seems logical: If the problem is based on factors we do not measure, surely we cannot do anything about it. We shall see that this logic is incorrect. Another reason is that few pollsters are trained to address nonignorable nonresponse. Even though tools that counter nonignorable nonresponse have been around for decades (e.g., the Heckman selection model that I discuss in Chapter 8), they are seldom emphasized in the training of survey researchers. The low profile of these tools may have arisen in part because they often proved unreliable in practice. I describe in the second half of this book the considerable methodological progress that has been made beyond the traditional tools. More importantly, perhaps, I emphasize that even the older tools can work well if we design our surveys to produce the kind of data they require.

1.3 THE LIMITS OF CONVENTIONAL PRACTICE

What should we do about the nonresponse bias that can arise in modern nonrandom samples? The appropriate methods depend on the nature of the nonresponse. If nonresponse is ignorable, the conventional polling toolkit provides excellent options. That is, conventional tools are good at adjusting for nonresponse when the differences between respondents and the full population can be explained by variables that (1) we observe for respondents and (2) for which population distributions are known (Mellon and Prosser 2017, 772). These tools adjust the sample data such that the distribution of these observable variables in the sample matches the population distribution. Weighting is the most widely used tool; Chapter 4 discusses other tools that perform the same task based on the same assumptions, tools such as quota sampling.

Conventional polling practice has less to say about how to counter nonignorable nonresponse. As discussed earlier, the most common approach to nonignorable nonresponse is to ignore it. Ignoring the problem is defeatist; the goal of social science should be to identify and fix problems. Other options in the standard toolkit include eliminating nonresponse, weighting and increasing sample size (Lohr 1999, 256). None of these options is appealing. Eliminating nonresponse, for example, is almost never feasible.

Weighting is the most common way to attempt to deal with nonignorable nonresponse. Does weighting as conventionally practiced at least help fight nonignorable nonresponse? Sadly, no. Weighting can even exacerbate bias. As we alluded to above, weighting only works if respondents are random samples of their demographic groups (Groves et al. 2009, 350). We've seen that if a survey sample doesn't have enough young people, a pollster using weights will use the responses of the young people who did respond to speak for those who did not. *If the young people in the sample are representative of all people in the population, weighting is great.* But what if nonresponse is nonignorable, meaning that the young people who answer polls are not a random sample of their peers? In this case, weighting does not correct for nonresponse bias. In fact, if the young respondents are particularly unusual, up-weighting them may make things worse because weighting attributes beliefs to the nonrespondents that do not reflect their opinions (Agiesta 2021). Ken Goldstein (2016) summarizes the problem: "Usually we assume the problem is that group X is too small, but the actual problem may be that group X is too weird." Placing *extra* weight

Modern Polling: Challenges and Opportunities 13

on members of these group X weirdos will make our estimates worse, not better.

Within the weighting paradigm, one counters nonignorable nonresponse by finding weights that absorb the heretofore unmeasured sources of bias. If someone can find a way to measure the characteristic at the root of the nonignorable nonresponse in *both* the sample and population, they could add the variable to their weighting protocols and defang the nonignorable nonresponse. For example, if one believes that low levels of trust are associated with both nonresponse and support for populist politicians, one could theoretically measure trust among survey respondents and among the population at large and use it as a weighting variable. The limits of this strategy are clear, however: The only way to measure trust in the population is with a survey, which itself would be subject to nonresponse bias. Such circularity makes it hard to believe that finding new variables to include in weights will definitively solve nonignorable nonresponse.

In recent years, we have been awash in big data and it is tempting to think that these large data sources offer a way to counter nonignorable nonresponse. This doesn't work either. Not only do large sample sizes not address nonignorable nonresponse, they may make matters worse (Meng 2018). Bradley et al. (2021) provide a vivid example related to vaccination rates. The specter of nonignorable nonresponse looms over vaccination studies because it may be easier to contact and get response from people who do socially acceptable things like getting vaccinated.

Bradley and colleagues compared the following three surveys about Covid vaccination to US government baselines.

1. A Facebook survey produced more than 4.5 million responses across multiple waves over time. This survey weighted on age and gender but not education or race/ethnicity. Because the survey was conducted on Facebook, it was limited to Facebook users.
2. A Census Household Pulse survey produced more than 600,000 responses across multiple waves. This survey was an experiment by Census designed to rapidly measure pandemic-related behavior. They randomly sampled people for whom they had cell phone or email contact information, a population that included approximately 81 percent of US households. Response rates were under 10 percent (Peterson, Toribio, Farber, and Hornick 2021). This survey weighted on age, gender, education, and race/ethnicity.
3. An Axios-Ipsos survey of around 1,000 respondents per wave based on samples from all addresses in the United States. The survey firm provided internet access to respondents who lacked internet access (accounting for about 1 percent of the final sample). This survey weighted on age, gender, education, and race/ethnicity.

14 *Part I: Polling in Context*

What should we expect from these surveys? A big data enthusiast would love the large samples of the first two surveys. A technically oriented pollster might be attracted to the Axios-Ipsos survey because they had the strongest argument that they were sampling from the whole country, not just Facebook users or people for whom the Census Bureau had contact information.

The Axios-Ipsos survey, small sample size notwithstanding, consistently tracked best with the government baseline with the reference data from the CDC in or nearly in the confidence interval produced by the Axios-Ipsos survey for the January through May 2021 period that was analyzed. Despite their much larger sample sizes, the confidence intervals of the Facebook and Census surveys did not contain the CDC reference estimates, meaning they were inaccurate. And the problem grew over time. By March 2021, the Census measure of vaccination take-up was 9 percentage points higher than the CDC measure and the Facebook measure was 16 percentage points higher than the CDC measure. These differences were even larger by May 2021.

Why did the smaller sample size Axios-Ipsos survey perform best? Bradley et al. (2021) argue that survey methods are more important than sample size. That is, the smaller-sized survey performed best because it was less likely to suffer from nonignorable nonresponse bias than the big data surveys (Meng 2018).

Given the dearth of tools in the conventional toolkit that deals with nonignorable nonresponse, some advocate simply coming clean: Polls will be imperfect and the public needs to accept this (Leonhardt 2020). In this approach, pollsters should emphasize that errors are inevitable, especially today because there are so many ways for the nonrandom samples produced by modern polling to go sideways. In other words, polls will sometimes be wrong. Get over it.

1.4 THE ROAD AHEAD: A PREVIEW

As social scientists, we should resist this polls-will-be-polls attitude. I advocate another option: Constructing a polling paradigm that accounts for ignorable nonresponse (the nonresponse that weighting can fix) and nonignorable nonresponse (the nonresponse that weighting cannot fix). This paradigm can broaden our intuitions about when polling does and does not work. It also helps us focus attention on designing and analyzing surveys in ways that are less vulnerable to all types of nonresponse that can arise in modern nonrandom samples.

There are, broadly, three approaches to dealing with nonignorable nonresponse. The first involves documenting how vulnerable any given survey is to nonignorable nonresponse (Hartman and Huang 2023). Suppose that we are concerned that our survey has too many politically interested people. We cannot weight for political interest because we don't measure political interest among nonrespondents. We can, however, posit different possibilities (e.g.,

Modern Polling: Challenges and Opportunities 15

"what if 30 percent of people are interested in politics? Or 20 percent?") and for each possibility generate weights.

Such sensitivity analysis enables us to estimate how vulnerable a survey is to nonignorable nonresponse. If our conclusions change dramatically over the range of posited population averages, the results are indeed vulnerable to nonignorable nonresponse and we need to inform our readers accordingly. Even better, we should implement surveys following the ideas outlined in this book. If the results do not vary much across the posited population values, we can move our survey out from under the cloud of suspicion with regard to at least that source of nonignorable nonresponse. Chapter 7 discusses sensitivity analysis.

A second approach to dealing with nonignorable nonresponse involves using existing data in new ways. The 2020 American National Election Study (ANES) provides an interesting case. The ANES is a long running and widely respected academic poll. In the ANES preelection survey data, Biden led Trump by 11.8 percentage points (53.4 to 41.6), a lead that exceeded Biden's actual 4.4 percentage point margin victory in the popular vote.[8]

Figure 1.1 displays ANES results by political interest. The top panel shows support for Biden organized by interest in politics. Among respondents very interested in politics, Biden support was 61.9 percent. Support for Biden among somewhat interested people was 56.5 percent, while support for Biden among respondents who indicated they were not very or not at all interested in politics was 51.1 and 49.0 percent, respectively. In short, support for Biden among the most interested respondents was 12.9 percentage points higher than among those least interested in politics.

The bottom panel presents a similar breakdown for feeling thermometers, answers people give when asked to rate a politician on a 0 to 100 scale. Among people very interested in politics, the feeling thermometers for Biden averaged 19.3 points higher than the feeling thermometers for Trump. Among people somewhat interested in politics the gap was 9.3, while among people who said they were not very or not at all interested in politics, average feeling thermometer differences between Biden and Trump were only 2.8 and 0.7, respectively.[9]

If we believe that people who are more interested in politics are more likely to answer a poll about politics – which hardly seems farfetched – then it seems natural to worry that the ANES suffered from nonresponse bias. The response

---

[8] Using ANES's weights actually increased Biden's margin to 12.6 percentage points. The ANES was not alone in suggesting Biden's lead was large. The final preelection FiveThirtyEight.com margin based on many polls indicated that Biden led by 8.3 percentage points. Across respected large-scale polls from the ANES, the Cooperative Election Study, Nationscape and Pew, the average Biden lead was 17.9 percentage points unweighted and 14.7 percentage points when weighted (Jacobson 2022, 9).

[9] Controlling for demographics does not change the patterns reported in the figure. I'm grateful to Leonie Huddy for suggesting this example.

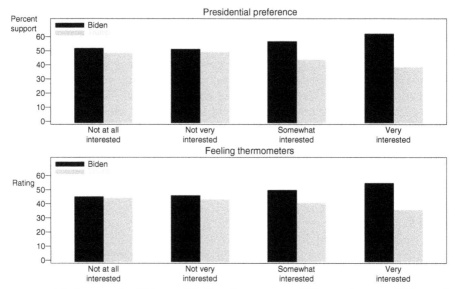

FIGURE 1.1 Support for Biden and feeling thermometer difference between Biden and Trump

rate for the ANES poll was 36.7 percent, so a lot of people didn't respond. If those nonrespondents were less interested in politics, then we should probably extrapolate lower support among nonrespondents than among respondents. Doing so would adjust Biden's lead downward toward the actual result.

While conceptually simple, no pollster that I know of made an adjustment based on interest in politics. Why? As we have already discussed, using non-demographic variables in weighting is difficult – if not impossible – because weighting requires us to know the distribution of weighting variables in the population. Because we don't know the actual distribution of political interest in the population, we don't weight for it, leaving us to disregard this seemingly obvious possible source of nonignorable nonresponse.

It need not be this way. Part III of this book describes tools that measure and correct for nonignorable nonresponse using such data. Peress (2010) did this to model turnout in the 1980s. As is often the case, surveys at that time overestimated turnout: Even though only 50 percent of adults turned out to vote at that time, 70 percent of ANES respondents voted.[10] Weights took a chunk out of the bias – turnout in the weighted data went down to around 60 percent – but did not eliminate the problem. Using the approach discussed in Chapter 9, Peress incorporated information about response interest, information that is akin to the political interest variable discussed plotted above and

---

[10] The ANES validated whether people voted so this was not simply a case of people saying they voted when they didn't. See Jackman and Spahn (2019) for excellent deep dive into this issue.

Modern Polling: Challenges and Opportunities   17

was able to bring estimates to within 1 percent of actual turnout in 1980 and 1988 and within 2 percent in 1984.

A third type of tool for tackling nonignorable nonresponse involves survey design. The importance of survey design is deeply embedded in polling DNA; after all, in random sampling the design of the survey is much more important than the number of responses. The centrality of design persists in the new paradigm as the goal is to create data that make it easier to diagnose and potentially correct for nonignorable nonresponse.

To explain how this works, let's start with a classroom scenario. Suppose that we are interested in knowing how many students know the answer to a test question. We'll assume there are two classes, each with 50 students, half of whom know the right answer. The teacher in the first classroom randomly selects five students and gives them the quiz. The teacher in the second classroom asks for volunteers and has the first five students who raise their hands do the quiz.

Will the quiz scores be the same in both classes? Probably not. In the first class, we should expect that 50 percent of the students will answer correctly because they have been randomly selected. In the second class, it seems likely that the students who volunteer will be more likely to get the correct answer.

Now suppose the teachers increase the number of students taking the quiz to 15, which is 30 percent of the class. In the first class, we should still expect 50 percent correct answers. In the second class, the scores may go down. We're still getting volunteers and volunteers are more likely than nonvolunteers to know the answer, but now we're going deeper in the pool. So even as the percent correct would likely exceed 50 percent, it would not be as high as when only five students took the quiz. If we keep increasing the number of students who take the quiz, eventually everyone in both classes will take the quiz and both classes will generate 50 percent correct answers.

The nonresponse in the first class is ignorable because students are randomly selected. In other words, in that first class there could be no systematic relationship between who responded and whether they knew the answer. In that class the percent correct was 50 percent in expectation whether 5, 15, or all 50 students took the quiz. In the second class, nonresponse is nonignorable because whether a student knew the answer influenced whether they volunteered. In that class, the average quiz score declined as the number of quiz-takers went from 5 to 15 to 50.

Figure 1.2 illustrates the scenario. On the y-axis is the percent correct. On the x-axis is the response rate. The line on top shows that the expected percent correct declined as the response rate increased for the voluntary classroom in which nonresponse was nonignorable. When 10 percent of the students volunteered, the percent correct was clearly higher than when 30 percent of the class volunteered, which was higher than when everyone answered. The flat line at 50 percent shows the expected percent correct for the randomly selected class. It was always the same regardless of response rate.

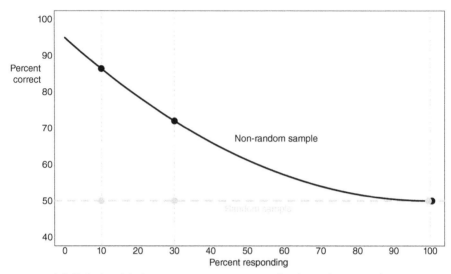

FIGURE 1.2 Relationship between response rates and quiz performance for two types of nonresponse

Now we can extend the logic to polling. Suppose we field two surveys simultaneously, one with a low response rate and one with a high response rate. Cohn (2022b) reports one example in which the *New York Times*/Siena pollsters fielded a conventional phone survey with typical low response rate around 1 percent and another high response survey in which respondents were paid to respond (and did so at a 30 percent rate). If the percent "correct" – which in this case could be support for a given political candidate – comes back different in the two arms of the survey, which line in Figure 1.2 would that be consistent with? If the percent supporting the candidate were the same, which line in the figure would that be consistent with?

Following our logic so far, different results across survey arms would accord with nonignorable nonresponse and similar results across surveys would accord with ignorable nonresponse. This, then, is the core logic for pulling out evidence of nonignorable nonresponse. There is work to be done, of course, in moving from the intuition to statistical models and survey design, work we do in Chapters 10 through 12. Once one understands the core intuition, however, the rest is mostly detail.

1.5 THE PLAN OF THE BOOK

This book is divided into four parts. Part I contextualizes the state of polling today. Chapter 2 tells the story of how the survey world has lurched from paradigm to paradigm, typically jolted from a consensus view by failed predictions in presidential elections. Chapters 3 and 4 provide an overview of the

Modern Polling: Challenges and Opportunities

current state of polling. Chapter 3 dives into weighting, an important tool to deal with nonresponse in contemporary polling. Parts of Chapter 3 are technical and can be skimmed by those readers less interested in such details. Chapter 4 broadens the lens to consider the entire range of contemporary polling, including use of nonprobability survey methods. For all the creativity and innovation in modern polling, it is striking the degree to which polling continues to rely on the assumption that nonresponse is ignorable.

Part II of this book builds the case that we need a new paradigm that will encompass modern polling realities. Chapter 5 presents a model that incorporates both ignorable and nonignorable nonresponse without privileging either. At its core is Harvard statistician Xiao-Li Meng's Big Data Paradox: "The larger the data size, the surer we fool ourselves when we fail to account for bias in data collection." That is, if the data collection process is problematic, having a lot of data may not only lead us to the wrong answer, but it may lead us to have misplaced confidence in the wrong answer (Meng 2018).

Chapter 6 fleshes out further implications of this paradigm. One major implication is that *random contact* surveys are incredibly valuable. Random contact surveys are what we mostly have today: People are contacted, and then of the contacted individuals, there is a (presumptively) nonrandom process that governs who actually responds. Random contact surveys do not produce random samples, but the Meng framework makes it clear that they limit the damage that nonignorable nonresponse can inflict.

Part III explains how to fight nonignorable nonresponse. Chapter 7 explains tools that assess the vulnerability of a survey to nonignorable nonresponse. These tools are extremely clever and provide a minimal analysis that anyone can do; they do not, however, diagnose or correct for nonignorable nonresponse and may therefore by skipped by readers eager to diagnose and correct for nonignorable nonresponse.

Chapter 8 introduces the logic underlying models that diagnose and correct nonignorable nonresponse. The key insight is that nonignorable nonresponse can leave traces in survey data, especially if we have the rights kinds of survey data. Understanding this insight helps us appreciate just how distinctive these models are from weighting approaches and how they desperately require certain kinds of data.

Chapters 9 and 10 describe the modern selection model toolkit in more detail. Researchers working not only on surveys, but also on economics and epidemiology have made excellent progress fighting nonignorable nonresponse. Chapter 9 presents a range of parametric and semi-parametric selection models. We see, for example, how one can generate weights that account for nonignorable nonresponse when it exists. Chapter 10 emphasizes how randomized response instruments produce the data that give these selection models the best chance to identify and correct for nonignorable nonresponse if it exists. In order to make sense of the many models and data types, Chapter 11 provides an integrated discussion of the models, their strengths and weaknesses. It culminates with a flowchart that can assist analysts seeking to use these models in practice.

Part IV of this book applies the tools. Chapter 12 describes multiple political polls that were designed to identify and correct for nonignorable nonresponse. The goal is to both explain *how* to implement the tools and reveal *what* the tools can uncover. There are strong signs that polls may provide distorted views of attitudes about race, while also exaggerating partisan divides.

Chapter 13 extends the toolkit beyond political polling to public health, another area where nonignorable nonresponse presents major challenges. It is highly likely that the people who choose to test for a given disease such as Covid will have different probabilities of being sick than the rest of the population, making it hard to generalize from observed testing data. This chapter suggests how randomized response instruments can improve estimates of disease prevalence and how the logic of nonignorable nonresponse can be leveraged to better compare prevalence across jurisdictions.

1.6 WHO SHOULD READ THIS BOOK

Asked to describe the media's understanding of polls, the Cook Political Report's Amy Walter said that "journalists talking about polls are like preteens talking about sex. They know all the words. They talk about it a lot. But they have no idea what they're talking about" (Grynbaum 2019). This description may cut a little close even for us nonreporters; certainly, we all recognize how it is easy to lose the thread of what polls mean when we face a barrage new methods and new results.

This book seeks to help people step back to understand the whole story of how nonresponse makes polling difficult, especially in today's post-random sampling environment. It is particularly useful for people who want to understand the limits of conventional methods and how to overcome them. I'll explain where we are – and how we got here. I'll explain the theory behind polling and what has been lost by ignoring the ironically named nonignorable nonresponse. I'll also show that we are not helpless; it may not be easy in practice, but via simple pictures I will make it clear that nonignorable nonresponse can leave traces and that new approaches offer promising avenues for countering the problem.

If you are a student or a politically engaged citizen, the book will give you deeper knowledge of how polls work, helping you know whether to be convinced or skeptical of the latest poll. If you are a polling professional or an academic researcher, the book will help you address that nagging worry that your weights have assumed away potentially important flaws in your survey samples. I provide specific suggestions for how to improve polls, suggestions that are grounded in theory and a broad academic literature.

Modern Polling: Challenges and Opportunities 21

The book centers on politics, but is broadly relevant. Nonignorable non-response can affect *any* effort to extrapolate from a sample to a population, meaning that researchers in health, business, economics, and demography will recognize the problems and benefit from the new solutions.

The book does not cover all aspects of survey research. As characterized by the total survey error approach, survey research can go wrong in coverage, response, question formulation, insincere or unthoughtful responses, social desirability, and poor analysis (Biemer 2010; Groves 2004). All of these are important topics; the focus here is on one of them, nonresponse bias. I also avoid some interesting, yet fundamentally distinct, topics. For example, polit-ical polling is often used to anticipate or explain election outcomes. Doing so requires not only a model translating survey responses to the population at large, but also a model mapping the population at large to turnout (see, e.g., Sturgis et al. 2018). Often the biases in survey response and turnout reinforce each other (because the kinds of people who answer polls are the kind of people who are more likely to vote), but I do not attempt here to model turnout.

This book can be read in different ways depending on your background. I present all the main arguments textually, visually, and mathematically. The purpose of the math is to *simplify* the arguments and reduce clutter, but I appreciate that not everyone thinks in such terms. Rest assured, therefore, that if you do not like equations, you will see a story and a picture for everything that matters.

1.7 CONCLUSION

Polling fulfils a valuable function in society, but has become increasingly dif-ficult in recent years. Modern survey samples are nonrandom samples. This is abundantly true for pollsters who do not randomize contact. It is also true of pollsters who randomize contact but hear from only a few of the people they contact.

Nonrandom samples risk two kinds of bias. Ignorable nonresponse bias occurs when the sample distributions of characteristics differ from known population-level distributions. Nonignorable nonresponse bias occurs when the propensity to respond is related to the item being measured even when we control for demographics. Dealing with ignorable nonresponse is rela-tively easy. Dealing with nonignorable nonresponse is not. In fact, weight-ing or generating large samples can aggravate bias when nonresponse is nonignorable.

I argue in this book that we need to build from a starting point that rec-ognizes both kinds of biases. We can then build tools and models that are more robust to the full set of risks facing the nonrandom samples produced by all modern polling. The payoffs can be substantial. Writing *before* the 2020 election, Isakov and Kuriwaki (2020) used Meng's 2018 framework to antici-pate how polling would perform. They noted that if nonignorable nonresponse occurred on the order it had in 2016 and if weighting hadn't improved (both true, as it turned out), then the 2020 polls were underestimating Trump by around 1 percent in key battleground states and, perhaps more importantly, were vastly underestimating the uncertainty in the numbers. While even their methods understated Trump's performance, their conclusion written before the 2020 election was prophetic: "Our approach urges caution in interpreting a simple aggregation of polls.... Our scenario analysis confirms [Biden's lead] in some states while casting doubts on others."

The point is not that all polls are terrible or that we should never believe polls. For all the problems outlined above, polls often perform well – remarkably well in light of the challenges (Jennings and Wlezian 2018; Silver 2021a). In 2018, Nate Silver famously declared that "the polls are all right," echoing the Who's song "The Kids Are Alright" (Silver 2018). If we think of polls as kids, we should acknowledge that yes, polls are going to school, getting decent grades, and eating their vegetables.

But that doesn't mean the kids are totally fine. Every few elections a packet of heroin falls out of one of their backpacks. We probably shouldn't look the other way. Instead, we need more work, more theory, and more innovation to keep polls from veering down the wrong path.

2

The Story of Polling in $2\frac{1}{2}$ Fiascos

> Governor Thomas E. Dewey will be elected the thirty-fourth President of the United States in November.
>
> *Fortune Magazine* (1948)

Three times in the last one hundred years, pollsters have failed to predict a presidential election. In the 1920s and 1930s, a popular magazine called *The Literary Digest* collected literally millions of survey responses before presidential elections. Their predictions were quite good … until 1936. In that year, their legions of respondents heavily supported Republican Alf Landon, leading the magazine to predict Landon would win in a landslide. He did not, to put it mildly. Landon lost to Franklin D. Roosevelt by the largest margin in US history. With Landon's failed campaign died the idea that big polls were good polls.

Pollsters shifted to quota sampling, a technique in which pollsters divided the population into subgroups and targeted their sample to match the proportions of the population in each subgroup. Quota sampling avoided *The Literary Digest*'s skewed sample, but it too had a weakness: Quota sampling gave massive discretion to surveyors in the field, leading to samples heavy with people similar to the survey takers. The quota sampling era ended with the famous "Dewey Defeats Truman" election of 1948 in which polls predicted Republican Thomas Dewey would easily defeat President Truman. He did not. With Dewey's loss died the idea that quotas were sufficient to produce accurate polls.

And, of course, there is 2016. The performance of polls that year was actually a bit nuanced – hence the $\frac{1}{2}$ fiasco in the chapter title. National polls accurately predicted that Clinton would win the popular vote. At the same time, though, state polls in crucial battleground states suggested Clinton would win there as well, contributing to the broad consensus that her victory was assured. It was not. Clinton's loss led many to wonder about the future of polling.

24   *Part I: Polling in Context*

Philosopher of science Thomas Kuhn provided a useful framework for thinking about evolution like this in a scientific endeavor (Kuhn 1970). Kuhn documented the important role played by paradigms in scientific progress. A paradigm is set of assumptions and techniques accepted by scientists in a field at any given point in time. During periods of paradigmatic stability, scientists deal with findings inconsistent with the paradigm by tweaking, but not abandoning, the dominant paradigm.

Sometimes, though, an anomaly is so large that no amount of patching the existing paradigm can save it. This creates a crisis, resolved by a scientific revolution that replaces the existing paradigm with a new one, after which scientists settle back into a new period of normal science. These revolutions are partially objective, in the sense that the new paradigm typically better explains the anomalous phenomena. Paradigmatic revolutions are also sociological, however, in the sense that the new paradigm emerges from very human and sometimes subjective interaction of leading scientists.

Survey research is remarkably Kuhnian (Bethlehem 2009). It has lurched from one paradigm to another after crises induced in large part by failures to predict elections. This chapter tells the tale of three paradigms in particular: Large-scale polling, quota sampling, and random sampling. The first two paradigms came crashing down after pollsters made poor predictions for presidential elections. The third paradigm remains vibrant intellectually, but is increasingly difficult to implement. We do not yet know if the bad polling predictions in 2016 and 2020 will push the field to a new paradigm, but certainly they raised doubts about the current state of the field.

The history of polling is interesting as intellectual history. It is also relevant today. The core challenges of polling have always been with us, and contemporary pollsters are now revisiting old tricks as they struggle to conduct accurate surveys in a post-random sample world.

2.1 MASS POLLING

Early seekers of information, such as governments eager to conscript soldiers or tax citizens, sought to implement a full census based on responses from every person in a target population. In 1086, England's new king, William the Conqueror, famously commissioned the *Domesday Book* to provide detailed information about people in 13,000 different locales (Bethlehem 2009, 4).

It did not take long for governments (and others) to realize that conducting a complete census is expensive, often prohibitively so. Hence, they looked to use samples from subsets of a population to generalize about a broader population, a practice that is both efficient and intuitive. After all, the idea of sampling soup with a sip or cheese with a small slice is "as old as mankind" (Bethlehem 2009, 1).

The story of modern political polling begins with the *Literary Digest* straw polls of the early twentieth century. The *Literary Digest* was a national

The Story of Polling in $2\frac{1}{2}$ Fiascos

magazine with nearly two million subscribers, more than any other magazine (Converse 2009, 118). Asking every voter how they would vote was impossible, of course. But asking *as many* voters as possible how they would vote seemed like a smart move. Hence from 1916 to 1936, the *Literary Digest* conducted large-scale straw polls before elections, based on their efforts to hear from as many people as possible. These polls were reasonably successful predictively and, it appears, quite successful commercially, as the magazine continued to pour massive resources into them.

The *Literary Digest* approach was built around an intense hunger for data. They didn't have deep theory about how the data were generated or how to analyze it. They were motivated by the intuitive idea that if data are good, more data are better. In modern terms, they had the big data bug. They sought out lists of Americans wherever they could, finding telephone directories and registers of automobile owners particularly useful. But they took data however they could and used other sources such as rosters of clubs and associations, voter registration rolls, occupational records, classified mail-order and city directories (Lusinchi 2012).

The scale of *Literary Digest*'s operation was astounding. At their peak scale in 1930, they mailed surveys to 20 million people, a large number even today, and an almost inconceivable number for those precomputer times. From 1916 to 1932, they sent out over 350 million pieces of mail (Moore 1995, 38). By 1930, they had 400 clerks tabulating 5 million returned questionnaires (Converse 2009, 118). In 1932, they described their process

the rumble of activity is beginning for what has been called 'the second greatest event of a presidential year' ... twenty million envelops to be addresst [sic] by hand. Twenty million ballots to be printed. Twenty million letters to be prepared, folded and inserted in those envelops ... paper by the car-load ... Just the addressing of envelops furnishes a real harvest of welcome work to some 2,500 women and men of superior penmanship. (Moore 1995, 39)

Their efforts paid off as the *Literary Digest* built a reputation for providing accurate intelligence about elections. Their surveys correctly anticipated victories by Calvin Coolidge in 1924, Herbert Hoover in 1928, and Franklin Roosevelt in 1932. In 1932, the *Literary Digest* final poll showed Roosevelt with 59.9 percent support and winning in 41 states with 474 electoral votes (Moore 1995, 42). The actual results were that Roosevelt received 59.1 percent of the votes and won and 41 states with 472 electoral votes. The average error for the predictions in each of the 48 states was 3 percent (Moore 1995, 42). Even today, a pollster would be proud of such accuracy.

There were some signs, however, that the *Literary Digest* might have some structural weaknesses. In 1916, they claimed to have predicted Woodrow Wilson's victory, when in fact this prediction was based on a survey of labor leaders. Their poll of voters that year indicated that Charles Evans Hughes would defeat Woodrow Wilson (Converse 2009, 118). In 1924, the magazine downplayed the fact that they had Progressive Party candidate Robert LaFollette coming in second, when he actually finished a distant third (Converse 2009, 119). And their polls were not particularly accurate in 1924 and 1928, years in which their state results were off by an average of 12 percentage points (Erikson and Tedin 2001, 8).

In 1936, the *Digest* sent out 10 million postcards with a "ballot" for the upcoming presidential election. They received 2.4 million back (Lusinchi 2012, 26). Their survey responses indicated that Republican Alf Landon would garner 55 percent of the vote and easily defeat President Roosevelt. These results were widely known and may have encouraged the Landon campaign (Squire 1988, 126) (an episode that may trigger Hillary Clinton's 2016 campaign staff).

How did the *Literary Digest*'s 1936 poll perform? Not well. Not well at all. Roosevelt not only won in 1936, but he won in a historic landslide, winning 61 percent of the vote and all but eight electoral votes.

The failed poll was a disaster for the *Literary Digest*. By 1938, the magazine was bankrupt. It had been suffering declining circulation since the 1920s, and the 1936 election fiasco certainly did not help (Converse 2009, 121). The failed poll was also a shock to the nascent polling field more generally, as people felt betrayed by an organization and method that had seemed reliable in the past.

The explanations of what went wrong fell into two general categories, categories that are useful to understand in light of current polling challenges (Squire 1988). The most widely recounted explanation was that the *Literary Digest* had a *sampling frame* problem: They reached out to an unrepresentative sample of Americans. Their contact list came primarily from automobile and phone registrations. At the time, these were relatively new technologies: Around 40 percent of households had phones, and 57 percent had cars (Lusinchi 2012, 34). The people possessing these items were on average wealthier, and wealth was a clear predictor of support for the Republican Party.

Lusinchi (2012, 28) quotes statistician Samuel S. Wilks summarizing a widely held view:

The names of people to be polled were selected from such lists as telephone directories, automobile registration lists, etc. It is quite obvious that such a system of selection will be biased by having too large a proportion of the higher income and social groups, which in the 1936 presidential election were known to be heavily weighted in favor of Landon.

If talking to the wrong mix of people was the flaw in the *Literary Digest* poll, they had an *ignorable* nonresponse problem. That is, if pollsters could adjust the mix of people they talked to, either proactively with quota samples or retrospectively with weights, they could avoid the *Literary Digest*'s disastrous errors.

A second explanation for the *Literary Digest*'s failure was that they had a *nonignorable nonresponse* problem. That is, even after accounting for

The Story of Polling in $2\frac{1}{2}$ Fiascos 27

demographics, Landon supporters were more likely to return their survey ballots (Bryson 1976; Squire 1988; and Lusinchi 2012). This explanation got less attention at the time, but even the *Digest* staff worried about it. Writing just after the 1936 election, staff at the *Literary Digest* noted that they had noticed in 1928 that Republicans seemed more inclined to respond to the survey. "Do Republicans live nearer mailboxes?" they asked plaintively (Squire 1988, 127).

There are two pieces of evidence that support the idea that nonignorable nonresponse was the main cause of the *Literary Digest*'s problems. The first arises from the fact that the *Literary Digest* actually had a varied approach to finding people to send ballots to. In *most* cities, the *Digest* used the much-maligned telephone and automobile records to build their sample. In *some* cities, however, they used voter registration lists, a technique that is respected even today.

If a skewed sample was the main flaw in the *Literary Digest* survey, then one would expect their results to be more accurate in the cities where they sampled only registered voters (Allentown, Scranton, and Chicago). In fact, however, their results in these places were also strongly skewed toward Landon, something the *Literary Digest* editors emphasized in their postmortem (Lusinchi 2012, 27, 45). In Allentown, 53 percent of the *Literary Digest* responses favored Landon, which was much higher than the 41 percent support Landon received in Allentown on Election Day (Moore 1995, 52). In Chicago, 49 percent of the *Literary Digest* responses favored Landon, which was much higher than the 32 percent support Landon received in Chicago (Moore 1995, 52). In other words, even when the sampling frame was registered voters, the *Literary Digest* results were heavily biased toward Landon, suggesting that the decision to respond was related to the content of the response, a sure marker of nonignorable nonresponse.[1]

The second piece of evidence for differential nonresponse emerged from a Gallup survey conducted in May of 1937. The survey asked people about their vote, if they got a *Literary Digest* ballot and if so, whether they returned it. (Respondents were also asked whether they changed their mind after they returned the survey ballot.) This survey was not perfect: It was conducted with the quota sampling method discussed below and also, as a postelection survey, displayed the typical pattern of more support for the winner than in the election. But, these data were produced given the contemporary state of the art and, as both Squire (1988) and Lusinchi (2012) argue, there is no obvious reason to suspect bias with regard to partisan differences in who said they responded to the *Literary Digest* poll.

---

[1] One possible explanation is that changing voter preferences over the course of the campaign accounted for the gap. However, the arguably better polls conducted by the Gallup organizations that we discuss later showed no significant movement in voters' views (Moore 1995, 52).

Two patterns were clear in the Gallup postelection poll. First, the differences in presidential preferences between those who did and did not own cars and phones were modest. Among those who had either a phone or a car (but not both), 68 percent supported Roosevelt (Squire 1988, 130), which while lower than the 79 percent support Roosevelt had among those who owned neither was still a very clear majority. Even those who owned *both* a car and a phone supported Roosevelt by 55 percent to 45 percent for Landon. This evidence cuts against the idea that the overrepresentation of phone and car owners was the core problem.

Second, Landon supporters indicated a much higher propensity to send back their *Digest* ballots than Roosevelt supporters. Seventy-five percent of Landon supporters who received a *Literary Digest* ballot reported returning their ballots, compared with only 57 percent of Roosevelt backers (Lusinchi 2012, 31–32). An additional survey in Cedar Rapids, Iowa, using similar questions also found that Landon's followers were twice as likely to return their straw ballots as Roosevelt's. This survey used a telephone-based contact list similar to the *Literary Digest* list and produced an estimate of 53 percent for Landon and 47 percent for Roosevelt, which was not far from the 50–50 split the candidates received in the city (Lusinchi 2012, 32).

Such behavior is puzzling, but not inexplicable. The set of cultural and political characteristics seemed to come together in a way that the types of people who were Democrats in 1936 felt less comfortable expressing their views. Many suspect we're seeing the same thing today in the United States; only now, it may be that cultural and political factors render Republicans (or, at least Trump supporters) less likely to engage with pollsters.

The evidence led Squire (1988, 130) and Lusinchi (2012, 44) to both conclude that the *Literary Digest* would have called the correct winner if everyone who received a ballot had returned it. In other words, even though they sent ballots to a skewed population, the *Literary Digest* would have, in Lusinchi's words, "done probably as well as two out of the three new 'scientific' pollsters" who famously outperformed the *Literary Digest* in 1936 if there had been no nonignorable nonresponse.

2.2 QUOTA SAMPLING

The stakes of adjudicating between the two explanations for *Literary Digest*'s woes may seem modest as sampling and differential nonresponse may not seem terribly different. To the survey field, however, the stakes were enormous, as the sampling frame explanation implied the problem was ignorable nonresponse while the differential nonresponse explanation implied the problem was nonignorable nonresponse. These competing perspectives, in turn, pointed the field in different directions. If the problem was simply that the people the *Literary Digest* queried were too wealthy, the solution was to get fewer rich people by using quotas or weights. If the problem was that Roosevelt supporters

The Story of Polling in $2\frac{1}{2}$ Fiascos

were less likely to respond than Landon supporters, however, the solution was less clear as the intellectual infrastructure for dealing with nonignorable nonresponse problem was poorly developed at the time.

The sampling frame explanation won out (Lusinchi 2012, 25–30). Scholar Claude Robinson summarized the conclusion effectively: "The *principal flaw* in the poll was that the sample was drawn primarily from higher income groups." This view was echoed across the polling and academic community; even to this day, sampling frame bias in the *Literary Digest* poll is a chestnut in modern political science (Lusinchi 2012, 27–30).

Quota sampling was well suited to solve sampling frame problems. And publicity savvy quota samplers George Gallup, Elmo Roper, and Archibald Crossley provided an appealing public face for the new method, presenting themselves as opening a window into the minds of Americans with samples only one-thousandth the size of the samples used by the *Literary Digest*.

Gallup, in particular, was a high-profile advocate of the new approach to polling. He had been using quota sampling to forecast elections since 1934 and was an outspoken critic of nonquota methods, especially the *Literary Digest*'s approach. In a July 1936 column, Gallup directly contradicted the *Literary Digest* and boldly predicted that Roosevelt would win 54 percent of the two-party vote (Converse 2009, 117). *Time* magazine put Gallup on its cover and provided breathless coverage of this new science of polling.

The key insight behind quota sampling was to set targets for categories of people to talk to, targets that were proportional to population sizes. This insight meshed naturally with the sampling explanation of the *Literary Digest*'s travails: If the sample had too many car– and phone-owning rich people, the solution is, of course, to not query so many owners of cars and phones. Pollsters using quota sampling identified strata of society and made sure to interview people in proportion to the size of these strata. As Gallup put it,

if 20 percent of the adults of the nation are engaged in farming, then obviously 20 percent of the total sample of the nation must consist of farmers. If 20 percent of all the adults of the country are between the ages of 21 and 29 years of age, then 20 percent of the total sample must come from this group. By following this procedure, every group and every area of the country can be properly represented in the sample. (Rogers 1949, 102)

Converse (2009, 93) provides a snapshot of how quota sampling worked by describing the approach of a market research firm in the 1920s. Interviewers were told to select respondents in specified proportions from four classes of citizens, categories that reflect the language and the biases of the time:

- Class A: Home of substantial wealth above the average in culture that has at least one servant. The essential point, however, in this class is that the persons interviewed shall be people of intelligence and discrimination.
- Class B: Comfortable middle-class homes, personally directed by intelligent women.

30 *Part I: Polling in Context*

- Class C: Industrial homes of skilled mechanics, mill operators, or petty trades people (no servants).
- Class D: Homes of unskilled laborers or in foreign districts where it is difficult for American ways to penetrate.

By the late 1930s, standard quota models targeted state, urban versus rural, gender, income, and political party, a fairly comprehensive list comparable to the factors used in modern weighting and related approaches today (Lusinchi 2012, 40).

Some critics were skeptical that the relatively small samples generated by Gallup and his peers were sufficient to characterize the entire country. An author in the *Literary Digest* itself wrote before the 1936 election that "we have not been able to find any resident of Michigan who has even been mailed a ballot by any of the (other) services. On the other hand, we do find at least one out of every twenty, in all walks of life, have received their *Literary Digest* ballots" (Moore 1995, 49).

The predictive power of quota sampling won many people over. Gallup's success in predicting the 1936 presidential results was followed with a stream of successes. In 1944, for example, Roper predicted Roosevelt would get 53.6 percent of the vote, remarkably close to the 53.8 percent Roosevelt actually received (Rogers 1949, 118). Gallup and Crossley's results were within 1.8 percentage points of the actual results.

Converse (2009, 394) captures the impact of these pollsters:

From their original success in predicting the 1936 election, they went on for ten years from one triumph to the next. Their names became household words, not only in this country but abroad. They became in some sense the vanguard of the infant social sciences and were seen by some as proof that the study of society, like the study of less diffuse and more controllable phenomena, could also be scientific.

Although quota sampling handily dispatched the hapless *Literary Digest* approach, it was far from perfect. In 1936, Gallup's polls indicated 54 percent of the public supported Roosevelt when Roosevelt actually received 61 percent of the two-party vote. There was also considerable error at the state level, with errors ranging as high as 28 percent for Arizona and 24 percent for Minnesota, with a median error of 12 percentage points (Converse 2009, 119). These state errors led Gallup to predict Roosevelt would get 292 electoral votes, which was substantially less than the 432 Roosevelt actually received (Katz 1944). And errors in later elections caught the attention of a congressional committee that called on Gallup to explain why his polling forecasts for Democrats were lower than the share they received in two-thirds of states in both 1940 and 1944 (Converse 2009, 207).

Quota sampling suffered from several weaknesses. Although Gallup and his peers liked to contrast their "scientific" approach to the "practical" approach of *Literary Digest* (Converse 2009, 148), quota sampling was not deeply scientific. The approach lacked foundations in theory and did not provide

The Story of Polling in $2\frac{1}{2}$ Fiascos 31

assessment of uncertainty (Converse 2009, 202). The results also depended heavily on decisions about the underlying population being sampled. Roper's quotas sought to match the U.S. Census data, while Gallup's quotas sought to match the voting population, which was, at that time, highly unrepresentative in terms of race, gender, and region due to laws and norms that prevented or hindered Black and Brown people and women from voting.[2]

Most problematic, however, was the extraordinary discretion left to interviewers. One Gallup interviewer described how he would fill his quota by

walk[ing] around town until I saw a WPA construction gang and I would get them on their lunch hour, three or four men sitting around eating their sandwiches and drinking their beer. I'd pull out my questionnaire and say "Do you approve or disapprove of a treaty with Germany?". Or whatever it was, and then I'd say, "How about you, and you, and you." (Converse 2009, 126)

The pitfalls of interviewer discretion were recognized at the time. Katz (1944, 472–3) argued that "the interviewer does not bring back randomly selected people to fill up his quotas. He characteristically tends to select the more articulate, better informed people who can answer his questions and with whom he finds it easier to establish rapport."[3] Rogers (1949, 135) pointedly framed this as a problem related to "the difficulties interviewers encounter in questioning the unshaven and sweaty." These tendencies manifested themselves quite baldly with regard to education: While the 1940 census indicated that about 10 percent of the population had at least some college education, almost 30 percent of respondents to a 1940 Gallup poll had that level of education (Berinsky 2006, 507).

The vast discretion left to quota sampling interviewers has led many modern researchers to reject the data produced by quota sampling.[4] We will revisit this point in Chapter 4 because some of the most innovative pollsters today have revived quota sampling.

The quota sampling era did not last long. In 1948, Democratic President Truman faced a strong Republican opponent in New York Governor Thomas Dewey. And, to make things virtually untenable for Truman, South Carolina Governor Strom Thurmond challenged Truman from the right on a pro-segregationist platform while former Vice President Henry Wallace challenged Truman from the left on a platform sympathetic to the Soviet Union.

---

[2] In 21 Gallup surveys in 1936–1937, men constituted 66 percent of the sample, at the direction of Gallup himself (Moore 1995, 62). African Americans constituted only 1.9 percent of Gallup samples, vastly unreflective of evidence from the 1930 and 1940 censuses that 10 percent of the population was African American (Igo 2007, 136). Berinsky (2006, 504) summarizes the specific procedures used by the major quota sampling organizations.

[3] Berinsky (2006, 507) notes that several studies in the 1940s found that respondents who were easily reached "differed from respondents who were contacted only after several attempts, even though the two groups had similar demographic characteristics."

[4] Berinsky (2006) reassesses this conclusion and provides weighting tools to make quota-sampled surveys more comparable to modern polling results.

32 *Part I: Polling in Context*

In the fall of 1948, the celebrity pollsters showed Dewey leading Truman by at least 10 percentage points (Moore 1995, 69). For example, in October 1948, Roper's surveys showed that Dewey had the support of 44.2 percent of voters while Truman only had the support of 31.4 percent of voters, leading *Fortune* magazine's editors to write

Barring a major political miracle, Governor Thomas E. Dewey will be elected the thirty-fourth President of the United States in November. Such is the overwhelming evidence of Elmo Roper's fifth pre-election survey in recent months... So decisive are the figures given here this month that *Fortune* and Mr. Roper, plan no further detailed reports on the change of opinion the forthcoming presidential campaign unless some development of outstanding importance occurs.

No development rose to their standard, and Roper and *Fortune* stuck with their prediction. Gallup was cocky as well. In the week before the 1948 election, he declared "we have never claimed infallibility, but next Tuesday the whole world will be able to see down to the last percentage point how good we are" (Rogers 1949, vi).

After a feisty campaign featuring Truman attacking a "do-nothing" Republican Congress, Truman won, leading to perhaps the most famous picture in American politics, that of a smiling (and victorious) Truman holding the *Chicago Daily News* with a banner headline declaring "Dewey Defeats Truman." And it wasn't particularly close, as Truman won 49.6 percent to Dewey's 45.1 percent, garnering 303 electoral votes.

Not only were the quota samplers' national numbers off, the state-level polling was inaccurate as well. Gallup gave Dewey a "substantial lead" in California, Illinois, Iowa, Ohio, and Wisconsin, all states won by Truman. Gallup also indicated Dewey led in nine other states where Truman won as well, leading Gallup's tally of electoral college votes to be off by 170 (Rogers 1949, 126).

The 1948 results were deeply embarrassing for the major pollsters: "Flushed with success and too over-confident to heed the portents of disaster, they plunged down together to public humiliation and ridicule" (Converse 2009, 394). And, as happened after the 1936 election, a "traumatic November episode" led to a period of deep reflection (Igo 2007, 153). The postmortems have a familiar feel to those who have lived through recent presidential elections:

The failure of the public opinion polls to predict correctly the outcome of the 1948 presidential election created wide confusing and misgivings about the reliability of polls... Reactions of experts ranged from condemnation for carelessness, unintentional bias, errors of judgment, and use of outmoded techniques to a determination to make use of this experience to enlarge our knowledge of political behavior and to improve survey methodology. After an initial period of shock and embarrassment, the main reactions of pollsters who forecast national and state elections was to initiate objective studies designed to find out what went wrong. (Mosteller et al. 1949, 1)

The Story of Polling in $2\frac{1}{2}$ Fiascos

Two themes emerged. On one side were George Gallup and others who saw the 1948 misfire not as a problem with the paradigm, but with the implementation of the methods. In particular, Gallup focused on the decision by pollsters to stop polling early and to treat undecided respondents as breaking in the same way earlier respondents had (Moore 1995, 71; Rogers 1949, 134).[5] In this view, the solution was simple: Continue quota sampling, but do so through Election Day. And, although it was awkward to emphasize the point too much, Gallup could be justified in saying that the 1948 polls really weren't that bad; after all, the size of error by Gallup in 1948 was only 5.3 percent which was smaller than the 7 percent error in Gallup's widely celebrated polls from 1936 (Moore 1995, 71). (The difference, of course, was that Gallup was right about the winner in 1936 and wrong in 1948.)

On the other side were those who blamed quota sampling itself. In particular, Mosteller et al. (1949, 115) concluded that the "major portion" or the errors could be linked to "the selection of respondents by interviewers." In particular, the samples underrepresented the least and most wealthy, the less educated and possibly rural voters (p. 304). It is not clear if this was differential nonresponse that could be re-weighted or nonignorable nonresponse. One sign that weighting would not be sufficient was that the errors were not fixed when Gallup redid his proportions so that his survey sample had same educational distribution as his estimated voting population. In addition, the biases against Democrats were recurring even as the pollsters adjusted their sampling, with election predictions in 1936 and 1944 also underestimating Democratic vote shares (Mosteller et al. 1949, 62; Delli Carpini 290).

2.3 RANDOM SAMPLING

The result of the polling catastrophe of 1948 was that many people were eager to move beyond the quota sampling. And, as in 1936, a competing paradigm had been developing in the shadows. This paradigm was random sampling.[6]

The idea behind random sampling was simple. Instead of letting interviewers choose whom to talk to, polling organization would preselect a random sample of people to talk to, thus reducing the chances that people with certain views would be more likely to make their way into samples. This approach was well suited to address both ignorable and nonignorable nonresponse because the pool of people they talked to would, in expectation, be indistinguishable from the overall population, with respect to everything – whether demographics or the very beliefs being surveyed. Random sampling was particularly well-suited to avoid the interviewer bias that may have led quota sampling

---

[5] History repeated itself in 2016 as late-deciding voters broke heavily for Donald Trump (Kennedy et al. 2018).

[6] Bethlehem (2009, 4) calls the rise of the random sampling paradigm an "intellectually violent revolution" akin to the rise of quantum physics.

techniques to overrepresent people who were more socially outgoing or who had more affinity with the interviewers.

The ideas underlying random sampling had been developing for some time. In 1906, Arthur Bowley established that means of random samples from a distribution are normally distributed (Bethlehem 2009, 12). In 1934, Jerzy Neyman established the superiority of random sampling over nonrandom sampling (Bethlehem 2009, 14). These techniques had been used in the Census Bureau and other government agencies since the late 1930s (Converse 2009; Berinsky 2006, 501). In 1944, Congress convened an expert committee to examine polling and advocated moving to random sampling (Moore 1995, 67). By 1952, Horvitz and Thompson had generalized the theory for constructing unbiased estimates based on random sampling (Bethlehem 2009, 16).

The main attraction of random sampling was its elegant and powerful theoretical foundation. Suppose that we take a random sample of n observations from a population of size N where each person in the population has an equal probability of being chosen.[7] We then calculate $\overline{Y}$, the average for some quantity of those observations. For example, suppose we are interested in the percent support for the incumbent president, which will be the average of a variable indicating whether someone intends to vote for the incumbent president.

We do not know whether the calculated mean from the sample will be the true mean in the population. But via the magic of the central limit theorem we know certain properties about the distribution of $\overline{Y}$. The central limit theorem states that if we take a sufficiently large random sample from a population, the distribution of the mean of these samples will be centered on the population mean and will be normally distributed. In other words, the central limit theorem allows us to characterize the distribution of $\overline{Y}$ if we were to repeatedly draw a random from the population and record and plot the value of $\overline{Y}$ each time.

Suppose, for example, that we use the computer to select a random sample of 2,000 people from a population of 5 million in which 52 percent of the people support the president. Now suppose that we do this a total of 50 times. Figure 2.1 shows a histogram of results for one such simulation. We see that in 4 of the samples, $\overline{Y}$ was between 0.49 and 0.50. Six samples produced $\overline{Y}$ values that were between 0.50 and 0.51, eleven samples produced $\overline{Y}$ values that were between 0.51 and 0.52, and so on.

Even with the small number of samples, we can see that random sampling is doing pretty well. We never observed a $\overline{Y}$ below 0.5 or above 0.55. In other words, a sample of 2,000 is giving us a decent picture of the actual percentage of people who support the president.

---

[7] We can generalize this to cases in which people have different probabilities of being chosen by using sampling weights. See, for example, Lohr (1999, 1030).

The Story of Polling in $2\frac{1}{2}$ Fiascos

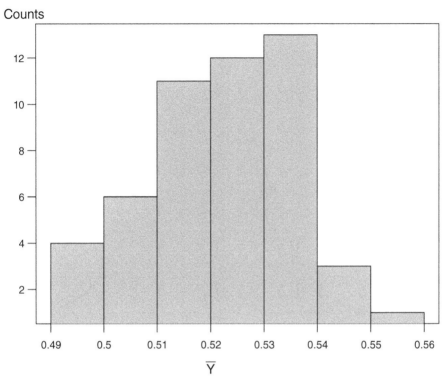

FIGURE 2.1 Distribution of the sample average of $\overline{Y}$ for a small number of samples, each of size 2,000

Now suppose that instead of taking 50 random samples, we take 10,000 different random samples, each one a sample of 2,000 people. We can again produce a histogram of these outcomes producing something like Figure 2.1. On the horizontal axis are possible values of $\overline{Y}$, and on the vertical axis is the relative probability of observing those values. The shape looks more regular, as the large number of samples led the samples that had slightly high values of $\overline{Y}$ to be offset by a similar number of samples that had a slightly low value of $\overline{Y}$.

The magic of statistical theory is the histogram we produce with our simulations can be generalized to a continuous probability density, which is the black curve in the figure. Mathematically, the density characterizes the relative probability of the values of $\overline{Y}$ we will observe as we take a very large number of samples from the full population.

There is a bit of a trick to thinking about survey samples in these statistical terms. For any single survey, we do not know the truth. But the statistical logic behind random sampling tells us the characteristics of polls in general. That is, if we have a random sample with a given sample size we know that the mean of that random sample will be "drawn" from a normal distribution like

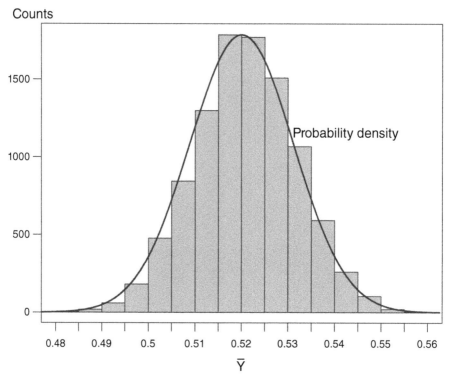

FIGURE 2.2 Distribution of the sample average of $\overline{Y}$ for large number of samples, each of size 2,000

the one traced by black line in Figure 2.2. We know that our random sample won't systematically produce an average that is above or below the population average, and based on the sample size we can characterize the probability that the average of our sample will be a given distance from the truth. This allows us to say a lot about the properties of our procedures, but it does not eliminate uncertainty. For any given poll, it is possible (albeit relatively unlikely) that we are rather far from the truth. In Figure 2.2, we see that it is still possible to produce an average of 0.55 or 0.49. These outcomes are relatively unlikely but definitely possible.

There are four remarkable features of the distribution of averages from a random sample. The first is that the middle of the sampling distribution is the true value of the parameter. That is, if the true mean in the population is 52 percent support for the president, then the mean of the sampling distribution is 52 percent as well. That does not imply, of course, that every sample will produce 52 percent support for the president; we can see in Figure 2.2 that there are nontrivial probabilities on a range of possible values of $\overline{Y}$. But we can say that we will not see a bias toward values that are too high or too low. For every probability that $\overline{Y}$ is a value that is too high, there is a corresponding and

The Story of Polling in $2\frac{1}{2}$ Fiascos

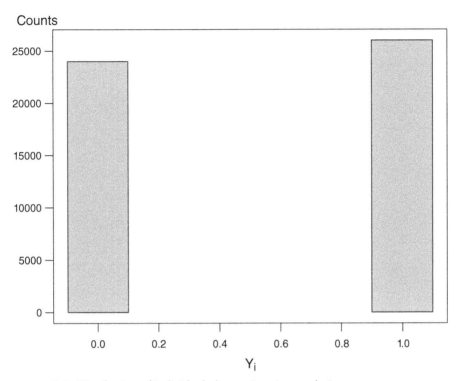

FIGURE 2.3 Distribution of individual observations in population

equal probability of seeing a value of $\overline{Y}$ that is equally too low. Formally, we can say that $\overline{Y}$ is an *unbiased* estimator of μ, the mean of the entire population.

Second, we not only know the middle of the $\overline{Y}$ distribution, but also know the shape of this distribution. It is the famous normal distribution, whose familiar bell-shaped curve has thrilled (and perhaps tortured) generations of students in statistics. Remarkably, the distribution of $\overline{Y}$ will be normal even if the distribution of Y_i in the population is not normal. Suppose, for example, we want to estimate support for the president in a particular state. Even if the underlying distribution of responses looks like Figure 2.3, the distribution of the *mean* of responses from samples will look like Figure 2.2.

Third, we not only know the middle and shape of the $\overline{Y}$ distribution, but also know its width. This is a simple function of number of observations in our sample: The bigger the sample, the narrower the distribution. (And just to be clear, we are now talking about the number of people in each sample, *not* the number of samples taken.)

Formally, we can say that the sample average based on n observations, $\overline{Y}_n$, is normally distributed with a mean equal to the mean in the population, μ, and a standard deviation equal to $\frac{\sigma}{\sqrt{n}}$. The parameter σ is the standard deviation of Y in the population; it measures how far observations are on average from

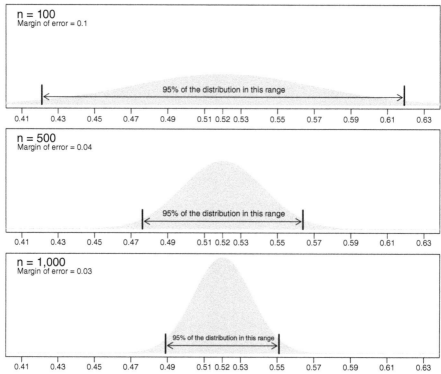

FIGURE 2.4 The distribution of the sample average of $\overline{Y}$ changes as the sample size changes

the mean. A high σ means that the values of Y are quite spread out, while a low σ means the values of Y tend to be closer to the average of Y. For continuous variables, the population variance is $\sigma = \sqrt{\sum_i \frac{(Y_i-\mu)^2}{N}}$. For dichotomous variables (such as a variable measuring whether someone approves of a politician or not), the population $\sigma = \sqrt{p(1-p)}$ where p is the probability in the population of whether Y equals 1; for more details, see Lohr (1999, 49).

Figure 2.4 shows the distribution of $\overline{Y}$ for three different sample sizes. In the top, the sample size is 100 and the distribution of sample means is quite broad. In this case, because the sample size is small, just a little bad luck can lead to a streak of supporters or opponents of the president appearing in the sample, leading to a sample mean that is quite far from the true sample mean. We can see that the relative probabilities of getting a value such as 0.43 or 0.61 are pretty high, even though the true percentage is 0.52.

The middle panel of Figure 2.4 shows the distribution of $\overline{Y}$ when the sample size is 500. The distribution of $\overline{Y}$ is now narrower as it is less likely to get a skewed sample. It's highly unlikely that we observe an average value of Y of 0.43 or 0.63, unlike the case where the sample size was 100. But values around

The Story of Polling in $2\frac{1}{2}$ Fiascos   39

0.47 or 0.57 are still relatively plausible. The bottom panel of Figure 2.4 shows the distribution of $\overline{Y}$ when the sample size is 1,000. The distribution of $\overline{Y}$ is even narrower as it is even less likely to get a skewed sample.

These examples illustrate several key ideas in random sampling. First, the random sample produces unbiased results even for small survey sizes. Note that all three of the panels in Figure 2.4 show probability distributions centered on the true value. Second, sampling distributions become more precise as the sample size increases; that is, the more people interviewed, the narrower will be the distribution of $\overline{Y}$. Third, the width of the sampling distribution depends on the *sample* size, not the *population* size. That means that a sample of 1,000 will produce estimates with the precision illustrated in the bottom panel, whether the target population is the 600,000 people living in Wyoming or the 39 million people living in California or the 1.4 billion living in China. The reason is that the random sample will give you the same probability of drawing any given person meaning that you'll get a selection of above average folks equally balanced in expectation by below average folks no matter what how big the underlying population is.[8]

Pollsters often characterize sampling uncertainty with the so-called margin of error. The margin of error characterizes the interval around the sample average that is likely to contain the population average. Pollsters typically focus on a 95 percent confidence interval which is approximated by $2 \times \frac{\sigma}{\sqrt{n}}$. If the margin of error is 4 percentage points (as in the middle panel of Figure 2.4), then we can say that if we fielded a survey 100 times, 95 of them would produce an average that is within 4 percentage points of the true mean (Mercer 1996). This is a useful measure of the precision of a sample, but is hardly perfect: For any given random sample, we cannot be sure that we have not just observed one of the five in hundred samples that is further than the margin of error from the true mean.

Figure 2.5 shows the margin of error for various sample sizes, assuming that the variable being measured is dichotomous with a probability of 0.5 in the population. Think of this as the margin of error when polling a very close election where half the population supports reelecting the incumbent. For small samples, the margin of error is around 10 percentage points, which is pretty

---

[8] We are assuming that the sample is a small percentage of the population and is drawn "with replacement" meaning that when we select the first person in the sample, we keep them in the pool so theoretically this person could be selected more than once. If the sample size is large relative to the population, one can add a so-called finite population correction which is multiplied times σ discussed earlier. This correction is $\sqrt{\frac{N-n}{N-1}}$ where N is the total population and n is the sample. If $n = N$, then we have observations from everyone in the population and the sampling variance must be zero. If n is very small relative to N, then $\sqrt{\frac{N-n}{N-1}} \sim 1$, which is the assumption we will use in this book. One can also consider sampling "without replacement" which occurs when person cannot be selected twice in a sample. For large populations, the probability of selecting someone twice is so small that the extra complexity added by ruling out such selection is not worth it. Lohr (1999, 37) does a good job discussing issues arising when sampling without replacement.

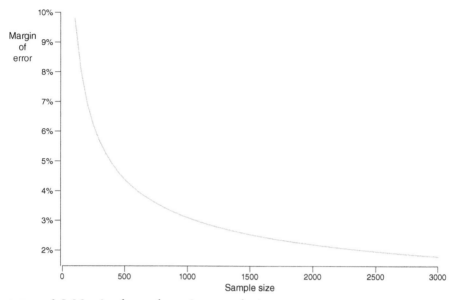

FIGURE 2.5 Margin of error for various sample sizes

high. The margin of error is 4.5 percentage points for $n = 500$, around 3 percentage points for $n = 1,000$ and around 2 percentage points for $n = 2,000$.

The intellectual power of random sampling was not, by itself, sufficient to propel it to dominance. There were two sources of resistance. The first was garden-variety ignorance. In particular, people resisted the idea "that the way a sample is selected is more important than the size of the sample" (Bethlehem 2009, 21). How, many asked, could a sample of only a few thousand people characterize the vastness American public opinion? For example, in 1952 the chair of the campaign of Ohio Senator, and candidate for the Republican presidential nomination, Robert Taft dismissed Gallup's results suggesting widespread support for Dwight Eisenhower as being "of the Ouija board variety. Gallup freely admits his poll is based on what he calls 'cross-section sampling' of somewhere between 1,500 and 3,000 people ... so even at the maximum Gallup polls average less than one voter in each county" (Igo 2007, 163).

While contemporary pollsters naturally accept that "the way a sample is selected is more important than the size of the sample" (Bethlehem 2009, 21), this was fairly nuanced insight when modern polling emerged in the form we now know it. And even in the modern era, this view has not penetrated the public's mind: In 1996, only 28 percent of respondents said a sample of 1,500 to 2,000 could accurately reflect the views of the nation's population (Erikson and Tedin 2001, 23).

A more substantial factor that held back the widespread adoption of random sampling was its cost. The "scientific" quota samplers were aware of

The Story of Polling in $2\frac{1}{2}$ Fiascos   41

random sampling, but balked at the challenge of devising a protocol that would identify the entire population and then enable speaking in person to a random subset of this population. Given the technology of the early and middle twentieth century, this was a daunting task (Igo 2007, 131). As Moore (1995, 67) relates, random sampling

was a much more complicated technique than quota sampling, because it required the pollster to specify precisely which houses, and which person within each household, would be included in the poll. To do that, the pollster first divided the state into numerous regions, from which several regions were selected use a "probability" method – such as every fifth region going from west to east and north to south. Within each region, several cities and towns would be selected. And within each city and town, several blocks would be selected. On each block, the interviewer would be instructed to visit every 'nth' house (every fifth or tenth house, for example). Within each household, the interviewer would have to select the respondent based on a table, issued by headquarters that took into account the number of males and females in the household and what their ages were.

Consider, for a moment, a pollster who wanted a national random sample in 1930. Even if they had access to a list of addresses for every adult in the country, how would they contact the randomly selected people? Phones were not a possibility because they were still far from universal. Their only options were mail or visiting each targeted individual, a daunting prospect today, which was likely even harder in the 1930s when travel was more difficult (Mosteller et al. 1949, 86, 117). Mail was slow. So, for many years, Gallup, Roper, and Crossley viewed the vast increase in costs associated with random sampling as too high to justify what they saw as only modest benefits of the technique (Moore 1995, 68; Mosteller et al. 1949, 303).

And the survey world was already concerned about nonresponse in random samples. Mosteller et al. (1949, 92, 306) discussed how identifying a random sample in Elmira, New York, for in-person visits was a nontrivial task. And even with this hard-won list, interviewers were unable to elicit responses from 20 percent of the people on the list. An 80 percent response rate today would make any pollster ecstatic, but at the time this raised some eyebrows for the deviation from true random sampling suggested by the nonresponse.

Technological and societal changes allowed random sampling to flourish. By the 1950s, the telephone had become nearly universal in American homes. This made random sample immensely more practical and cost-effective. Pollsters could simply randomly sample from a master list of phone numbers and call virtually anyone, anywhere in the country from a single location. And pollsters worried about unlisted phone numbers, and other inaccuracies on phone lists could simply call randomly dialed phone numbers, often geographically identifiable based on certain digits in the phone number.

Once pollsters could marry the theoretical power of random sampling with the practical ease of random sampling from phone lists, the Golden Age of Surveys commenced. Nonresponse rates were often under 10 percent

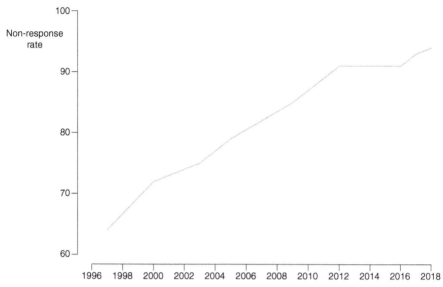
FIGURE 2.6 Nonresponse rates in political surveys

(Groves 2011, 863), and academic, government, and private organizations built impressive infrastructures that could crank out high-quality polling on virtually any topic.

Random sampling had a good run, but three factors have weakened it substantially. As we have seen, it has never been the case that response rates are 100 percent. But nonresponse has gone from worthy-of-note, to eyebrow raising to troubling to potentially devastating. Figure 2.6 shows the steady rise of nonresponse rates in the US since 1998. The polling community was nonplussed in the late 1990s when a clear majority of randomly selected potential respondents did not respond. Now we are in a hair-on-fire state as nonresponse rates are now over 94 percent for many political surveys (Kennedy and Hartig 2019; see also Dutwin and Lavrakas 2016). Nonresponse tends to be less severe in academic surveys, but is high and rising for them as well.

The declining response rate is not directly a source of problems. It is perfectly possible to have high nonresponse rates and highly accurate polling (Groves and Peytcheva 2008). After all, a US national poll with 2,000 randomly selected respondents could be considered as a survey in which 99.999 percent of the people have not responded. If the sample is truly random and everyone responds, this is a great poll, for the reasons discussed earlier.

The challenges created by nonresponse occur when respondents systematically differ from nonrespondents. If the differences can be completely explained by measurable demographics, weighting will solve the problem, as we shall see in Chapter 3. But if the nonresponse is nonignorable (meaning the likelihood of responding is related to the content of the survey response), not

The Story of Polling in $2\frac{1}{2}$ Fiascos 43

only do we have a problem, but the magnitude of the problem interacts with the degree of nonresponse as we shall see in Chapter 5.

The second factor weakening random sampling has been technological shifts and the behavioral changes accompanying them. We saw that in the early years of polling, random sampling initially could not quite get off the ground because random sampling for in-person visits was very costly, especially at a national scale. When telephones became nearly universal, however, calling random samples from phone lists or even randomly selected digits in a phone number made it remarkably cheap to contact randomly selected people.

This golden age was hostage to technology, however. As phones became more complicated, random sampling based on phones becomes more complicated. It is no longer the case that every family has a single landline. Many people have multiple phone numbers; others may be off-the-grid using other means of communication.[9]

These differences are behavioral as well. People answered the phone in the 1960s. There was no caller id, and any call could be from a family member or friend or other desirable interlocutor. People could – and did – decline to respond once they were on the phone, but at that point, one of the major impediments to response was already solved. Now, phones are cameras we use to text; responding to a call from an unknown phone number is unusual; honestly, you need to be pretty bored or pretty weird to do so regularly.

The third factor weakening random sampling has been simple: Polling has failed or, at a minimum, has been perceived to have failed. The irony of 2016 polling is that in many respects polls that year were accurate. In the lead up to the election virtually every poll showed Hillary Clinton ahead, usually by around 3 percentage points. And this was quite close to the result – she won the popular vote by around 2 percentage points, meaning that the polls were actually "among the most accurate in estimating the popular vote margin in U.S. elections since 1936" (Kennedy et al. 2018, 9).

The partial fiascos appeared at the state level. One problem that is no fault of polling methods is simply that there were not a lot of polls in some key battleground states, meaning that late-breaking trends toward Trump were hard to see (shades of 1948!). But the polls in the final days of the campaign consistently suggested that Clinton's lead in national polls would roll down to key states, showing her up by four points in Michigan and Pennsylvania and by six points in Wisconsin (Kennedy et al. 2018; Shepard 2016). Clinton even spent the last days of the campaign in places like Arizona, apparently

---

[9] Pollsters make great efforts to identify cellphone numbers for specified regions. For example, Washington Post (2020) reports that they used "a database of out-of-state cellphone numbers whose users are billed within the state along with landlines with in-state area codes and exchanges. The cell/landline allocation is proportional to the share of residents who mostly or exclusively use cellphones, per the most recent state estimates from the federal National Health Interview Survey."

trying to solidify her (perceived) lead in those states. In the end, she lost these key midwestern states narrowly; Clinton also lost by quite a bit in other states such as Iowa, Florida, North Carolina, and Arizona where polls suggested she was competitive.

After determined soul-searching in the polling community, a consensus emerged that the problems of 2016 were largely fixable: Pollsters need to poll at the state level right up to election day, weight by education, and refine their turnout models (Kennedy et al. 2018). The hope was that if pollsters did these things, all would be well. And, in 2018, things went great: Polling errors in the midterms were about as small as one could hope for (Silver 2018).

As we have already seen, reality slapped back in 2020. Despite the lessons learned in 2016, the United States came quite close in 2020 to a repeat of 2016. Biden led easily in national polls; he also led in state polls. On Election Day, Biden won a majority of votes nationally, as had Clinton. But, as with Clinton, many key states were substantially closer than polls would suggest. In Wisconsin, credible polls suggested Biden would win by double digits, when in fact, he just squeaked by. Trump's postelection lies, and shenanigans make it easy to overlook the fact that he would have won in the Electoral College if 40,000 votes shifted in a handful of states. Biden's comfortable polling leads at national and, more importantly, state levels were anything but. In 2016, we at least had the cold comfort of knowing that in strictly quantitative terms, the national polls were quite accurate.

Polling in 2020 was problematic for congressional races as well (Leonhardt 2020). Republican Senator Susan Collins from Maine won by almost 9 percentage points even though every poll from October onward recorded in the FiveThirtyEight polling aggregator had Collins losing, sometimes by as much as eight points. The North Carolina Senate race had more polls, and Republican Senator Thom Tillis of North Carolina trailed in the 10 final polls in the FiveThirtyEight polling aggregator, but won by almost 2 percentage points. In the House, major pollsters predicted the Democratic margin to be about double what it actually was (Jacobson 2022, 5).

The polling errors may have influenced the outcome (Leonhardt 2020). After the 2016 election, many worried that the poll-inspired confidence of the Clinton campaign in the "blue wall" in the Midwest may have led to complacency and poor decisions. In 2020, the Trump campaign pulled back from campaigning in Michigan and Wisconsin, states where polls said he had little chance, but where he was actually close to winning. Biden campaigned in Iowa and Ohio, states where polling indicated he could pull off a victory but where he lost by almost 10 points. At the congressional level, "Democrats poured money into races that may never have been winnable, like the South Carolina Senate race, while paying less attention to some of their House incumbents who party leaders wrongly thought were safe. The party ended up losing seats" (Leonhardt 2020).

The Story of Polling in $2\frac{1}{2}$ Fiascos   45

As with 2016, the fallout after the 2016 election was brutal. Leading pollsters noted that the polling errors gave the industry a "black eye" (Leonhardt 2020). David Wasserman of the Cook Political Report concluded that "district-level polling has rarely led us – or the parties and groups investing in House races – so astray" (Leonhardt 2020).

Leading pollsters and scholars from the American Association for Public Opinion Research (AAPOR) spent more than a year analyzing more than 2,800 polls for the 2020 election and found a grim reality (Clinton et al. 2021, 3; see also Panagopoulos 2021):

> The 2020 polls featured polling error of an unusual magnitude: It was the highest in 40 years for the national popular vote and the highest in at least 20 years for state-level estimates of the vote in presidential, senatorial, and gubernatorial contests. The polling error was much more likely to favor Biden over Trump. Among polls conducted in the last two weeks before the election, the average signed error on the vote margin was too favorable for Biden by 3.9 percentage points in the national polls and by 4.3 percentage points in statewide presidential polls. The overstatement of the Democratic-Republican margin in polls was larger on average in senatorial and gubernatorial races.

The AAPOR team paid considerable attention to nonresponse bias as a source of the 2020 polling errors. There are two ways in which nonresponse could be a problem. First, perhaps too many Democrats and too few Republicans responded to polls (Clinton et al. 2021, 5). Clearly, such a pattern of nonresponse would skew results toward Biden. However, this was not likely to be a primary source of error because the polls that re-weighted their samples to partisan benchmarks produced similar errors as those that did not (Clinton et al. 2021, 69). Second, there may have been nonignorable nonresponse. For example, the Republicans who responded to polls may have been less likely to support Trump than Republicans in the population, a possibility that is not unreasonable

> considering the decreasing trust in institutions and polls especially among Republicans … statements by Trump could have transformed survey participation into a political act whereby his strongest supporters chose not to respond to polls. If so, self-identified Republican voters who participated in polls may have been more likely to support Democrats than those who chose not to participate in polls. (Clinton et al. 2021, 5; see also Cox 2020, Cramer 2016 and Leonhardt 2020)

Democratic political consultant David Shor focuses on trust. It's hard to know what percent of people in the population believe that, in general, people can be trusted, but it seems that the percent of trusting people in survey samples runs higher than in the population. Specifically, Shor uses the General Social Survey (GSS) as a baseline. The GSS has a 70 percent response rate, and while this sample may well be biased, it is likely less biased than the political and commercial surveys used by campaigns and news outlets that have response rates of 5 percent or lower. In the GSS, only 30 percent of respondents say people can be trusted, but in a typical phone survey 50 percent of respondents say people can be trusted (Matthews 2020).

The interesting thing about trust is that its relationship to survey bias appears to be dynamic. As Shor tells it

It used to be that once you control for age and race and gender and education, that people who trusted their neighbors basically voted the same as people who didn't trust their neighbors. But then, starting in 2016, suddenly that shifted. If you look at white people without college education, high-trust non-college whites tended toward [Democrats], and low-trust non-college whites heavily turned against us. In 2016, we were polling this high-trust electorate, so we overestimated Clinton. These low-trust people still vote, even if they're not answering these phone surveys. (Matthews 2020)

2.4 CONCLUSION

Polling has ground through three paradigms over the last hundred years. The first two paradigms, large data and quota sampling, each failed when pollsters using these tools incorrectly predicted presidential elections. Their problems arose from nonresponse, some of which was ignorable and likely fixable with modern weighting techniques and some of which was likely nonignorable and therefore beyond the ken of modern weighting.

The random sampling paradigm solved these maladies and did so in a theoretically elegant manner. The key idea was that how one gathered a sample of respondents was more important than the size of the sample: As long as a sample is random, we can produce unbiased estimates of population averages. *And* we can even characterize our degree of confidence. And as if that wasn't enough, random sampling was cheap after telephones become standard in virtually every US household.

Almost 70 years into the random sampling era, the paradigm has begun to show its age. Changes in society have made it harder and harder to implement surveys according to the tenets of the paradigm. Most people are unlikely to respond to phone calls or other outreach. And identifying a random sample is complicated by the complex and evolving mix of technologies people use to communicate.

And the shockingly misleading state-level polls in 2016 and the near miss on state-level polls in 2020 have – as in 1936 and 1948 – raised serious doubts about the credibility and viability of survey practices. While it is clearly an exaggeration to say that polls are always wrong, good results in some races in some years are not enough: The *Literary Digest* had some good years, too, and that did not protect their approach over the long term. People in politics, certainly, but in other areas as well cannot ignore the objective failures of polling and therefore hunger for something better. To understand where we stand, Chapter 3 explores the key paradigmatic tweak of random sampling, the use of weighting to try to undo nonrandom patterns in nonresponse.

3

Weighting

An Appreciation and Critique

> Survey weighting is a mess.
>
> Andrew Gelman (2007)

The Golden Age of random sample-based polling was not perfect. Response rates were never 100 percent, and pollsters fretted about the how errors could sneak in (Mosteller et al. 1949; Groves and Lyberg 2010). Nonetheless, pollsters were confident that well-placed weighting could patch over many of the nonresponse problems. As nonresponse rates rose, however, weighting moved from patch to crutch and maybe something more (Peytchev 2013, 106).

Although weighting is widespread, it is far from simple. The process involves numerous steps involving many judgment calls as the *New York Times* illustrated brilliantly in 2016 (Cohn 2016). They gave four respected pollsters *identical* survey data about the 2016 presidential election race in Florida and asked them each to produce an estimate of where the race stood. To an outsider, this seems like a pointless exercise, perhaps akin asking four different people to add $7 + 4$.

But insiders, including the *New York Times*, knew better. They knew that every pollster does things differently, especially with regard to weighting. And the *Times* was not disappointed: The pollsters' answers ranged from Clinton up by 4 percent to Trump up by 1 percent. These are big differences! And given that Trump actually won Florida by 1.2 percentage points, it is possible that the results were not only highly varied, but they may have been biased as well, an unappealing prospect for those who want to believe in polls.

The upshot is that weighting is hard.[1] Some decisions relate to technique, and others relate to variable choice. None are completely straightforward, and some are highly fraught.

---

[1] A little shout-out to *New York Times* readers.

48   *Part I: Polling in Context*

And weighting does not guarantee accuracy. When comparing weighted results to known baselines, Tourangeau, Conrad, and Couper (2013) found that weighting removed up to 60 percent of bias. But the remaining bias was substantial, and weighting sometimes made estimates *less* accurate.

How things play out varies considerably across applications. Jacobson (2022, 10) assessed performance of several major polls during the 2020 presidential campaign. Weighting helped by lowering Biden's average predictive margin from 14.9 percentage points in the unweighted results to 9.6 percentage points in the weighted results. But even with weights, Biden's average predicted margin was more than double his actual margin.

The purpose of this chapter is to explain weighting in a manner that allows us to appreciate both the power and vulnerability of the technique and, by extension, other techniques that rely on similar assumptions. In other words, once we understand *how* weighting works, we will better understand *when* it works. The chapter opens by discussing weighting in general terms. The subsequent sections get more granular. Sections 3.2 and 3.3 cover widely used weighting techniques: Cell-weighting and raking. Section 3.4 covers variable selection, a topic that may well be more important than weighting technique. Section 3.5 covers the effect of weighting on precision, a topic that frequently gets lost in polling reporting.

This chapter mixes intuitive and somewhat technical descriptions of weighting. The technical details in Sections 3.2 and 3.3 can be skimmed by readers focused on the big picture how weighting works. For deeper dives into the technical aspect of weighting, see Lohr (1999), Dorofeev and Grant (2006), and Valliant, Dever, and Kreuter (2013).

3.1 THE BIG PICTURE

The problem weighting sets out to solve is that survey samples often have too many people from some groups and too few people from other groups. This is common in probabilistic polls and endemic in nonrandomly sampled internet polls. These imbalances can also occur by design. Researchers interested in specific groups – perhaps young people or Hispanics – oversample people from these groups to ensure that the sample contains enough information to make accurate claims about them, a process referred to as stratified sampling.

The imbalances will bias the sample averages if they are related to the outcome of interest. For example, if college graduates are more liberal, raw polling averages will likely be more liberal than the population when the proportion of college grads in the sample is higher than in the population. Weighting takes on this problem by giving more weight to the people in the "too few" category and less weight to people in the "too many" category.

The concept of weighting is so intuitive that many in the polling community take it for granted. We should not, however, lose sight of how audacious it is: Weighting essentially involves making up some data points and cutting others.

Weighting: An Appreciation and Critique

Imagine the conversation in which the first pollster to weight came up with the idea: "We were supposed to talk to 100 young men, but only heard from 50 of them? Umm ... let say we heard from 100." "And we were supposed to hear from 20 women with graduate degrees, but heard from 40? Let's make it 20."

Weighting is not only audacious, but also complicated. Pasek (2010, 1) notes

Survey weighting is a methodological black box. While survey research firms are often acutely aware of the large number of arbitrary decisions that go into the production of survey weights, they often provide researchers with a single [set] of weights that represent only one such set of decisions. Researchers have typically been removed from the process. While most practitioners have been taught to include weighted data in their analyses, few know where those weights come from or what kinds of decisions are involved.

Angrist and Pischke (2009, 91) expressed similar sentiments, noting

Few things are as confusing to applied researchers as the role of sample weights. Even now, 20 years post-Ph.D., we read the section of the Stata manual on weighting with some dismay. Weights can be used in a number of ways and how they are used may well matter for your results. Regrettably, however, the case for or against weighting is often less than clear-cut, as are the specifics of how weights should be programmed.

And, despite its importance and complexity, weighting goes unremarked surprisingly often. Many commercial and political polls refer to their weighting only in passing. In the academic world, weighting is discussed shockingly rarely: Franco, Malhotra, Simonovits, and Zigerell (2017) found that weighting wasn't even mentioned in approximately 75 percent of studies published in three top political science journals using online survey data sources (see also Mutz 2011).

TYPES OF NONRESPONSE   Before exploring approaches to weighting, it is useful to clarify two conceptual dimensions related to nonresponse. The first relates to the scale of nonresponse. An individual can provide no information whatsoever; this is "unit nonresponse" meaning that the "unit" (which is the bloodless term researchers sometimes use to refer to a person) did not respond at all. Or, an individual can respond to some, but not all questions. The lack of data for such an individual on specific questions is "item nonresponse."[2]

A second dimension of nonresponse relates to the source of the nonresponse. Ignorable nonresponse is, as we have seen, nonresponse that can be attributed to a factor or factors that we know about all the respondents and the general population. Typically, these factors are demographics such as age, region, gender, and education, all of which are well documented in Census data. The term

---

[2] Calculating nonresponse is not always straightforward. How should we count partially completed surveys? Do we know that the respondents who did not respond were even eligible for the poll? What if the phone number or address is not valid? Tourangeau and Plewes (2013, 11) and Groves et al. (2009, 184) explain various standards AAPOR has created to address these issues.

50   *Part I: Polling in Context*

TABLE 3.1 *Examples of different types of nonresponse*

	Ignorable (conditionally exogenous)	Nonignorable (endogenous)
Unit	People with less education do not respond to survey request	Trump supporters do not respond to political survey request
Item	Highly educated people do not answer income question	Racially conservative people skip questions about racism

ignorable is meant to suggest that once we model it, we do not have to worry about this kind of nonresponse as a source of bias. As we discussed in Chapter 1, ignorable nonresponse is not a great label. For some, it may be helpful to think of such nonresponse as "demographically based nonresponse" or, more precisely, "conditionally exogenous nonresponse."

Nonignorable nonresponse is nonresponse that occurs when an unmodeled factor that affects nonresponse also affects the outcome of interest. In academic parlance, we could also refer to nonignorable nonresponse as *endogenous* non-response if the decision to respond is "internal to" (meaning endogenous to) the process that also produces respondents' answers to the question being polled.

The distinction between ignorable and nonignorable nonresponse depends on context. If the decision to respond and the response are related only to factors that we have measured in the population and survey sample, then the nonresponse is ignorable because we can account for the factor. If the decision to respond and the response are related to factors that we have not measured in either or both of the population and survey sample, then the nonresponse is nonignorable because we cannot account for the factor. Suppose, for example, that education is literally the *only* attribute that affects response and that it also affects Y, our outcome of interest. If we have measured education in our sample and the population, nonresponse is ignorable. If we have not measured education, then we can't control education in our analysis and nonresponse is nonignorable.

Table 3.1 shows examples of unit and item nonresponse for a case in which we know the education levels of all potential respondents but do not know their presidential preferences or their views on race. Ignorable unit nonre-sponse would occur if, as is common, people with no college education are less likely to respond at all to a survey request. Ignorable item nonresponse would occur if, as is common, highly educated people (who tend to make more money) respond to polls at the same level of others but do not respond to specific questions about what their income level is. Nonignorable unit non-response would occur if, as many fear, people who supported Donald Trump for president were less likely to respond at all to a survey request. Nonignor-able item nonresponse would occur if, again, as many fear, people with racially

Weighting: An Appreciation and Critique 51

conservative views generally answered surveys at the same rate as others but declined to answer specific questions about race.

An important point is that nonignorable nonresponse is a question-level property. This is obviously true for item nonresponse for which the kinds of people who, for example, do not provide their income, are different than those who do. This is also true even for unit nonresponse because the unit nonresponse may have different relations across questions. It could be that the types of people who do not respond are more racially conservative, causing bias for race-related questions. But the types of people who do not respond may have the same tastes in ice cream, meaning there would be no nonignorable nonresponse bias for questions about mint chocolate chip ice cream on the same survey with the same respondents.

These distinctions are useful when thinking about weighting. First, the most common use of weights is to provide a single set for an entire survey, but one could imagine contexts in which one may wish to create weights for a specific item, given potential differences associated with item nonresponse and potential differences in the variables needed in the weights across question topics. Second, weighting is grounded on an assumption that nonresponse is ignorable. The methods discussed here assume that nothing outside the weighting model affects both response and the outcome of interest. We'll see an example of weighting that addresses nonignorable nonresponse in Chapter 9; suffice it to say that such models look very different than the standard weighting approaches we discuss in this chapter.

3.2 CELL-WEIGHTING

In order to help us understand the role weighting plays in contemporary polling, we describe in some detail two widely used algorithms for generating survey weights: Cell-weighting and raking. We begin with cell-weighting, a process in which the population is divided into groups and weights are chosen so that the proportion in the weighted sample matches the proportion in the population for each group. This is perhaps the most intuitive approach to weighting.

Let's begin with a simple example. Suppose we are polling feeling toward the Republican Party by sampling from a population that looks like Figure 3.1. The panel on the left shows that there are three young people and three old people. The young people aren't very keen on Republicans, with feeling thermometer ratings of 0, 20, and 40. The older folks feel good about the Republicans, with feeling thermometer ratings of 40, 60, and 80. The average rating of Republicans across the whole population is 40.

The middle panel highlights respondents to a survey with darker shading. One young person and all three old people responded. (Young people responding less is a thing, by the way.) The young person who responded rated the Republicans as 20. The average in the four-person survey sample is 50, which

52   *Part I: Polling in Context*

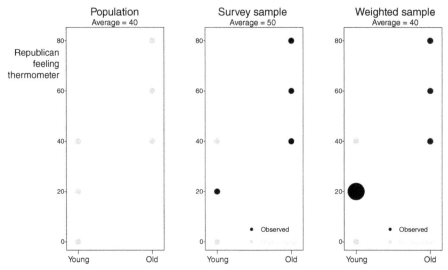

FIGURE 3.1 Hypothetical population and survey sample for which weighting works

is higher than it should be because there are too few young people, a group that feels cold toward the Republicans.

The trick of weighting is to devise a way the that sample is demographically representative of the population. Specifically, we calculate the weight on observations from demographic group g as $w_g = \frac{\text{PopulationPercent}_g}{\text{SamplePercent}_g}$. The values of weights are intuitive. If the population percent of a given group is twice as high as the sample percent of that group (meaning there are too few members of that group in the sample), the weight placed on that group will be 2. If the population percent of a group is half as high the sample percent (meaning there are too many members of that group in the sample), the weight placed on that group will be 0.5.

In the example depicted in the middle panel of Figure 3.1, young people are half the population, but only one-fourth of the sample. Hence, the weight on young people will be $\frac{0.5}{0.25} = 2$. Old people are half the population, but fully three-fourths of the sample, meaning that the weight on old people will be $\frac{0.5}{0.75} = 0.67$. The panel on the right of Figure 3.1 shows the observations with their circle sizes drawn proportionally to their weight. The young person gets a dot that is three times the size of the dots for the older people in order to make up for the fact that we have too few young people in our sample.

The weighted average is

$$\overline{Y}_{\text{weighted}} = \frac{\sum_i w_i Y_i}{\sum_i w_i} = \frac{\sum_i w_i Y_i}{n_{\text{sample}}} \tag{3.1}$$

Weighting: An Appreciation and Critique 53

where the difference from the sample average is that we sum over each observation of Y_i multiplied by its weight.[3]

The weighted average for the panel on the right is $\overline{Y}_{\text{weighted}} = \frac{\sum_i w_i Y_i}{n} = \frac{2 \times 20 + 0.67 \times (40 + 60 + 80)}{4} = 40$, which is, in this case the population average. At the cost of fairly modest calculations, this is quite an accomplishment. We have taken an unrepresentative sample from the population and nonetheless produced an accurate estimate of the population mean.

There are two useful features of cell-weighted samples. First, the proportions in the sample for each group will be the same as the proportions in the population. This is, of course, by design. (See the online appendix for the calculations.)

Second, the weighted averages will be the sum of the averages in each group weighted to the proportion of each group in the population (see, e.g., Berinsky 2006, 512):

$$\overline{Y}_{\text{weighted}} = \sum_{g=1}^{G} P_{g,\text{pop}} \overline{Y}_g$$

where $P_{g,\text{pop}}$ is the proportion of group g in the population (see online appendix for details).

While we don't necessarily need this equation to actually calculate weighted averages (we'll leave that to the computer), this is the equation we should use conceptually when thinking about weighting. It shows that cell-weighting is a process whereby we calculate the average of Y for each group and patch these averages together in proportion to the groups' population proportions. This is exactly what stratified samplers build into their research design and what weighters do as a matter of course. If the population averages are good for each group, then patching them together is super smart.

If, however, the averages within groups are wrong, the patched-together sum will be wrong. Hence, weighting solves unrepresentativeness *across* subgroups, but is vulnerable to unrepresentativeness *within* subgroups (Agiesta 2021).[4]

We should be clear, therefore, that weighting is not guaranteed to produce the population average. Notice that in Figure 3.1 the average value of

---

[3] The sum of the weights calculated in this manner is the sample size. To see this, note that $\sum_{i=1}^{n_{\text{sample}}} w_i = \sum_{i=1}^{n_{\text{sample}}} \frac{\frac{n_{g,\text{pop}}}{N}}{\frac{n_{g,\text{sample}}}{n_{\text{sample}}}}$. Because the weights are the same for all observations within a given group, we can rewrite this as $\sum_{g=1}^{G} n_{g,\text{sample}} \frac{\frac{n_{g,\text{pop}}}{N}}{\frac{n_{g,\text{sample}}}{n_{\text{sample}}}} = n_{\text{sample}} \sum_{g=1}^{G} \frac{n_{g,\text{pop}}}{N}$ which is n_{sample} because $\sum_{g=1}^{G} \frac{n_{g,\text{pop}}}{N} = 1$.

[4] Thinking in these terms also draws attention to the implications of weighting for precision; if some groups have only a small sample size, we would want to take that into account when we calculate the overall precision of our estimate. We discuss this topic in Section 3.5.

54   *Part I: Polling in Context*

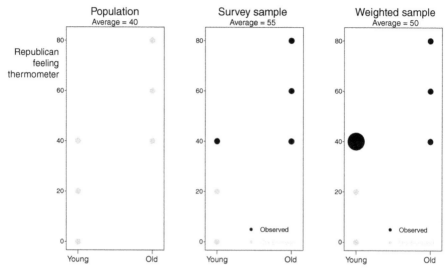

FIGURE 3.2 Hypothetical population and survey sample for which weighting does not work

Y observed in each group is equal to the average in the population. The average of young people is 20, and our sample average for young people was also 20. The average among old people was 60, and our sample average for old people was 60. This is ignorable nonresponse: Conditional on observed variables with known population distribution, there is no relationship between responding and the value of the response. That's a mouthful, but boils down to the average in each demographic category in the sample equaling the average in the population in each demographic category.

Suppose we violate this condition. Figure 3.2 shows the same population in the panel on the left. The sample depicted in the middle panel is different, however, as the youthful respondent in this case is the person who rates the Republicans at 40. The survey average is 55. The weights are the same, but since the observed values are different, the weighted average is $\overline{Y}_{weighted} = \frac{\sum_i w_i Y_i}{n} = \frac{2 \times 40 + 0.67 \times (40+60+80)}{4} = 50$, which is higher than the population average of 40. The reason weighting has not solved the problem is that response is nonignorable. Among young people, the proclivity to respond *is* related to the value of Y. Specifically, the young person who responds runs warmer toward the Republicans than young people in general.[5]

Weighting did not undo the damage from nonresponse in Figure 3.2, but at least it made things better compared to using the simple average from the

---

[5] A different problem arises if the only young person to respond was the one who rated the Republicans as 0. In this case, the weighted average would be too low: $\overline{Y}_{weighted} = \frac{\sum_i w_i Y_i}{n} = \frac{2 \times 0 + 0.67 \times (40+60+80)}{4} = 30.15$.

Weighting: An Appreciation and Critique

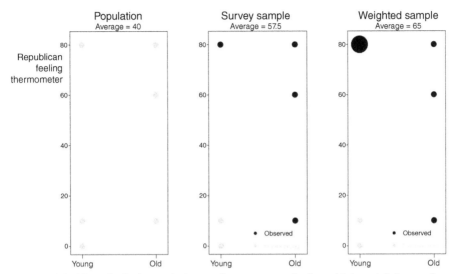

FIGURE 3.3 Hypothetical population and survey sample for which weighting makes things worse

survey sample. Sadly for weighting, however, this need not be the case. Figure 3.3 shows a case in which weighting is *worse* than doing nothing at all. The young people in the population rate the Republicans as 0, 10, 80; the old people rate the Republicans as 10, 60, and 80. The population average is 40. The sample in the middle Figure shows that among young people, only the young person most favorable to Republicans answered. All older people responded. The sample average was 57.5, which was much higher than the population average.

The panel on the right of Figure 3.3 shows what happens when this sample is weighted. As before, the young person gets a weight of 2 and the older people get weights of 0.67. The weighted average is $\frac{2 \times 80 + 0.67 \times (10+60+80)}{4} = 65$, which is not only far from the population average of 40, but is also *further* from the population average than the simple sample average of 57.5 depicted in the middle panel. In other words, weighting was worse than doing nothing.

This is a simple example. Is it an extreme example, unlikely in practice? Perhaps, but we saw in Chapter 1 that ANES weights increased their overestimate of Biden's lead in 2020 (see also Tourangeau, Conrad, and Couper 2013). Two more stories show how weighting can make things worse. Discussing his polling in Iowa in 2008, Goldstein (2016) recounts that

we didn't have enough 18 to 29-year-olds in our sample – and we knew how many there should be in the general population – so we up-weighted them. The results went from a slight Obama lead to a McCain lead. We thought: That doesn't make sense. How, if we gave more weight to the responses of the young people we did have, did it get better for McCain? We failed to consider that the 18 to 29-year-olds we did have, whom we had reached on their landlines, were living at home in Iowa with their parents and were more likely to be religious and conservative. We didn't have enough young people, but the ones we had were too Republican. So when we fixed their size, we made it worse; we amplified their impact. ...Usually we assume the problem is that group X is too small, but the actual problem may be that group X is too weird.

The polls in the United Kingdom in the mid-2010s careened about a bit, in no small part due to weighting challenges. In 2015, polls underestimated the Conservatives lead over Labor by 7 percentage points. Sturgis et al. (2018, 773) show evidence that this may have occurred because of biases within weighting cells; in particular, "it seems likely that a key reason that the polls underestimated the Conservative lead over Labour is that their sampling procedures systematically under-represented Conservative voters within.... Conservative supporting demographic groups." Feeling burned by having underestimated Conservative support in 2015, pollsters seem to have overcorrected in 2017 when they predicted that Conservatives would easily win the June national elections based on weighted survey results that showed Conservatives leading by 8.3 percent over Labor. On election day, Labor came within 2.3 percentage points of the Conservatives in the popular vote and to the surprise of most observers picked up 30 seats in parliament (Enten and Silver 2017). Ironically, weighting had made the results *less* accurate: In the unweighted results, the Conservative lead was 2.6 percent, which was remarkably close to the actual outcome.[6]

As a general matter, cell-weighting involves more than just the two demographic cells in our simple example. To provide a more realistic examples of what this looks like, we calculate cell weights for the 2012 American National Election Studies (ANES) and a 2016 online poll conducted by Lucid. The population values for each cell come from the Census Bureau's American Community Survey. The ANES survey is based on a probability sample with considerable effort made to contact each person in their random sample. The Lucid poll is a nonprobability survey of an internet sample of respondents. Both polls had around 5,900 observations.

We create cells based on

- three categories of age (younger than 40, between 41 and 65, and older than 65),
- two categories of education (people with and without college degrees),
- four categories of race/ethnicity (White, Black, Other, and Hispanic), and
- two categories of gender (female and male).

The total number of cells is $3 \times 2 \times 4 \times 2 = 48$. For each of these categories, we calculate the proportion in the population and the sample and create a

---

[6] Gittelman et al. (2015) had similar experiences in a marketing context. Of the 17 nonprobability samples they assessed against known benchmarks, demographic weights reduced bias in five while demographic weights *increased* bias in eight.

Weighting: An Appreciation and Critique 57

weight which is the population proportion divided by the sample proportion. Once we have this information, cell-weighting is simple. Observations in each cell are weighted by the ratio of the proportion of the population in that cell to the proportion of the sample in that cell.

Table 3.2 shows selected demographic groups that were underrepresented in at least one of the two survey samples sorted from highest to lowest population proportions. The top line shows young, noncollege White men. They constitute 8 percent of the population but only 4.9 percent of the ANES sample and 2.9 percent of the Lucid sample, leading to weights of 1.62 and 2.73 for the ANES and Lucid data, respectively. The second line shows young, noncollege White women. They constitute 7 percent of the population and only 4.8 percent of the ANES sample. They are actually overrepresented in the Lucid sample, constituting 9.2 percent of that sample.

The bottom four lines show information on noncollege educated young and middle-aged Black and Hispanic men. In the ANES data, they tend to be *overrepresented* as their ANES proportions equal or exceed their population proportions. In the Lucid data, on the other hand, these groups are decidedly underrepresented. For example, middle-aged Hispanic men without college degrees constitute 1.6 percent of the population, but only 0.5 percent of the Lucid sampling, meaning that men in this category are weighted 3.56 times in the cell-weighted Lucid sample.

It's a good exercise to step back and appreciate what is happening here. In the ANES survey, there were 284 young White men with no college degrees in the sample, which is substantially short of the $284 \times 1.66 = 471$ that we would observe if young White men with no college degrees answered the survey in proportion to their presence in the population. The imbalance is even clearer in the Lucid survey where there were 175 young White men with no college degrees in the sample, which is substantially short of the $175 \times 2.73 = 477$ that we would observe if young White men with no college degrees answered the survey in proportion to their presence in the population.

Weighting will lead us to lean heavily on the young White men without college degrees in our sample. If these men are a random sample of all such young men, we'll undo bias caused by having too few of them in our sample. If, however, the young White men with no college degrees in our samples are themselves somehow distinctive – perhaps they are more politically aware or more socially trusting, for example – then placing extra weight on their answers could push us *further* from the truth than not weighting.

Table 3.3 shows selected demographic groups that were overrepresented in at least one of the two survey samples sorted from highest to lowest population proportions. College grads tend to be overrepresented, even as there is variation across polls within this category based on the other demographic characteristics. Older White men and women with college degrees are slightly overrepresented in the ANES sample but very overrepresented in the Lucid sample. Older White men with college degrees are 3.4 percent of population

TABLE 3.2 *Selected groups underrepresented in at least one sample*

Age	College grad	Race/ethnicity	Gender	Pop. pct	ANES			Lucid		
					n	Pct	Weight	n	Pct	Weight
Young	No	White	Male	8.0	284	4.9	1.62	175	2.9	2.73
Young	No	White	Female	7.0	277	4.8	1.46	550	9.2	0.76
Young	No	Hispanic	Male	2.8	186	3.2	0.86	64	1.1	2.59
Young	No	Black	Male	2.0	115	2.0	1.0	42	0.7	2.84
Middle	No	Black	Male	1.6	137	2.4	0.66	29	0.5	3.21
Middle	No	Hispanic	Male	1.6	118	2.0	0.79	27	0.5	3.56

TABLE 3.3 *Selected groups overrepresented in at least one sample*

Age	College grad	Race/ethnicity	Gender	Pop. pct	ANES			Lucid		
					n	Pct	Weight	n	Pct	Weight
Old	Yes	White	Male	3.4	218	3.8	0.9	422	7.1	0.48
Old	Yes	White	Female	2.7	165	2.9	0.96	335	5.6	0.49
Young	Yes	Hispanic	Female	0.4	42	0.7	0.6	56	0.9	0.46
Young	Yes	Hispanic	Male	0.3	36	0.6	0.5	51	0.9	0.36
Middle	Yes	Black	Male	0.3	46	0.8	0.37	14	0.2	1.26
Middle	Yes	Hispanic	Male	0.3	36	0.6	0.45	17	0.3	0.99

but more than double that in the Lucid sample, meaning their cell weights in that sample are 0.49. Middle-aged Black men with college degrees are 0.3 percent of the population, but 0.8 percent of the ANES sample, meaning that cell-weighting will put a weight of 0.37 on each individual in that group. Meanwhile, middle-aged Black men with college degrees are underrepresented in the Lucid sample, meaning they will get extra weight in the Lucid sample.

The good news is that cell-weighting takes the edge off of the disproportionality of response. Not enough people without a college education? Cell-weighting bumps up our effective sample in that category. Too many people with college education? Cell-weighting effectively reduces the numbers of such individuals in the sample. The result is that our weighted sample will have proportions equal to the population proportions.

The bad news is that the limitations of the method are abundantly clear. We see that the number of observations in some cells is very small. Looking at Table 3.3, we see, for example, that there were only 14 middle-aged college educated Black men in the Lucid sample. We know that estimating any quantity will be less accurate when we have only a few people and many of the cells could therefore be quite imprecisely estimated.

Equally noteworthy is how coarse our categories are. Could there be differences within our rather broad education categories? That is, could it be that people with some college and those who did not graduate from high school are systematically different? In our example, we lumped both of those groups into the noncollege group. And categories for race and ethnicity are especially hard to accept. The "other" category contains a multitude of different groups. A substantial range of politically relevant backgrounds are subsumed in the Hispanic category as well; people with Cuban, Puerto Rican, Mexican, and other backgrounds often have different political attitudes. This issue arises in polling in Florida, in particular where political pros know that Cuban–Americans often have different views that other respondents classified as Hispanic.

One solution to the coarseness of our cell categories is to use more fine-grained groupings. This runs into data limitations quite quickly, however. Suppose, for example, that we thought the following demographic breakdown was attractive:

1. Age – six categories (under 25, 25 to 34, 35 to 44, 45 to 54, 55 to 64, and 65 and over).
2. Region – five categories (Northeast, South, Midwest, Mountain, and West).
3. Gender – two categories (female and male).
4. Education – five categories (less than high school, high school, some college, college, graduate school).
5. Income – five categories (from low to high).
6. Race – five categories (Asian, Black, Hispanic, Non-Hispanic White, and Other).

Weighting: An Appreciation and Critique 61

Cell-weighting based on these demographic categories would mean that we would have $6 \times 5 \times 2 \times 5 \times 5 \times 5 = 7,500$ cells. If we had a survey with 2,000 responses, it is literally impossible to have a single respondent in every cell, let alone the multiple respondents in cells that we would want. And this overly ambitious cell-grouping may not even capture other subgroupings that are relevant. A White person with no college living in Philadelphia may, on average, have quite different views than a White person with no college living in a small town in rural Pennsylvania. Someone with a job may be different than someone looking for work. Being married, having kids, attending church, being a regular voter ... the list of potential characteristics that one might want to weight for is extensive.

This means that groupings will need to be merged, a solution that is practical, but undermines the attractiveness of the cell-weighting approach. Lohr (1999) recommends devising the cell-weighting protocol to ensure that each call has at least 20 observations in the survey sample. For a survey with 2,000 respondents, this means we would have at most 100 cells, and probably many fewer such as we had in our cell-weighting described in Tables 3.2 and 3.3.

A second weakness of cell-weighting is that it can lead to weights that are very high or very low. This problem is not unique to cell-weighting, but arises regularly. A striking example occurred in a panel survey conducted by the *Los Angeles Times* during the 2016 US presidential campaign. The *Los Angeles Times* was getting very few responses from young Black men, meaning that any young Black man that did answer would be treated as more than one respondent. The approach got a bit out of hand though as one young man was weighted "30 times more than the average respondent, and as much as 300 times more than the least-weighted respondent" (Cohn 2016). The consequences of the weighting were jarring, as the large weight placed on this young man (who happened to support Trump) was "enough to put Mr. Trump in double digits of support among Black voters [and to] improve Mr. Trump's margin by 1 point" in the national survey.

Many pollsters avoid such an outcome by trimming their weights which involves placing minimum and maximum values on weights. Means from trimmed weights will not be as close to population averages as with untrimmed weights, but the benefit is that no single observation will be given very large (or very small) weight.

3.3 RAKING

Raking is an alternative weighting technique that proceeds on a variable-by-variable basis. It is a relatively simple algorithm, and it typically allows for more variables than cell-weighting. It is used widely and has a solid track record. Dutwin and Buskirk (2017) found that raking performs as well as other weighting methods (see also Mercer, Lau and Kennedy 2018, 4).

The term raking refers to the fact that the method involves iteratively smoothing out imbalances on one variable at a time. The raking technique involves smoothing ("raking") the data by each variable in turn, repeating until the data are representative in terms of the marginal distributions for all variables.

The advantage of raking is that it enables researchers to proceed through a potentially large list of variables without worrying about cells that have very few or even no observations. The process may require many steps, but can be expected to converge to sensible weights. Berinsky (2006, 513) and Little and Wu (1991) outline formal algorithms for raking.

To see how raking works, we will rake the Lucid data based on the college education and gender variables used above. The Lucid is very heavily skewed toward college graduates and women. College grads are only 27 percent of the population, but 56 percent of the Lucid sample. Women are 52 percent of the population, but 65 percent of the Lucid sample.

Raking involves iteratively adjusting the proportions for each variable. First, we re-weight the data to fix the education imbalance. We'll see that is easy to do, but doing so will of course not fix our gender proportions. So, given what we did to fix education, we then calculate weights that fix the gender proportions. But these new weights may throw off our education balance. So we re-weight the data for education in light of the weights on gender. As we iterate back and forth across these variables, eventually we'll get to weights that produce weighted data that have the correct proportions for both education and gender. We'll show the first two iterations manually, but in practice, one would likely use an automated package such as the "anesrake" package (Pasek 2018).

Based on the calculations in Table 3.4, we implement weights in the first round of raking that set the education proportions to equal the population proportions. In our case, we multiply the sample sizes in the noncollege educated row (the top row) by $\frac{0.73}{0.56} = 1.3$ and we multiply the sample sizes in the college-educated row (the second row) by $\frac{0.27}{0.44} = 0.62$. This step allows us to undo the substantial imbalance in the sample toward college graduates. This produces weighted sample sizes reported in Table 3.5.

We have fixed the education proportions, but the gender proportions in Table 3.5 are still way off, with a much higher proportion of women in the sample than in the population. Therefore, we multiply the columns by the values needed to align gender. Specifically, we multiply the sample sizes in the women's column by $\frac{0.52}{0.67} = 0.78$ and we multiply the sample sizes in the men's column by $\frac{0.48}{0.33} = 1.45$. The result is the weighted sample size reflected in Table 3.6.

We are now getting close to the population averages for both variables. The marginal distributions for gender are correct, and the marginal distributions for education are close to the population marginals. To get even closer, we repeat the process of raking the rows and the columns until we get within some prespecified margin of the actual population.

TABLE 3.4 *Distributions in Lucid sample and population*

| | Women | Men | Proportions | |
			Sample	Population
Noncollege	2,343	1,015	$\dfrac{2,343+1,015}{5,970}=0.56$	0.73
College	1,528	1,084	$\dfrac{1,528+1,084}{5,970}=0.44$	0.27
Sample proportion	$\dfrac{2,343+1,528}{5,970}=0.65$	$\dfrac{1,015+1,084}{5,970}=0.35$		
Population proportion	0.52	0.48		

TABLE 3.5 *Distributions after first round of raking*

	Women	Men	Proportions	
			Sample	Population
Noncollege	$2,343 \times 1.3 = 3,046$	$1,015 \times 1.3 = 1,320$	$\dfrac{3,046 + 1,320}{5,970} = 0.73$	0.73
College	$1,528 \times 0.62 = 947$	$1,084 \times 0.62 = 672$	$\dfrac{947 + 672}{5,970} = 0.27$	0.27
Sample proportion	$\dfrac{3,046 + 947}{5,970} = 0.67$	$\dfrac{1,320 + 672}{5,970} = 0.33$		
Population proportion	0.52	0.48		

TABLE 3.6 *Distributions after second round of raking*

| | Women | Men | Proportions | |
			Sample	Population
Noncollege	$3,046 \times 0.78 = 2,376$	$1,320 \times 1.44 = 1,901$	$\dfrac{2,376 + 1,901}{5,970} = 0.72$	0.73
College	$947 \times 0.78 = 739$	$672 \times 1.44 = 968$	$\dfrac{739 + 968}{5,970} = 0.28$	0.27
Sample proportion	$\dfrac{2,376 + 739}{5,970} = 0.52$	$\dfrac{1,901 + 968}{5,970} = 0.48$		
Population proportion	0.52	0.48		

66 *Part I: Polling in Context*

TABLE 3.7 *Raking weights after two steps for Lucid sample*

	Women	Men
Noncollege	$1.30 \times 0.78 = 1.02$	$1.30 \times 1.44 = 1.87$
College	$0.62 \times 0.78 = 0.48$	$0.62 \times 1.44 = 0.89$

If we keep track of the values we have multiplied the rows and columns by, we end up with raking weights as depicted in Table 3.7. Women without college degrees are given weights close to 1, while noncollege men are given very substantial weights of 1.92, which makes sense given that the Lucid sample underrepresented both men and noncollege graduates. Women with college degrees are substantially underweighted, and men with college degrees are slightly underweighted. The resulting weighted sample will have the same distributions as the population with respect to both gender and college education.

Raking has two weaknesses. First, raking disregards any interactions among the variables (Dutwin and Buskirk 2017). For example, when raking by gender, the weights on observations in all education categories are bumped up or down by the same proportion depending on gender. For example in going from Table 3.4 to Table 3.5, we multiplied both the college and noncollege rows for men by one number and for women by another number. Doing so could suppress potentially real differences within education group by gender. Such concerns are real in many practical circumstances. Among people over 75, for example, women are much more numerous than men due to the fact that men tend to die at a younger age (Pasek 2010, 4) so if we were raking by age we could wrongly boost both men and women when perhaps only women needed boosting given their higher proportions at older ages. When raking by race and gender, one may end up increasing weights for all people of a given race up or down even though men and women within a given racial category may be quite different on average (Berinsky 2006, 514). Ackerman (2016) shows that race and age interacted strongly in the Lucid data: 91 percent of their respondents over 65 years old were White, while only 64 percent of their respondents under 35 were White. Raking by race would adjust all age categories by the same amount, which does not match the diversity of ages with racial categories.[7]

Table 3.8 shows the proportions for each group in the population and the raking-weighted sample. These values are reasonably close, but not exact as they would be with cell-weighting. Specifically, the raking-weighted sample has more noncollege women and college-educated men. The disparities are not big, but in other contexts could be larger and could lead to weighted sample

---

[7] See additional discussion in Dorofeev and Grant (2006, 58). One can deal with this problem by creating raking groups based on joint characteristics such as age and gender.

Weighting: An Appreciation and Critique

TABLE 3.8 *Group proportions in population and raking-weighted Lucid sample*

	Population		Raking-weighted sample	
	Women	Men	Women	Men
Noncollege	0.38	0.35	0.40	0.33
College	0.14	0.13	0.12	0.16

values that poorly reflect population values if groups within rows or columns have distinctive views.

Second, as with cell-weighting (and any other weighting technique) it is possible that some weights are very high or very small. Such weights are necessary to produce the right descriptive statistics for the sample, but are nonetheless unsettling. Trimming weights to be above some minimum and below some maximum eases the concern about giving any observation too much or too little weight, but produces results that are not as closely aligned with the target population as untrimmed weights.[8]

3.4 VARIABLE SELECTION

An important and tricky step in the weighting process is deciding which variables to use in the weighting algorithm. This might even be the most important decision in the weighting process. Mercer, Lau, and Kennedy (2018, 4) compared weighting and other adjustments for questions where the population values were known from high-quality federal surveys and concluded that "choosing the right variables for weighting is more important than choosing the right statistical method." They found that while weighting techniques tended not to matter much, including more politically oriented variables tended to reduce bias substantially. Despite the importance of the matter, "few texts, however, provide much concrete guidance on how exactly to select [weighting] variables" (Caughey et al. 2020, 8).

When selecting variables, we should begin with the three criteria of a good weighting variable (Caughey et al. 2020, 19):

---

[8] There is also an unsettling possibility that raking weights may be negative (Dorofeev and Grant 2006, 57). This issue is rare and can be ameliorated by trimming the weights at some minimum above zero with the cost, as usual with trimming, being that the weighted marginal distributions will not match the population as closely as they could with untrimmed weights. This will induce the weighted sample to be at least mildly unreflective of the target population. A deeper question is what to make of a technique that could potentially produce negative weights as such weights lead us to infer certain respondents said the *opposite* of what they actually said. It's one thing for weights to make up people to fill in demographic gaps. It seems to be quite another thing to flip people's answers.

68   *Part I: Polling in Context*

1. The variable predicts response probability.
2. The variable predicts Y.
3. The distribution of the variable in the population is known.

To see why these criteria matter, consider what happens when each one is not satisfied. Consider first a variable that does not affect selection and does affect opinion. For example, suppose that a person's region does not predict whether they are more likely to respond, but does predict their response. Recall that weights are a ratio of the proportion of people for a given category in the population to the proportion of people in that category in the sample. If these groups' proportions are the same in the population and sample, then the weights will all equal one. Those ain't weights. At that point, the fact that opinions vary across regions is irrelevant.

Next, consider a potential weighting variable that predicts response probability but does not predict Y, the outcome of interest. Suppose, for example, that we are analyzing survey data that came from a phone-based survey that was much easier for right-handed people to fill out. Suppose also that the political views of right-handed people are not systematically different than left-handed people. Our sample will be crawling with righties, but it will not lead us astray as their views will be representative of the whole population. Weighting by handedness will produce a sample with the correct proportion of right- and left-handed people but will not change our estimate of $\overline{Y}$ because the respondents we weight up have on average the same views as the respondents we weight down. And not only will including handedness not avoid bias, but also it will likely reduce the precision of the estimate (Little and Vartivarian 2005). (We'll come back to how weighting affects precision in Section 3.5.)

The fact that a weighting variable needs to predict Y introduces a wrinkle that is usually ignored in weighting approaches. For any given poll, there are multiple variables of interest (multiple "Y"s). A variable that may predict one response (such as presidential preferences) may not predict another response (such as intention to turnout). Hence, if we really want to do weighting right, we should create weights targeted to each outcome of interest. Pollsters do not do this and instead rely on a single all-purpose weight provided by the survey vendor. This may be fine in general, but should be recognized as a convenience rather than a theoretically motivated choice (Caughey et al. 2020, 19).

The third criterion for a weighting variable is that we know the distribution of the variable in the population. Suppose we have identified a variable that predicts response and outcome, but for which we lack a population-level benchmark. We simply can't proceed as the cell weights and raking procedures do not get off the ground without benchmarks as the weights are literally built using population-level information.

Although this third criterion is easily satisfied for many demographic attributes such as age, gender, race, education, and income by region, it is actually a tricky criterion. When polling election outcomes, for example, this

Weighting: An Appreciation and Critique

criterion is hard to satisfy. Yes, we may know the demographic attributes of a population in any given region reasonably well, but do we know the demographic breakdown of *voters* by region? For example, the Lucid poll described earlier weighted results to the US population, which is standard practice. But do we really expect the electorate to match the population? Exit polls (as flawed as they are) suggested that the electorate may have differed substantially from the population in 2016 on race and other characteristics (Ackerman 2020).

Getting the right polling benchmarks even for relatively straightforward weighting variables such as demographics is a long-standing challenge in polling (Caughey et al. 2020; Bradley 2022). We saw in Chapter 2, for example, how the quota samplers of the 1930s used markedly different benchmarks, with Roper seeking to match population data and Gallup seeking to match the voting population, targets that were quite different given the systematic exclusion of non-whites from voting.

And even if we accept population-level benchmarks as the right target, there will be many factors that affect both response and survey outcomes that are not reliably measured in the population. Religious people, trusting people, outgoing people, and many other kinds of people may be distinctive both in their willingness to respond and how they respond. Often we will not be able to benchmark these attributes in ways needed for weighting.

Debates about specific potential weighting variables highlight the complexities of variable selection in weighting. The most famous example, at least in recent years, is the question of whether to weight by education. Given our discussion earlier, it seems natural to weight be education given strong relationships to response and to a host of possible polling questions, from politics to Covid. In addition, education data are available for national and many subnational areas.

The aftermath of the state-level presidential polling fiasco of 2016 provides a case study of the promise and reality of fixing polling with good covariates. As we saw in Chapter 2, a consensus finding in postmortems was that

many polls – especially at the state level – did not adjust their weights to correct for the over-representation of college graduates in their surveys. The concern was that voters split fairly dramatically by education levels in their support for Donald Trump and surveys tended to get disproportionately more white respondents with college degrees, thereby skewing the samples against Trump. (Kennedy et al. 2018)

The disparities in response related to education can be huge. (We'll see an example in Figure 4.2 in Chapter 4.) And yet, many pollsters had not weighted by education.

The hope was that after 2016 every pollster would weight by education, thereby undoing the overrepresentation of college grads, and, *voila*, polls would be ok again. The generally accurate polls of 2018 validated this hope. The near-catastrophe of 2020 polling crushed the dream, however, as polling again underestimated support for Donald Trump, especially in key states. In the final two weeks of the 2020 campaign, there were 317 state-level presidential polls that described their weighting; virtually, all of them (92 percent) accounted for education (Clinton et al. 2021, 4). And yet, as we have seen, 2020 state-level polls were among the worst in modern presidential polling history. And, some of least accurate polls weighted on education. A *Washington Post*/ABC News poll of Wisconsin in late October 2020 weighted their results based on education, phone type, gender, region, age, and race. Their results suggested that Joe Biden was up by 17 percentage points over Donald Trump (*Washington Post* 2020). To say that they were off hardly does justice to what happened: Biden only beat Trump by 0.6 percentage points in Wisconsin.

Other potential weighting variables are plausible, but much debated. Region within states may be important because people living in urban, suburban, exurban, and rural areas may have distinctive views. Consider a hypothetical noncollege White respondent in Pennsylvania. Picture that person as living in the middle of Philadelphia, and then, picture them living in a small rural town. Our expectations for these scenarios are quite different, and if the respondent pool leaned toward people living in urban or rural areas, we may need to weight on this variable. Regional weighting may be part of the secret sauce of at least one pollster; *Des Moines Register* pollster Ann Selzer has had remarkable success polling Iowa, sometimes producing distinctive – and correct! – poll results for the state. One of her techniques is to weight by congressional district in the state, a tool that ensures that the various regions are balanced in survey samples.

As pollsters searched for better weights, they faced important constraints. First, they need to have population-level data, something that is often difficult as we move away from the standard demographics. And this problem is harder than it sounds: The "population" of interest for campaign polling at least is the voting electorate. Even if we have great Census or registration data for weights, we will never have definitive data on the population that actually votes until (perhaps!) after the election.

The challenges of weighting become clear as we explore some of the promising – but not perfect – alternatives that pollsters have explored. A particularly controversial weighting variable is party identification. The influence of partisan identification on political views – and likely other views – is undeniable. It is also plausible that party identification could influence propensity to respond in at least two respects. First, the attribute could be related to underlying propensities to respond to polls. Many suspect that Democrats may be more socially trusting, which could make them more likely to respond to polls. Or, during Covid, it was possible that Democrats tended to be more likely to have jobs they could do from home, which made them easier prey for pollsters than Republicans who may have been more likely to be working in person somewhere. Second, partisan identity could have changing effects over time (Clinton, Lapinski, and Trussler 2022). Clinton (2021) showed that the Democratic advantage in party identification over Republicans went from +9 to −2

Weighting: An Appreciation and Critique

in one year. Was this due to changes in response patterns or changes in party identification?

The issue with party identification is that it is hard and possibly impossible to measure population-level benchmarks. First of all, this variable is not something that high-quality government surveys such as the Census tend to ask, as government polls typically avoid explicitly political topics. More fundamentally, partisan breakdowns are a moving target. Suppose we had a national benchmark for Democrats and Republican partisans in November 2020. Is that the right breakdown in November 2022? Politics is dynamic and people could change their partisan identification. In fact, one of the goals political polling is to measure changes in partisan identification over time. Therefore, most pollsters do not weight on partisanship. In AAPOR's comprehensive study of 2020 polling, only 10 percent of the state-level polls in the last two week of the campaign reported weighting on partisanship (Clinton et al. 2021, 69).[9] And, perhaps most importantly, although weighting party improves accuracy, "it is no panacea" (Clinton, Lapinski, and Trussler 2022). In particular, Clinton, Lapinski, and Trussler found that Republicans and independents who responded to surveys differed from Republicans and independents who did not; in other words, response was nonignorable because even within group, the respondents had different views than nonrespondents.

Some pollsters weight on previous vote; for example, in a 2020 survey they asked people who they voted for in 2016. If political variables tend to improve results, well, this is about as political as one could get. Using this as a weighting variable likely fulfills the three criteria for weighting variables in ways that speak directly to concerns about contemporary political polling. First, previous vote may well predict whether someone responds. We do not know for certain, but the major concern has been that Trump voters are less likely to respond so this is a rather direct way to account for that possibility. Second, surely previous vote predicts current preferences. And finally, the distributions are known quite well based on vote outcomes in each state (or other geography).[10]

And for all their complexity, weights based on highly political factors such as past vote and partisanship do not generally fix the biases we've seen in recent US elections. Clinton et al. (2021, 68) found that the 69 polls in 2020 that weighted by partisanship and 2016 vote were not more accurate than polls that were weighted only with standard demographic variables. Similar to the finding about party identification, nonignorable nonresponse may be

---

[9] Not all polls described their weighting. Among those that did, 46 reported weighting on party identification and 249 reported a weighting scheme that did not use party identification.

[10] Cohn (2022) notes that using recalled vote choice may be biased because voters are less inclined to recall voting for the losing candidate, which will mean that people who say they voted for the loser may get larger weights than they should and those who said they voted for the winner may get smaller weights than they should. It is also possible to weight by vote choice in the year in question. This, of course, is infeasible prospectively as the population values are unknown. But it can be done after the fact and – unsurprisingly! – doing so produces excellent predictions (Jacobson 2022).

an important impediment. Doug Rivers, a Stanford University political science professor and chief scientist for YouGov, noted that

the 2016 Trump voters who still approved of Trump in December of 2019 had declining participation rates in 2020, and 2016 Trump voters who . . . disapproved of him at the end of 2019 actually had increasing participation rates, the only group that actually went up in its participation rate over time. So our weighting on 2016 Trump vote unfortunately had the effect that we had too many 2016 Trump voters who were not enthusiastic about him and too few who were enthusiastic about him. (Agiesta 2021)

In addition, personality traits likely affect both response propensity and political views. For example, the many polling professionals suspect that people with low social trust may be less likely to respond but more likely to support Republicans. For example, David Shor uses the General Social Survey's (GSS) social trust question, which is "Generally speaking, would you say that most people can be trusted or that you can't be too careful in dealing with people?" Given the high response rate of the GSS, he treats their finding that 30 percent of respondents think people can be trusted as a population measure (Matthews 2020). His experience was the following.

If you do phone surveys, and you weight, you will get that 50 percent of people say that people can be trusted. It's a pretty massive gap. . . . people who don't trust people and don't trust institutions are way less likely to answer phone surveys. Unsurprising! This has always been true. It just used to not matter. It used to be that once you control for age and race and gender and education, that people who trusted their neighbors basically voted the same as people who didn't trust their neighbors. But then, starting in 2016, suddenly that shifted. If you look at white people without college education, high-trust non-college whites tended toward [Democrats] and low-trust non-college whites heavily turned against [Democrats].

Pollsters were listening to a disproportionately high-trust and, therefore, pro-Clinton sample. But the low-trust people were still voting, leading to election results that did not match the polls (Matthews 2020).

If Shor's weights based on trust or others' additional weighting variables lead to samples that are, conditional on these variables with known population-level targets, representative by subgroup, then weighting or poststratification approaches offer familiar, intuitive, and relatively simple fixes to what ails polling.

The problem, of course, is that it is hard to know if our weighting and poststratification covariates have in fact cleared out potential nonignorability. It could be that our national averages of attitudinal variables (based on good, but nonetheless imperfect polls such as the GSS) are wrong. Or the correlations of response and outcome could lurk in unknown variables. Or it could be that response directly depends on the outcome of interest. If any of these possibilities still unnerve a researcher, they will need a selection model such as we cover later in this book.

Weighting: An Appreciation and Critique 73

Not only do we need to select variables when weighting, we also need to consider functional form. Among other possibilities, variables may interact in important ways. Kennedy et al. (2018) showed that simply accounting for race, ethnicity, region, and educational attainment is insufficient. They argued that survey analysts also needed to account for how some of these variables interact. Figuring out how best to select variables and their functional forms in weighting is an active area of research (Hartman, Hazlett, and Sterbenz 2021).

Taken together, these challenges mean that there is no single set of variables or techniques for weighting; each survey and, indeed, each question could theoretically require its own set of variables and functional forms. This leads to another challenge, one that is sometimes referred to as the researcher degrees of freedom challenge. The idea is that the more decisions a researcher can make, the more likely that they will make decisions that skew results toward their preferred outcomes. Of course, this is a concern with regard to partisan pollsters who always seem to find a way to produce results sympathetic to their co-partisans; their weighting decisions may be one of the reasons why. This may also be an issue for academic researchers. Their biases may not be partisan (and may well be toward publication), but they too may intentionally or unintentionally put a thumb on the scales as they weight (Franco, Malhotra, Simonovits, and Zigerell 2017).

3.5 WEIGHTING AND PRECISION

Weighting can be a good deal. Yes, it requires assumptions, assumptions that we probe throughout this book. But given those assumptions, weighting provides a relatively simple way to clean up the messy samples we often observe in practice. Weighting is not costless, however. In particular, "Weighting the results of a sample ... increases variability of responses and lowers the effective sample size and thus lowers the precision of the results" (Gittelman, Thomas, Lavrakas, and Lange 2015, 371).

To see why this happens, let us begin with the variance of the mean, a concept we introduced in Figure 2.4. For a simple random sample, the variance of the sample average is

$$var(\overline{Y}) = \frac{\sigma_Y^2}{n} \tag{3.2}$$

where σ_Y^2 is the variance of Y (the survey answer) and n is the sample size.

Using the properties of the variance function (see, e.g., Bailey 2021), the variance of a cell-weighted average based on Equation 3.1 is

$$var(\overline{Y}_{weighted}) = \frac{\sigma_Y^2(\sigma_w^2 + 1)}{n} \tag{3.3}$$

74   *Part I: Polling in Context*

where σ_Y^2 is the variance of Y, σ_w^2 is the variance of the weights, and n is the sample size.[11]

Equation 3.3 contains three important insights. The first insight is silly, but useful. Suppose we saw how useful making up data points is in the weighting enterprise and decide to push that logic by using weights to make up a ton of data. That is, suppose we have a sample of 200 and say, what the heck, let's give every observation in our sample a weight of 10. We'll have a sample of 2,000. Think of all the money we could save!

Intuitively, that seems sketchy. Equation 3.3 shows why. If we simply increase every weight by some factor, we will not change the variance of the weights (σ_w^2). If, as in our silly example, $\sigma_w^2 = 0$, the variance of our estimated average will be the same as if we put weights of 1 on every observation. This is reassuring because we shouldn't be able to cheat by pretending we have 10 times the data we have.

The second point is more serious. As the variance of the weights rises, so too does the variance of our estimate (Dorofeev 2006, 76). In other words, if our weighting steps described above lead us to have some weights near zero and others near 10, then σ_w^2 will be large and the variance of our $\overline{Y}_{weighted}$ estimates will be large. In other words, if our weights vary a lot, our weighted survey averages will be less precise than they would if our weights varied a little. So, while weights that vary widely do a lot of work to clean up imbalances, they are not a free lunch. And weights that vary only a little bit (meaning that they are all near 1) are not doing much work cleaning up bias, but have only a modest effect on the precision of our estimates.

In the Lucid weights described in Tables 3.2 and 3.3, some observations got a weight of above 3.5 and others got a weight below 0.4, meaning that σ_w^2 was relatively high which meant that the variance of the estimated sample mean was quite high, as well.[12]

Third, it is useful to think of how much weighting influences how much information we have. If we are leaning heavily on weights, we do not have as much information as we do in a random sample requiring no weighting. One way to see this is to calculate the effective sample size given weights. Consider two surveys. In the first, a pure random sample with n observations, no weights are needed. In the second, weights are needed and the weights have variance of σ_w^2. This weighted sample will need to have $n(1 + \sigma_w^2)$ observations in order to achieve the same precision as the unweighted random sample (Bradley, et al.

---

[11] Note that if the observations are independent of each other and weights are treated as fixed values, then $var(\overline{Y}_{weighted}) = var(\frac{\sum_i w_i Y_i}{n}) = \frac{\sigma_Y^2 (\sum w_i^2)}{n^2}$. Using the facts that $var(w) = E[w^2] - (E[w])^2$ and $\sum w_i = n$ for cell weights produces Equation 3.3.

[12] In these calculations, we are treating weights as known, fixed quantities. To the extent, there is uncertainty arising because they are estimated quantities or, even more concerningly, there is specification uncertainty, because the influence of weights on the uncertainty of our estimates will be larger. These considerations tend not to get the attention they deserve; see Caughey et al. (2020) and Gelman (2007, 157) for additional discussions of these issues.

Weighting: An Appreciation and Critique

2021, 43; Kish 1965). If the variance of the weights equals 1, then the weighted sample would need to be twice as large as the pure random sample in order to achieve the same variance for the estimated mean. If the variance of the weights equals 2, then the weighted sample would need to be three as large as the pure random sample in order to achieve the same variance for the estimated mean. In other words, as the variance of our weights rises, the effective amount of information per observation declines.

Precision is a topic that gets lost in the hustle-bustle of polling commentary all too often. As discussed in Chapter 2, pollsters typically report precision in terms of margins of error, which are simple functions of the variance of $var(\overline{Y}_{weighted})$. These reported measures are, sadly, usually wrong.

First, organizations rarely make the required adjustment for weighting when calculating their confidence intervals. Even if we do not know the variance of the weights the pollster used, we can tell when they do not account for weights if their numbers correspond to the variance calculations that do not include weights, calculations that are a function of sample size. Shirani-Mehr, Rothschild, Goel, and Gelman (2018) showed that only 20 percent of Senate surveys in 2012 reported margins of error higher than one would compute based on Equation 3.2; excluding YouGov (a firm that does account for weights), then only 6 percent of polls reported margins of error that accounted for weighting.

Second, even the correct equation that accounts for weights likely underestimates the true variability. Shirani-Mehr, Rothschild, Goel, and Gelman (2018) compared actual results to survey predictions and found that the error in the surveys was roughly twice as large as the margins of error would suggest. Kotak and Moore (2020) conducted a similar study more recently by looking at more than 1,400 polls. Their title tells it all: "Public Election Polls Are 95 percent Confident but Only 60 percent Accurate" (see also Kimball 2019).

Finally, the implications for precision of weighting in surveys are different in interesting ways from the implications of weighting in econometrics. All econometricians are familiar with weighted least squares (WLS) (Solon, Haider, and Wooldridge 2015). WLS is often used to counter heteroscedasticity, a condition that arises when errors in a model have unequal variance. The purpose of WLS is to place *more* weight on observations that have low variability. Doing so has no effect on expected bias, but gives more influence to the "better" observations that have less error and thereby produces estimates that are more precise than models that disregard heteroscedasticity.

Notice how the logic of weighted least squares differs from the logic of survey weighting. In survey weighting, observations from groups that are least likely to respond get the most weight, whereas in weighted least squares observations that are the most precise get the most weight. These two logics are not diametrically opposed, but the tension is clear as the goal of weighting in surveys is to place extra weight on observations that were unusually unlikely to respond while the goal of weighting in econometrics is to place more weight on observations that are expected to be more accurate.

3.6 CONCLUSION

Survey samples often don't quite look like the population. Sometimes, they stray considerably, especially when response rates are low. In the Lucid data explored in the chapter, fully *two-thirds* of the respondents were women. Simply reporting sample averages for such samples seems foolhardy.

Therefore, virtually every pollster weights their data. Weighting can clean up demographic imbalances in survey samples by essentially adding data for groups for whom we have disproportionately few observations and cutting data for groups for whom we have disproportionately many observations. It's an audacious solution to a difficult problem.

Survey weighting is not simple, however. As Gelman (2007, 153) puts it "weighting may be 'dirty' but it is not always 'quick': Actually constructing the weighting for a survey is more difficult than you might think." There are multiple techniques to choose from, and more importantly, there is a vast range of variables that could be used in the process. Creating weights is therefore one of the dark arts of polling; each pollster has a different alchemy of variables and techniques that they find most reassuring.

One key to successful weighting is finding the variables that slice the data into subgroups such that people in these subgroups are random samples of that subgroup. If we weight only on age, it may be that the respondents over 65 are more liberal than nonrespondents under 65 because the respondents have more education. If we weight on age and education, though, it may be that the over 65 age and college group is a random sample of the population and this weighting approach may be sufficient to produce accurate population estimates.

Nor is weighting costless. Estimates become less precise as weights vary more. In a more general sense, the weighting process creates "researcher degrees of freedom" that may allow bias to slip in. Perhaps most importantly, weighting does not solve – and could potentially exacerbate – nonignorable nonresponse bias.

For all its importance, weighting is not the only tool used by pollsters. In Chapter 4, we consider how the contemporary polling combines weighting and many other tools to try to address the challenges of declining response rates and changing technology.

4

The Wild West of Contemporary Polling

> Politics has become a high-stakes spectator sport at the same time that the country's ability to understand it has weakened.
>
> David Leonhardt 2020

If you saw a poll in the Golden Age of polling, you could pretty much bank on it being a random digit-dialed phone survey. Today, however, any given poll *might* be a random digit-dialed poll. More likely, it is a web-based or text message poll of respondents who opted-in on the internet.

And some polls are wild. None more so, perhaps, than Microsoft's 2012 Xbox poll (Wang, Rothschild, Goel, and Gelman 2015). It's an amazing story. Folks at Microsoft had the idea during the 2012 election campaign that they could sneak a quick political survey on their Xbox users who were waiting for their online games to load. They conducted 750,148 interviews with 345,858 unique respondents and figured that something useful could be learned.

Of course, they knew that these responses would not be representative. And they were right! Their sample was mostly a bunch of dudes playing video games: The sample was 93 percent male, and 65 percent were between 18 and 29 years old. Less than 1 percent of respondents were over 65 years old. They didn't ask if respondents were in a dark basement, but I think we can all guess what the answers would have been. Weirdly, Republican Mitt Romney led President Barack Obama by 10 percentage points in the unweighted data even though Obama won by 4 percentage points.

Viewed from the random sampling paradigm, the Xbox poll is, I assure you, insane. But the Xbox team adjusted the bejesus out of the data and came up with something, well, not crazy: Obama's lead was within 0.6 percentage points of how he actually performed on Election Day (Wang, Rothschild, Goel, and Gelman 2015, 984). The state-level results were good too. The Xbox pollsters note that even though women were a small percentage of the sample, the very large sample size meant that they had 5,000 women in the sample, a much

78   *Part I: Polling in Context*

higher number than a typical sample would have (Gelman, Goel, Rivers, and Rothschild 2014, 7).

Nonetheless, it's natural to worry about survey via Xbox. The small number of women and older people playing Xbox were heavily weighted. Were women playing Xbox representative of all women? And what kind 75-year-old was playing Xbox? Do we really believe that these old folks rocking their Xboxes were representative of all old folks?[1]

The fact that pollsters even tried something like this shows that polling has gone from the Golden Age to the Wild West. Pollsters are getting creative, often in very smart ways, but also often in ways that blow far beyond the comfortable confines of the random sampling paradigm. The goal of this chapter is to provide an overview of contemporary polling, from the random digit dialers still hanging on to the surging wave of pollsters who, like the Xbox pollsters, identify potential respondents via nonprobabilistic methods. Scanning the current landscape positions us to formulate a theory that better encompasses actual practice and to focus attention on weaknesses in modern polling practice.

Several themes emerge. First, even pollsters who aspire to random sampling are doing something quite foreign to the random sampling paradigm. Continuing to use the language of random sampling is therefore becoming increasingly untenable. Second, the energy and growth in polling are concentrated in nonprobabilistic polls that do not even pretend to adhere to the tenets of the random sampling paradigm. When we use, teach, and critique such polls, we need a new language for assessing them. Finally, one of the biggest vulnerabilities for both probabilistic and nonprobabilistic polling is nonignorable nonresponse, something largely ignored in the current state of the art.

Sections 4.1 and 4.2 of this chapter describe contemporary practices of probabilistic and nonprobabilistic pollsters. The Section 4.3 compares the accuracy of probabilistic and nonprobabilistic polling. Section 4.4 brings together themes, focusing in particular on the striking fact that despite the incredible diversity of techniques currently deployed, academic and commercial pollsters mostly continue to use models that assume away nonignorable nonresponse. These pollsters are, of course, well aware of the problem, but focus their efforts on improving response rates and weighting in ways that eliminate ignorable nonresponse. They pay little attention to the approaches we present in part two of this book that allow us to directly model nonignorable nonresponse.

4.1 PROBABILITY-BASED SAMPLES

Probability-based surveys retain a privileged position in the polling world. They hew as closely as feasible to the random sampling paradigm that

---

[1] What game do they play? "Grand Auto Theft: Home by 6:15 pm edition"?

pollsters cling too. And because they have been used for so long, pollsters and researchers have built up a large pool of shared wisdom about how to implement them. But they are hardly monolithic: Any specific probability-based survey will need to make a series of important decisions.

SAMPLING FRAME The first decision is how to identify the pool of respondents. In the Golden Age of polling, pollsters often used random digit dialing (RDD). The process begins, not surprisingly, with pollsters generating random phone numbers associated with a given geographical area. This means that both unlisted and listed phone numbers would be included. RDD excludes people without phones, but since most people had landlines, this was a fairly modest problem.

Things are more complicated now. It is difficult, if not impossible, to tell where a person lives based on their cell phone number, rendering random generation of phone numbers inappropriate. Roughly 75 percent of calls are to cellphones (Cohn 2022), and while it is possible to know where people are and other characteristics, cellphones are inevitably more complicated than landlines. For example, the Pew Research Center reports that in 2016 in California, 8 percent of people interviewed had a cell phone number from another state and 10 percent of those called on a California number lived in another state (McGeeney 2016).

There is no list, or "white pages," to fall back on, as no single compilation of people and their phones numbers exists. And the link between phones and people is complex. More than half of US adults have a cell phone and no landline, while many have both or even multiple cellphones. To make things even more difficult, it is illegal to call mobile phone numbers using automated dialing methods. This means that including cellphones – which seems unavoidable – requires costly manual dialing of numbers (Blumenthal 2005).

Some probability-based pollsters therefore use address-based sampling (ABS) or registration-based sampling (RBS) (Kennedy et al. 2021; Cohn 2022; Wilcox-Archuleta 2019). This information is fairly comprehensive and reasonably up-to-date and for RBS in particularly helpfully contains information about nonrespondents (Kennedy et al. 2016). The differences across sampling frames do not appear to be substantial: A Pew study conducted RBS and RDD polls simultaneously and found the RBS sample needed more weighting (and hence was less precise for the reasons we discussed in Chapter 3) and was just slightly more Democratic (Kennedy et al. 2016).

Voter files have some built-in challenges. They of course omit people who are not registered, an important population and one that varies from state to state based on registration laws and administrative practices. And even with the relatively high-quality voter registration lists, it is surprisingly difficult to know if the person contacted is the same as the person listed. A 2018 Vanderbilt survey based on Tennessee voter files found that only 36 percent of the people who answered the phone gave a name or initials that matched the voter file name of the person the pollster thought they were talking to (Clinton 2022; see also Kennedy at al. 2016 and Cohn 2022).

INTERVIEW MODE   A second major decision is how to interview respondents. Live calling respondents on phones is historically the mode of choice, but doing so has important limitations (West and Blom 2017). Most people do not like talking to a stranger, especially about personal and potentially controversial political views. And it is costly to have an interviewer calling and calling and calling and then walking through a script in real time. Some interviewers may inadvertently influence responses by their tone or the way they ask or answer questions.

The high cost of live phone calls has led some pollsters to contact respondents in other ways. One common approach is interactive voice response (IVR) polls. There are many variations, but the basic idea is to contact a respondent and play them an automated, recorded message. Respondents can respond by pressing a key or stating their answer. The automation makes the calls cheap and standardized. It is also possible that respondents are more willing to be honest on socially difficult topics when no human is directly involved (Tourangeau and Smith 1996).

IVR presents challenges as well. Some people are turned off by the impersonal nature of the exchange, and response rates tend to be lower for IVR polls. Speaking to a computer also makes some respondents more willing to cut short the interview (Tourangeau, Steiger, and Wilson 2002).

While probability sample surveys are generally conducted offline (Cornesse et al. 2020, 19), some pollsters have taken probabilistic polling to the web. Ipsos (formerly Gfk) maintains a panel of survey respondents who were recruited using address-based probabilistic sampling methods. Ipsos provides households without internet a web-enabled device and free internet service.

Other pollsters such as the high-quality American National Election Study (ANES) and the General Social Survey (GSS) use *more* expensive face-to-face interviews, sometimes considered the ideal mode of interview (Couper 2011). The advantage is the surveys can be longer and respondents are more likely to be fully engaged. This approach is incredibly costly, though, as pollsters must first engage in extensive recruitment and persuasion in order to get the person to agree to meet and then must travel and conduct the interview.

NONRESPONSE TRENDS IN PROBABILITY SAMPLES   Nonresponse is a sore spot for probability-based polling. This has always been true. We saw in Chapter 2 that the earliest probabilistic surveys had 20 percent nonresponse, a fact that made practitioners nervous. In 1992, the President of the American Association for Public Opinion Research Norman Bradburn described an article in a nonpeer-reviewed journal that presented results from a survey with a 69 percent nonresponse rate, noting that he was "sure that they would not have accepted an article based on that survey if it had to pass peer review" (Bradburn 1992).

The Wild West of Contemporary Polling 81

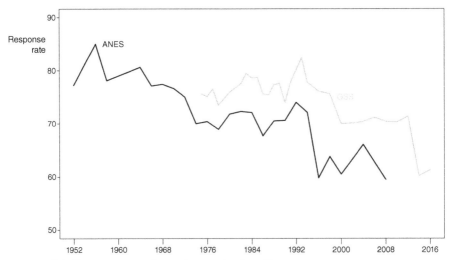

FIGURE 4.1 Response rates for major academic polls

Today, many pollsters would love to have such *low* nonresponse rates. Figure 2.6 in Chapter 2 showed the nonresponse for large polling firms since 1998 from Dutwin and Lavrakas (2016) and Kennedy and Hartig (2019). Currently, nonresponse rates above 95 percent are common. Simply by answering questions, survey respondents are indicating to us that they are willing to do something that the overwhelming majority of Americans are not willing to do: Respond to pollsters.

Nonresponse rates, while troublesome in all surveys, vary across surveys. In the *New York Times* Upshot polls discussed in Chapter 1, response rates were generally between 1 and 3 percent. In academic polls, the response rates are higher. Figure 4.1 shows the response rate for the high-profile academic surveys ANES and GSS. The general pattern is similar for both: 70 percent or higher until the 1990s, with a drop-off since then. Even now, though, their response rates are much higher than seen in most commercial and political polls due to much greater effort invested in getting responses and the longer period of being in the field. The GSS, for example, was "in the field" asking questions for more than six months in 2019.

Nonpolitical surveys tend to have higher response rates, especially when conducted by government or other well-established entities (Tourangeau and Plewes 2013, 17). The scope of such surveys is vast, including the National Household Education Survey, the National Immunization Survey, the Behavioral Risk Factor Surveillance System, the Survey of Consumer Attitudes, Panel Study of Income Dynamics, Survey of Consumer Finances, Census Bureau Household Surveys (such as the Consumer Expenditure Quarterly, the Current Population Survey, the National Crime Victimization Survey, the National

82   *Part I: Polling in Context*

Health Interview Survey, and the Survey of Income and Program Participation), and Bureau of Labor Statistics Surveys (such as the Consumer Price Index Housing Survey, the American Time Use Survey, National Longitudinal Survey of Youth). Patterns in levels and trends in nonresponse vary across these surveys. Generally, these high-quality surveys tend to get around 50 to 70 percent response rates, but that response rates have been declining even as the resources being put into gathering responses have increased (Tourangeau and Plewes 2013). And a recent effort by the Census to innovate with its "Pulse" survey fielded during the Covid pandemic met the reality that other pollsters have long-faced: Their response rate was under 10 percent.

Nonresponse can occur because of noncontact (the pollster was unable to reach the targeted respondent) or refusal (the pollster reached the targeted respondent, but the person declined to answer the survey). Peytchev (2013, 98) describes components of nonresponse for a phone survey of consumer attitudes from the 1980s to the early 2000s, noting that refusal rates were relatively flat while noncontact rates climbed steadily, a pattern consistent with the idea that people became less likely to answer calls from unknown sources. Face-to-face surveys, however, saw flat noncontact rates, but growth in refusal. Clinton, Lapinski, and Trussler (2022) found that while contact rates did not differ by demographics, cooperation rates did.

Noncontact is generally viewed as less problematic than refusal because there is less likelihood the nonresponse will be directly related to the content of the survey. Refusals, especially refusals that occur after the potential respondent becomes aware of the content, are generally viewed as more likely to introduce a relationship between response and the outcome being measured. Groves et al. (2006) show that when the topic of a survey is more obvious, "exaggerated population estimates of interests and activities related to the topic can be expected" (Peytchev 2013, 96).

DEMOGRAPHICS PATTERNS OF NONRESPONSE IN PROBABILITY SAMPLES We know a lot about who does and does not respond to polls. Much of what we know we can use to improve our inferences. After all, if nonresponse is ignorable, meaning that nonresponse is fully explained by available demographic variables, the patterns of nonresponse are interesting, but may not be particularly worrisome because the weights will adjust based on response patterns to produce an unbiased estimate of the outcome variable for the population. We should note, however, that having a sample that requires only a small amount of weighting is not associated with survey accuracy (Kennedy et al. 2016).

It is, nonetheless, interesting and potentially troubling to observe the actual variation in response across demographic groups. First, even within the ignorable nonresponse paradigm, large weights decrease the statistical precision of the estimates, as we saw in Chapter 3. And, seeing the variation in nonresponse across demographic groups may make us cautious about assuming response is ignorable. After all, if response varies dramatically by race, age, or gender,

The Wild West of Contemporary Polling

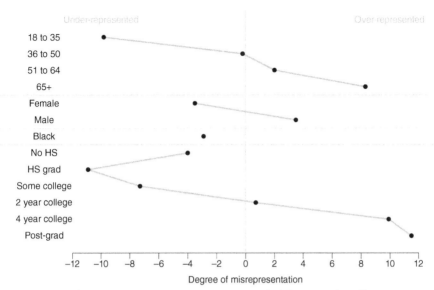

FIGURE 4.2 Relative representation in Pew 2016 probability sample poll

for example, isn't it at least plausible that other factors matter and that these factors could conceivably bear directly on our measured outcome?

Nonresponse patterns vary from poll to poll, but several patterns are common. First, people with less education tend to respond less. Second, people of color respond less in some, but not all, polls. Finally, response often differs by age, although this can depend on the mode and timing of the poll.

To illustrate the magnitudes of these demographic patterns, Figure 4.2 plots the relative representation for several demographic groups in a single random digit-dialed random sample poll fielded by the Pew Research Center just before the 2016 presidential election (Caughey et al. 2021, 40). For each group, the figure shows the difference between the actual proportion in the US population and the proportion in the unweighted survey sample. At the top, we see vast underrepresentation of young people, with the survey sample proportion of people between 18 and 35 (which was 19 percent) being almost 10 percentage points below the actual proportion (which was 28.8 percent). The proportions for people in the 26 to 50 and 51 to 64 age groups were not particularly off, but the proportion of people over 65 was far too high in the sample, as 28.4 percent of the sample was in that age group, compared to the true proportion of 20.1 percent. The differences for gender were modest, with a slight overrepresentation of men.

Nonresponse did not differ much by race, as Black people were only slightly underrepresented. This was the only racial and ethnic comparison data provided for this particular Pew study. In many polls, non-Hispanic White people are more likely to respond than other groups, but this pattern is not universal (Johnson, O'Rourke, Burris, and Owens 2002, 57).

The differences for education in the Pew study were stark. In particular, people with lower levels of education were vastly underrepresented while people with higher levels of education were vastly overrepresented. Such educational patterns in nonresponse are quite common. For example, Tourangeau (2019) reports a comparison of education levels in a probability-based survey and an internet poll. Census data at the time indicated that 16.9 percent of Americans had less than a high school degree while only 7 percent of the probability-based survey and 2 percent of the internet survey had that level of education. Census data indicated that 30.5 percent of Americans had a college degree or more while 42 percent of the probability-based survey and 50 percent of the internet survey had that level of education. This pattern seems timeless: Recall from Chapter 2 that Gallup polls vastly oversampled people with more education.

Chapter 3 discussed the controversy after the 2016 election about whether it was necessary to weight by education. The consensus was that it was, but this practice was not universally practiced – with the state-level polls being only half as likely to weight by education (Kennedy et al. 2018, 34). Pew is a cutting-edge polling organization and of course weighted by education. Can you imagine looking at the sample in Figure 4.2 and *not* weighting by education?

ACCURACY OF PROBABILITY SAMPLE SURVEYS   Theoretically, it should be easy to characterize the precision of polls based on random sampling. For example, as we discussed in Chapter 2, the margin of error for a poll of a close presidential election will be around 3 percentage points for a sample size of 1,000, meaning that 95 out of 100 polls will produce an estimate that is within 3 percentage points of the truth.

Characterizing the accuracy of polls in the real world, however, is a different matter. First is the issue of weights. When they are used – as they almost always are – polls are less precise. As discussed in Chapter 3, for any given sample size the margin of error goes up when weights are used. The more the weights vary, the greater the increase in margin of error. And yet, most pollsters report the smaller margins of error based on simple random sampling (Shirani-Mehr, Rothschild, Goel, and Gelman 2018), a tactic that lies in the gray area between lazy and unethical.

As we've discussed, however, polling in the real world deviates substantially in other respects from an idealized random sample. In addition to nonresponse, it is possible that the sampling frame (the enumeration of the total population from which the random sample was selected) is incomplete. It is also possible that people misrepresent their opinions either intentionally or perhaps due to question wording effects. This has meant that the measures of precision reported by most pollsters tend to be overoptimistic in the sense of reporting unrealistically small margins of error.

The 2018 study by Shirani-Mehr, Rothschild, Goel, and Gelman that we referenced in Chapter 3 compared hundreds of polls to election results and

The Wild West of Contemporary Polling

found that the errors were about twice what would be expected if the only source of error were variance due to random sampling. In theory, only 5 percent of polls should produce results outside the sampling 95 percent margins of error, but in reality 29 percent of senatorial polls, 28 percent of gubernatorial polls, and 13 percent of presidential polls were outside of the margin of error in 2016. This is a reminder that standard errors, for all their statistical sophistication, are reporting accuracy as if they are random samples drawn from the full population, something is not true in modern polling (and probably never true in large-scale polling).

4.2 NONPROBABILITY-BASED SAMPLES

Given the challenges of probability-based sampling, it is not surprising that nonprobabilistic surveys are booming. Cornesse et al. (2020, 6) conclude that "the majority of survey data collected online around the world today rely on nonprobability samples." Even the academy has embraced nonprobabilistic polls: Ansolabehere and Rivers (2013) note that even more than 10 years ago, the nonprobabilistic CCES poll had been used in over 100 publications, spread across more than 60 academic journals and publishers.

Sometimes, people use internet polling as a short-hand for polling with nonprobability-based samples. This is not quite accurate as there are online probability-based samples and many probability-based approaches that use address-based sampling are mail to web, meaning that potential respondents are contacted via postal mail and directed to an online link for the questionnaire. Nonetheless, among the higher profile polls, there is a reasonably strong connection between probability-based phone surveys and nonprobability web surveys.

The advantages of nonprobability internet samples are clear: "They are fast and cheap, and the technology is pervasive" (Kennedy et al. 2016). Figure 4.3 shows that national presidential polls went from 38 percent online (and mostly nonprobabilistic) in 2016 to 64 percent online in 2020 (Clinton et al. 2021, 11). Probabilistic random digit-dialed polls with human interviewers went from 36 percent of national polls in 2016 to just 6 percent in 2020. Probability-based phone surveys maintained their share at about 19 percent of state-level presidential polls in competitive states (Clinton et al. 2021, 11).

Most nonprobabilistic polls are conducted via the internet or text messages (Cornesse et al. 2020, 19). Beyond that, it is hard to generalize because nonprobabilistic polls span a vast range of protocols described below, ranging from simple convenience polls to sophisticated quota sampling enterprises (Kennedy at al. 2018). Even within a given category, there are numerous differences in how respondents are recruited, contacted, and analyzed.

CONVENIENCE POLLING At one end of the nonprobabilistic polling environment are pure convenience samples. One common approach is to use pop-up ads to initiate a survey; these surveys tend to be short and cheap. These

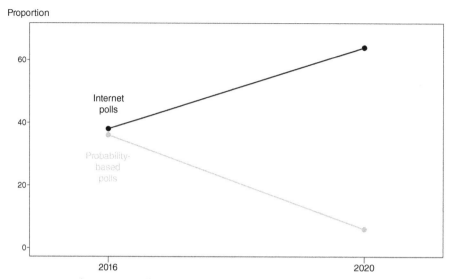

FIGURE 4.3 Changes in polling types from 2016 to 2020 for national US presidential polls

pop-up ads can be targeted to websites of particular interest or, as Change Research does, to people on phones in a highly specific geographic area.

Another approach to convenience polling involves paying people to take surveys. The most prominent example in academic circles is Amazon's Mechanical Turk, an online service that allows researchers to recruit and pay subjects to perform tasks such as answering surveys. Competitors include websites like Survey Junkie, Swag Buck, and InBox Dollars. The effective pay ranges from $0.41 to $2 an hour.

Mechanical Turk has been widely used in academic studies because it is much cheaper than hiring a pollster. In many respects, the service has been quite useful. While the samples are less representative of the US population than probability samples or even nonprobability samples (Berinsky, Huber, and Lenz 2012), they are quite similar to some widely used benchmarks for attributes such as occupation and urban–rural residence (Huff and Tingley 2015). Mechanical Turk samples also tend to produce experimental results similar to results conducted on nationally representative samples (Coppock 2019) making them attractive for efficiently conducting experiments (Berinsky, Huber, and Lenz 2012).

Concerns remain, of course. These surveys are based on respondents who are online, looking for tasks on Mechanical Turk, willing to accept a survey task and then complete the task to satisfaction. At every point, we would expect nonrandom selection. Mechanical Turk samples tend to have particular trouble attracting older and Black respondents. Surprisingly, older respondents in Mechanical Turk appear to vote less than individuals of a similar age in benchmark survey samples (Huff and Tingley 2015).

NONPROBABILITY INTERNET PANELS Nonprobability samples face "one fundamental problem: There is no comprehensive sampling frame for the internet, no way to draw a national sample for which virtually everyone has a chance of being selected" (Kennedy et al. 2016). Hence, nonprobability pollsters have to go looking for potential respondents, which they typically do by creating a panel of people who have volunteered to answer surveys from time to time. These potential respondents are typically recruited via ads on the internet or company loyalty programs or other sources of email or other digital contact information. After choosing to enroll, respondents provide demographic information that the polling firms use to sample and weight.

The specifics of how firms handle these processes vary substantially and are seldom fully transparent (Kennedy et al. 2016). Many on-line samples come from firms specializing in providing lists of potential respondents. These firms may aggregate pools across various sources. They also may rout potential respondents to polling organizations based on characteristics of the individual (Comer 2017). For example, an aggregator may first provide a list of potential respondents to an organization interested in polling people who watch news on TV. That organization will then screen the pool and return individuals who do not watch TV news back to the aggregator who will then provide a sample from the remaining potential respondents to another organization interested in another question. Unbeknownst to the second polling firm, this pool may overrepresent people who do not watch news on TV. The hope, of course, is that large sample sizes and a more-or-less random sequence of polling requests will limit the odds of bias, but nonetheless it is hard not to be a bit unnerved by the process.

Cleaning online samples is quite involved. Organizations providing potential respondents to polling firms need to validate identity, ensure that no children are in the sample, ensure that the respondents come from the desired region (a challenge for US surveys where payments are so small as to be unattractive to Americans but attractive to residents of lower income countries), prevent individuals from answering more than once, and assess whether respondents are answering extremely quickly and/or providing nonserious answers (ESOMAR World Research 2014).

Once an internet sample has been gathered, analysis raises its own challenges. Response rates are difficult, if not impossible, to ascertain, at least in any way that is comparable to probabilistic sampling approaches (Callegaro and Disogra 2008, 1010). Pollsters using internet panels can report what percent of the people they reached out to responded, but what are we to make of that information? In the random sampling paradigm, the contact list is a random sample which will include people willing and unwilling to respond. For internet panels, the people contacted have already said they will respond to polls. Of course, they do not always respond, but clearly comparing the response rate in these polls directly to the response rates of probability sample polls would be inappropriate.

Everyone recognizes that nonprobability internet panels are not representative:

No claim is made as to the representativeness of the panel, which exhibits obvious skews (not dissimilar to current telephone samples): It is disproportionately white, old, and overeducated. Panelists are, as may be expected, heavier users of technology than the overall adult population, and because all surveys are conducted using the Internet, they are composed entirely of Internet users. (Ansolabehere and Rivers 2013)

Unrepresentative panels are not, in and of themselves, a problem. As noted in our discussion of probability samples, highly variable demographic patterns of response are not particularly concerning if nonresponse is ignorable because the weights or other adjustments will simply change as needed. However, seeing substantial variation across surveys in observable demographics may make some people nervous that response depends also on unobservable factors, rendering nonresponse nonignorable.

Figure 4.4 depicts the representation of certain groups in raw unweighted data from a 2004 YouGov nonprobability internet sample (Krosnick and Malhotra 2007). This is a single poll at a single point in time from a single internet pollster. It should not be taken as a general characterization. Paired with the previous demographic patterns we saw in Figure 4.2, however, the figure helps us appreciate the extent to which response patterns can vary from poll to poll.

For the 2004 YouGov poll depicted in Figure 4.4, the age distribution was much different than we saw in the earlier poll. Here, younger *and* older voters were underrepresented. The underrepresentation of younger people is quite common. The underrepresentation of older people is less common today, but Figure 4.4 displays results from the early 2000s when older people were less active on the internet. Men and African-Americans were underrepresented in the YouGov sample. People with less education were also underrepresented (a common pattern) although the most overrepresented educational category was those with some college (an unusual pattern).

Of course, we should keep in mind that a representative sample does not guarantee an accurate poll. Kennedy et al. (2016) note that "it does not do much good to get the marginal distribution of Hispanics correct if the surveyed Hispanics are systematically different from Hispanics in the larger population." Across a broad range of nonprobability polls, they found that predictive accuracy was unrelated to the representativeness of samples.

QUOTA SAMPLING   Some internet pollsters, including YouGov and Civiqs, have moved to a modern version of quota sampling. This technique is the foundation for many important studies, including the Cooperative Congressional Election Study that is widely used by scholars studying American politics (Ansolabehere and Rivers 2013; Cooperative Congressional Election Study 2014).

The Wild West of Contemporary Polling 89

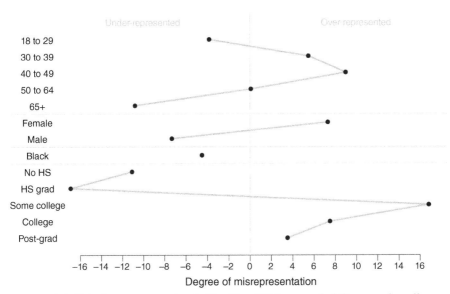

FIGURE 4.4 Relative representation in YouGov 2004 nonprobability sample poll

The modern quota sampling approach harkens back to quota sampling of the 1940s, but with improvements. The idea is to first recruit a large opt-in sample of potential survey respondents who are willing to respond to internet survey requests. For example, YouGov has identified more than one million US residents who have agreed to participate in web surveys. These people have been recruited primarily via web advertising based on keyword searches. For example, "a search in Google may prompt an active YouGov advertisement soliciting opinion on the search topic. At the conclusion of the short survey respondents are invited to join the YouGov panel in order to receive and participate in additional surveys" (YouGov 2014).

The recruited panel members are, in all likelihood, unrepresentative of the population given that the type of people willing to sign up are unrepresentative of the entire population. The quota sampling approach takes the edge off this concern by constructing samples that will demographically match a cross-section of the country. The implementation is clever: YouGov first enumerates the target population via decennial Census data or a high-quality representative survey such as the US Census Bureau's American Community Survey. They draw a random sample from this population-level data. For each member of the random sample from the population, they select someone who is as similar as possible from their pool of opt-in respondents. They base similarity on demographic variables such as age, race, gender, education, and state. They use standard statistical measures to calculate similarity.

For example, pollsters may randomly select a 48-year-old Hispanic woman from Maryland from a population-level data set provided by the Census

Bureau. The modern quota-sampling firm is not able, of course, to contact this person, as identifying information is not provided by the Census. They can, however, contact demographically similar women in the pool of potential survey respondents they maintain until they got a response from a demographically similar person. Doing so will produce a sample of respondents that "will have similar properties to a true random sample. That is, the matched sample mimics the characteristics of the target sample" (YouGov 2014).

There are several advantages of this approach. It is cost-effective as it can be done on-line and at scale. The method also provides samples that are demographically representative. And unlike the original quota-sampling approaches, the approach eliminates interviewer effects. Recall that the original quota-sampling interviewers were often tempted to go to places where people were more amendable to responding, which potentially skewed the pool toward more highly educated people or people who were more similar to the interviewer. In this modern version of quota sampling, the process of whom to query is automatic and based only on demographics.

In important respects, quota sampling is similar to weighting in that it assumes ignorable nonresponse and produces an effective sample that is representative for selected variables. For demographic groups that readily respond, quota sampling could be reframed as firms getting a large sample and only keeping the first number of observations depending on the groups' proportions in the target population. This is not too different from downweighting observations in such groups. For groups that do not produce many responses, the quota sampler keeps asking until they get the desired number of responses. This is different from weighting in that instead of simply repeating observations in these groups (which is what upweighting does), the quota sampler proactively keeps asking until a desired number of responses are received in a given category. This is akin to increasing outreach to underrepresented groups. Such an approach can make it easier to generate results for these subgroups, although Gittelman et al. (2015, 376) found the larger samples for subgroups did not decrease bias.

Our weighting-oriented paradigm is not well equipped to characterize uncertainty of quota samples. Yes, quota samples may be weighted, but these weights tend to not vary substantially because quota-sampling procedures produce samples with demographics that are similar to the target population. A more useful sign of the underlying uncertainty in quota samples may be a measure for each respondent of how deep the quota sampler needed to go get a response for a person with that demographic profile. Consider two different observations in the quota-sampled survey. For the first, the quota sampler randomly picked a 40-year-old White male with a graduate degree from the target population. They then selected a person matching that profile from their internet panel and that person responded. Easy. For the second, the quota sampler picked a 19-year-old Hispanic woman who did not graduate from high school. They found someone in their panel and sent them a survey, but got no response. So they asked another person matching that demographic profile ... and another ... and another until after asking 15 people, they finally got a response. The weights on these individuals in the reported sample may well both be near one, but clearly the nonresponse issues loom larger for the young Hispanic woman in our example. In a standard nonquota-sampled survey, the demographic profiles would be flagged with a large weight. For quota samples, consumers of survey responses often have no idea of how hard the sampler had to work to get each response.

Quota sampling does not eliminate nonresponse concerns. First, people who do not use the internet are, of course, excluded (Mercer, Kreuter, Keeter and Stuart 2017). Second, the recruitment process is a bit of a black box, meaning that nonresponse patterns in the process of joining the panel could be important, yet hard to track. Pettit (2015) showed that respondents varied in important ways in measurable and unmeasurable ways depending on the website they were recruited from. Consider, for example, the differences one would expect in people recruited from a video game site and a scrapbooking site, even if they were demographically similar. Third, even among those in the (potentially unrepresentative) opt-in panel, there can be differences in who is willing to respond. As is true for probability-based samples, some individuals may simply be less engaged and hence less likely to respond to an email asking for a response. Or, as we have seen, response patterns can change over time; when things are going well for Democrats or for Republicans, the types of people on the opt-in internet panel who choose to respond could be different than when things are going poorly for one party or another (Gelman, Goel, Rivers, and Rothschild 2014).

"PROFESSIONAL" ONLINE SURVEY RESPONDENTS   Because nonprobability samples are based on opt-in behavior by respondents, a concern is that a relatively small group of people are opting-in again and again, creating essentially a "professionalization" of survey respondents. Studies have found that online panelists tend to belong to multiple panels. Hillygus, Jackson, and Young (2014, 219) report one study that found that 1 percent of panel members in major market research panels were responsible for more than one-third of all completed surveys.

Professional survey panelists raise several concerns (Hillygus, Jackson, and Young 2014, 221). First, there are likely differences in personality and other traits of the kinds of people who engage in this behavior. One study that focused on professional respondents as survey samples for marketing research reports that so-called professional survey respondents are more likely to write positive or negative reviews but less likely to consult reviews when shopping. Repeat respondents are more likely to try new products and use coupons, Twitter, Tumblr, Instagram, and Pinterest. They like TV more and are more likely to take vitamins, recycle, and vote (Civic Science 2016).

Second, the act of responding to polls may change people, something pollsters refer to as panel conditioning (Mercer, Kreuter, Keeter, and Stuart 2017,

259; Baker et al. 2010). For example, seeing lots of polls about politics or social issues may inform respondents or may lead them to think more about these topics. This is especially true if some polls include information designed to change opinions, a common practice in academic, political, and commercial polling. Bartels (2000) found evidence that panel attrition and conditioning could be particularly relevant for political interest and turnout. Third, professional respondents – especially those doing it to make money – may answer polls in ways that prioritize speed over authenticity, although evidence is mixed on this question (Hillygus, Jackson, and Young 2014, 222).

The full implications of professional panelists are subtle. Of course, it is concerning that online surveys repeatedly hear from a small slice of the population. On the other hand, it is possible that professional respondents may be *more* representative of the overall population in some respects (Hillygus, Jackson, and Young 2014, 222). Consider a political survey. A person who seldom responds to polls may choose to respond because they have strong political views. A serial poll respondent, however, may respond because they like answering surveys. In this case, the one-and-done survey respondents may be responding to political events or politically extreme and therefore less representative than the so-called professional survey respondent. A similar pattern may play out in consumer behavior. Schoenmueller, Netzer, and Stahl (2020) found that people who leave few online reviews are much more prone to extreme ratings than those who leave many online reviews.

4.3 WHICH IS MORE ACCURATE? PROBABILITY VERSUS NONPROBABILITY SAMPLES

We saw earlier in this chapter that characterizing the precision of probabilistic polls is no walk in the park. Assessing the precision of nonprobabilistic polls is a walk in a swamp filled with alligators – at night. The people given a chance to opt-in to the panel are not random, in unknown ways. Those who opt-in to the panel are not random, in unknown ways. And the panelists who accept the chance to respond to a given poll are, again, not random in unknown ways. These are layers of nonrandomness, all unknown and all unmodeled. If we assume away nonignorable nonresponse, we will be able to get a handle on things but absent such assumptions "there is no general statistical theory of non-probability sampling that, justifies when and why accurate inferences can be expected" (Cornesse et al. 2020, 7).

Many evaluations of nonprobability polls are based on a proof-is-in-the-pudding approach. That is, while the theoretical connection of nonprobability samples to population samples is theoretically underdeveloped, perhaps we need not worry too much if they work in practice. Such evaluations compare how close probability and nonprobability polls come to predicting external benchmarks, such as those provided by the Census Bureau, high-quality probability polls or election results. This is a huge and hotly contested literature. In general, it is fair to say the literature is unsettled, just as is the entire polling ecosystem (Kennedy et al. 2016). Nonetheless, we can cautiously identify several patterns in the research:

1. Probability samples probably do a better job matching Census and other nonelection benchmarks.
2. Nonprobability samples are likely more variable than probability samples.
3. Weighting and other adjustments tend not improve the accuracy of nonprobability samples.
4. It is hard to discern whether probability or nonprobability samples better predict elections.

We consider each of these research areas in turn.

EXTERNAL BENCHMARKS Many studies that compare probability and nonprobability samples to external benchmarks find that probability samples perform better. Cornesse et al. (2020, 14) conclude that "the vast majority of these studies concluded that probability sample surveys have a significantly higher accuracy than non-probability sample surveys."

- Gittelman et al. (2015) compared 17 nonprobability samples to Census and high-quality survey benchmarks. They found that nonprobability samples performed less well than a random digit-dialed survey, with pronounced differences on matters relating to employment status, home ownership, smoking, and political ideology (Gittelman et al. 2015, 376). Similar previous studies had found that nonprobability sample respondents were more active on the internet, more likely to be early adopters, less traditional and more concerned about the environment (Gittelman et al. 2015, 369).
- MacInnis, Krosnick, Ho, and Cho (2018) compared estimates based on probabilistic RDD polls, probabilistic internet polls, and six nonprobability internet polls, all conducted in 2012. They found that the probability samples were more accurate than nonprobability internet samples.
- Yeager et al. (2011) compared probabilistic and nonprobabilistic polls to Census benchmarks across multiple modes and variables for surveys conducted in 2004. They found that error was consistently lower for the probabilistic surveys.
- Krosnik and Malhotra (2007, 311) compared nonprobability internet samples and the probability-based ANES to Census benchmarks across 16 variables; the ANES was more accurate for 14 of the comparisons (see also Dutwin and Buskirk 2017; Gutsche, Kapteyn, Meijer, and Weerman 2014).

Other studies are more optimistic about nonprobability samples. Ansolabehere and Rivers (2013) compare the nonprobabilistic Cooperative Congressional Election Study to the American National Election study. They found that the nonprobabilistic polls were accurate in predicting election outcomes and produced a correlation structure similar to the ANES. Ansolabehere and Schaffner (2014) compared internet polls to a probabilistic telephone RDD poll. They found that the nonprobabilistic survey was as accurate as the probabilistic survey. Ansolabehere and Schaffner (2014) also found differences between the probabilistic and nonprobabilistic surveys. Compared to Census data, the internet survey respondents reported significantly lower home ownership. The opt-in internet panelists were also more knowledgeable, a difference they attribute to using the internet and not to the opt-in nature of the nonprobabilistic process. And they found more than 10 percentage point differences in the percent of people who said that the government was always wasteful and the percent of people who supported affirmative action, with the phone survey respondents being more liberal.

While the issues with nonprobability samples may be due to the biases inherent in allowing people to opt-in to samples (and still getting less than 100 percent response), Ansolabehere and Schaffner (2014) argue that some of the poor showings of nonprobability polls may be due to the use of older data (that was gathered before internet use was nearly universal) and the fact that some internet polls may be of lower quality than others.

While most studies of nonprobability polls focus on population average estimates, some studies explore the ability of nonprobability polls to estimate relationships among variables. For example, do nonprobability polls produce accurate estimates of the effect of race and ethnicity on turning out to vote? Here, the evidence is mixed. Kennedy et al. (2016) compared the estimated effects of being Hispanic or Black on substantive outcomes such as turning out to vote and found that results based on nonprobability samples were quite different from relationships estimated with high-quality probability-based samples. On the other hand, Ansolabehere and Rivers (2013), Ansolabehere and Schaffner (2014), and Pasek (2016) report that the correlations across variables found in nonprobability samples are similar to correlations found in probabilistic samples. In addition, Coppock (2019) found similar results across sampling type when he compared the results for randomized survey experiments conducted on probability samples and Mechanical Turk convenience samples.

VARIABILITY OF NONPROBABILITY POLLS Nonprobability samples seem to be more variable. Yeager et al. (2011, 730) found that nonprobability internet polls were highly variable across firms, leading them to conclude that "it is difficult to anticipate whether a nonprobability sample internet survey will be somewhat different from a population benchmark or substantially different from it, whereas the probability sample surveys were consistently only minimally different." This pattern may not be surprising in light of the range of protocols used by these firms to recruit and interview respondents and to analyze results (Kennedy et al. 2016).

WEIGHTING AND NONPROBABILITY POLLS   One could argue that it is not a problem if nonprobability samples are not demographically representative. After all, weights can address demographic imbalances if response is ignorable. However, Cornesse (2020, 20–21) reviewed the literature and noted that most studies "found that weighting did not sufficiently reduce bias in non-probability sample surveys" and concluded that "the inaccuracy of non-probability samples cannot be reliably solved by weighting procedures." Gittelman et al. (2015, 375) found that weighting reduced bias for only five of the 17 nonprobability sample providers they examined while weighting increased bias for eight of the 17 sample providers. Pasek (2016) found that weights "extenuated rather than reduced" apparent biases, and Dutwin and Buskirk (2017, 213) found that "propensity weighting and matching did not improve things and sometimes made matters worse." Krosnick and Malhotra (2007, 296) noted that "weights did almost nothing to reduce the differences between modes/sampling methods in the distributions of the political variables." In a study of three online panel vendors using over 30,000 observations, Mercer, Lau, and Kennedy (2018) found that even the most effective weighting strategies were able to remove only about 30 percent of the original bias. And to the extent weighting was useful, the key factor appears to be variable selection, not weighting technique.

ELECTION BENCHMARKS   Perhaps nowhere is the research as unsettled as it is with regard to the question of whether probability or nonprobability polls do a better job predicting election results. On the one hand, studies in Sweden and the United Kingdom suggest "election polls based on probability samples usually reached more accurate predictions than election polls based on non-probability samples" (Cornesse et al. 2020, 6; Sohlberg, Gilljam, and Martinsson 2017; Sturgis et al. 2018).

On the other hand, major retrospective analyses of US elections organized by AAPOR, the preeminent organization of pollsters in the United States, found mixed results as to which mode most accurately predicted elections. Kennedy et al.'s (2018) comprehensive review of 2016 polling found that IVR polls did best, live phone based on registration-based sampling did well, and RDD live phone polls and internet opt-in polls did the worst.[2] In 2020, the AAPOR analysis of 2020 polls concluded that

No mode of interviewing was unambiguously more accurate. Every mode of interviewing and every mode of sampling overstated the Democratic-Republican margin relative to the final certified vote margin. There were only minor differences in the polling error

---

[2] One reason IVR may have done well is that an important flaw in their sampling may have countered nonignorable nonresponse. Specifically, federal regulation mandated that IVR only call landline numbers, creating an obvious sampling problem because the type of people with landlines was likely different than people with cell phones. But since the cell phone population was younger and less White, IVR samples effectively countered pro-Democratic response bias with a pro-Republican sampling frame. Do we conclude the IVR mode was better? Or just lucky?

depending on how surveys sampled or interviewed respondents. Regardless of whether respondents were sampled using random-digit dialing, voter registration lists, or online recruiting, polling margins on average were too favorable to Democratic candidates. (Clinton et al 2021, 3, 28, 42; see also Enns and Rothschild 2020)

Specifically, the average absolute polling error varied from 4.4 points for IVR and online polls to 6.0 points for live phone and registration-based sampling polls (Clinton et al. 2021, 27).

Using election results to evaluate survey modes is tricky. It seems like we have a lot of data: Hundreds of polls across dozens of pollsters. However, nonprobabilistic polls have emerged in force only since 2016, meaning that assessments of their accuracy are based on just four elections: Two presidential elections in which polls tended to undercount Trump support and the 2018 and 2022 midterm elections in which polls were quite accurate. In 2016 and 2020, polls that were relatively pro-Trump were the most accurate. Does that mean that these polls had the best methods? Possibly.

It also possible, however, that so-called house effects mattered. House effects measure the extent to which pollster results tend to skew toward one of the parties (Jackman 2017). Consider the example of Rasmussen Reports, a pollster that Real Clear Politics rated as the second most accurate in 2016 and FiveThirtyEight rated as the third most accurate in 2020 (Rasmussen Reports 2016; Silver 2021a). They use a combination of IVR and online sampling. They also have a reputation for having pro-Republican house effects (Jackman 2017). For example, in the 2020, Rasmussen reported results suggesting that one-third of African-Americans would vote for Trump (Leonardi 2020). Trump may have done a bit better than expected among African-Americans, but most pollsters found Rasmussen's number to be decidedly optimistic for Trump. When we observe Rasmussen reporting relatively accurate results in 2016 and 2020, it is hard to know if their methods were better or if those were simply good years to have a pro-Republican house effect (Silver 2021a). The Trafalgar Group did even better than Rasmussen in 2020; many of their clients are Republican campaigns, something they did not always report (Silver 2021a).

Clearly, there is no consensus on which single approach to polling is the best. Polling aggregators such as fivethirtyeight.com and realclearpolitics.com lean into this uncertainty by aggregating across a large number of polls. The idea is that doing so will produce results that may be more accurate for two reasons. First, aggregation simply increases the effective sample size. Suppose we had ten different random samples of 1,000 people on a given day. That's really like having a single sample with 10,000 people, and for random samples, we know that the results from the larger sample will on average be closer to the true results than any single poll of 1,000. Of course, surveys are anything but cloned versions of the random sampling ideal. We have seen that there is a cacophony of polls, each with their different takes on how best to measure

The Wild West of Contemporary Polling   97

the pulse of the population. For aggregators, this heterogeneity is a strength: Maybe one poll – intentionally or not – does something that produces a pro-Democratic bias. Hopefully, another poll may do something differently that won't produce that bias. We saw with IVR polls in 2016, for example, that an obvious flaw – they did not call cellphones – turned into a strength because not calling cellphones meant they had less pro-Democratic bias. Add this all up, and the result may well be more accurate; certainly a broadly accepted view among political professionals is that polling aggregators are better than individual polls.

Alas, as with so many innovations, polling aggregation is no panacea. There are unavoidable decisions about which polls to include, decisions that are not easy particularly because some of the polls that showed the most signs of partisanship or had the least transparency did quite well in 2016 and 2020 because they were more favorable toward Trump. In 2022, Republican-friendly pollsters were more numerous in the days leading to the election, leading to a skew in polling averages. In New Hampshire, for example, nine of the 10 final polls were from Republican-leaning pollsters, perhaps explaining why the final Real-ClearPolitics poll margin was 7.5 percentage points too low for Democratic Senator Maggie Hassan (Morris 2020b).

And, for any given selection of polls, there is no guarantee that the average will be right: If the individual polls run warm one way or another, the aggregate will as well as happen in 2016 for state-level presidential polls and 2020 pretty much everywhere. And the aggregation occurring may be overstated if some risk-averse polling organizations hedge their results by shading their results toward consensus results. So even as polling aggregators are useful, they should not distract social scientists from pushing forward for better theory and practice so that the individual polls are better.

4.4 CONCLUSION

Polling has evolved from its Golden Era into a Wild West of competing approaches. Many prominent pollsters such as the *New York Times* and ABC News/*Washington Post* use traditional live phone calls to randomly selected people. Other pollsters such as Ipsos, SSRS, Pew and NORC recruit people via probability-based sampling and then interview them via the web. Many polling firms use non-random samples, firms such as Lucid and Dynata. YouGov and Civiqs use targeted sampling from online panels. And if that is not enough variation, many pollsters offer a range of options: Emerson College "uses a combination of landline respondents, cellphone respondents, and online panels to create a representative artificial sample" (Emerson 2021). The Trafalgar Group uses live callers, IVR, text messages, emails, and "two other proprietary digital methods we don't share publicly" (Trafalgar Group 2021).

The good news is that polling innovations have kept polling affordable and produce results that have generally performed pretty well. The bad news is that polling practice has become untethered from theory, meaning it has become harder to articulate bias and precision. As a practical matter, it has meant that surprises may be more common. Climate change is a useful analogy: Increased greenhouse gases have not only changed the average temperature, but also changed the variability of weather and thereby produced more dramatic storms and draughts. For polling, low response rates and nonprobabilistic methods may have not only increased the average bias, but they may well have also increased the potential for dramatic polling miscues, as we saw for state-level polls of the presidential elections in 2016 and 2020.

Contemporary polling splits into two camps. The probability samplers have roots in random sampling theory, but their low (and falling!) response rates make it hard to know how the theory applies. Nonprobability samplers have the momentum in terms of market share. But they are weakly tethered to theory and seem particularly vulnerable to nonignorable nonresponse that can seep in at multiple stages of their processes.

For all their differences, the two camps are united in one sense: Both disregard nonignorable nonresponse. The probability samplers use weighting to save their polls from nonresponse, an approach that assumes away nonignorable nonresponse. The nonprobability samplers use weights or quota protocols that also require response to be ignorable. As we have suggested throughout this book, nonignorable nonresponse should not be so easily dismissed. In Chapter 5, we therefore lay out more clearly evidence that nonignorable nonresponse is a real phenomenon and then develop informal and formal ways to think about the damage it can do.

PART II

A FRAMEWORK FOR MODERN POLLING

5

Nonignorable Nonresponse

> Usually we assume the problem is that group X is too small, but the actual problem may be that group X is too weird.
>
> Ken Goldstein (2016)

Nonignorable nonresponse has long been with us. Perhaps no story better illustrates this than the tale of political scientists' efforts to understand who votes in national elections. This should be easy, right? We can ask people if they voted and then get busy breaking down the results by age, gender, education, or whatever else strikes our fancy.

The problem is that the data seem off. After every election since 1952, the ANES has asked people whether they have voted. Survey respondents said they vote at higher rates than the official statistics suggested. In 1952, the survey respondents reported voting at rates 11 percentage points higher than actual turnout. The gap grew to 24 percentage points in 1996. In 2012, the gap was about 14 percentage points (Jackman and Spahn 2019, 193). While there are multiple reasons why surveys overestimate turnout (people sometimes lie, it turns out), one consistent theme is that nonresponse bias infects the survey results: Something about the people who are more willing to turnout makes them more willing to respond to surveys. This really isn't surprising as we can imagine the combination of feeling civically responsible plus socially outgoing that could be associated with voting and answering polls (Jackman and Spahn 2019; Brehm 1993; Burden 2000; Tourangeau, Groves, and Redline 2010).

Such nonignorable nonresponse crops up elsewhere as well. As discussed in Chapter 1, Bradley et al. (2021) showed that surveys – including those with huge samples – overstated the number of people who were vaccinated. Weighting doesn't solve the problem, and it is quite likely that the types of people who respond to health surveys are also the types of people who get vaccinated (and vote, for that matter!).

The polling community is flummoxed by what to do in the face of these problems. Mostly, analysts try to weight their way out of the problem, but we've seen that weighting only works for ignorable nonresponse. Other times analysts simply acknowledge nonignorable nonresponse could bias their results and then perhaps offer a bit of hope – but little evidence – that they've dodged the nonignorable bullet.

This chapter seeks to lay the groundwork for a more systematic approach to the problem. The point is not that nonignorable nonresponse is everywhere – surely it is not. The point is instead that nonignorable nonresponse *could be* almost anywhere, especially when surveys are based on nonprobability samples. With a foundation that explicitly centers this possibility, we can better reason through when the problem may be larger, how to diagnose it, and how to fix or at least ameliorate it. Section 5.1 describes qualitatively when nonignorable nonresponse may be likely. Section 5.2 works through the intuition about how and why nonignorable nonresponse undermines polling accuracy. Section 5.3 presents a framework for modeling nonignorable nonresponse and culminates by describing Meng's (2018) model of sampling error. Section 5.4 raises the possibility that nonignorability varies across groups, over time, and even across questions.

5.1 NONIGNORABLE NONRESPONSE: A PERVASIVE CONCERN

As we saw in Chapter 4, survey nonresponse is endemic and nonrandom. If measurable and benchmarkable characteristics completely explained nonresponse, weighting and related measures would allow us recover unbiased samples of survey responses. There may be differences of opinion about specific variables and forms used in weighting or related approaches, but broadly they should all point us in the right direction.

The more disturbing source of nonresponse, of course, is nonignorable nonresponse, which arises when responsiveness depends on the very opinions being studied. As mentioned earlier, nonignorable nonresponsiveness is a serious concern when measuring any form of civic participation, as the types of behavior being assessed could be correlated with the decision to participate in a survey or not.

PRESIDENTIAL POLLS Nonignorable nonresponsiveness lurks as a real possibility in many other areas. In modern US politics, many pollsters are concerned that political conservatism – or at least the Trump-inflected version of modern conservatism – may be correlated with a broader sense of distrust of the political system, a distrust that would make people less inclined to respond to pollsters (Matthews 2020). Hence, the "shy Trump" voters may not be "shy" (nonresponsive) because they are embarrassed of their views, but rather because they reject certain modes of civic participation. One sign that this is a problem is that Hillary Clinton underperformed her state-level polls in states with large white working-class populations, a pattern that repeated itself for

Nonignorable Nonresponse 103

Biden in 2020 (Clinton et al. 2021, 3; Silver 2016; Enns, Schuldt, Lagodny, and Rauter 2016).

Notice that weighting does not solve this problem. Many polls have disproportionately few white working-class voters. If among white working-class people, those who supported Trump were less likely to respond to surveys, weighting up the white working-class observations we do observe would do nothing but make us overconfident in incorrect results.

Nonignorable nonresponse could also occur in other segments of the electorate. Kennedy et al. (2016) found that online pollsters had particular trouble accurately characterizing the views of Hispanic people. It may be the case that the Hispanic voters who respond to polls may be more comfortable speaking English to unknown people than the nonresponsive Hispanic voters, creating a less Democratic pool of respondents. A sign that this was happening was that even as Clinton underperformed her polls in 2016 in states with large numbers of noncollege White people, she overperformed her state-level polls in states with many Hispanic voters.

Whatever the exact source, it seems reasonable to worry that presidential polls suffer from nonignorable nonresponse. Isakov and Kuriwaki (2020) used error estimates from the 2016 election to estimate the degree of nonignorable nonresponse that could reasonably be expected in the 2020 state-level presidential polls. Presciently, they found that the race would likely be closer in many battleground states than the polls suggested.

Gelman, Goel, Rivers, and Rothschild (2014) present a fascinating case study of nonignorable nonresponse. They investigated changes in polling for President Obama after his widely panned performance in his first debate with Republican Mitt Romney. Obama's polling numbers fell, which many observers took to mean that some voters had switched allegiance from Obama to Romney. However, across several polls, ranging from a more traditional Pew Research survey to the Xbox poll we discussed at the start of Chapter 4, they found that the percentage of Democrats dropped markedly after the debate. In other words, the observed polling changes were due to changes in the composition of the sample, not due to changes in support levels. Weighting or stratifying based on standard demographics did not solve the problem. Stratifying based on party identification, ideology, and past vote would be needed to eliminate the composition effects. For pollsters who have access to panel data that include political attitudes from before an election campaign begins, the nonresponse can be rendered ignorable with appropriate inclusion of these variables. If pollsters do not have these data (which is common), these variables are unmeasured and to the extent they affect response propensity and candidate preferences the omission of these variables will cause nonignorable nonresponse bias.

HEALTH SURVEYS Nonignorable nonresponse is also a common concern in health. Fry et al. (2017) found that participants in a large British health survey were less likely to be obese, to smoke, and to drink alcohol than the broader population. These differences added up to a situation in which people in their early 70s who responded to the survey were 50 percent less likely to die than people in that age cohort in the general population. Similarly, Hill, Roberts, Ewings, and Gunnell (1997) found that survey respondents smoked and drank less and exercised more than nonrespondents. If we're trying to measure healthy behavior, surveys will be corrupted as the behavior being measured (e.g., smoking) will be correlated with the propensity to respond. A study of glucose intolerance found that nonrespondents "were 59 percent more likely to report being in poor or fair health than respondents to the main survey" (Tourangeau and Plewes 2013, 42).

Nonignorable nonresponse comes up often in Covid-related research. As we have seen already, Bradley et al. (2021) showed how hard it was to use polls to assess vaccine take-up. Early in the pandemic when people desperately wanted to know how widespread the disease was, it was incredibly difficult to generalize from testing results to community-level infection rates because getting tested was a classic nonignorable response mechanism: Those who get tested were more likely to test positive, because they either had symptoms or had been in close contact with infected people (Bailey 2020).

One story where weighting and nonignorable nonresponse crashed together came from Santa Clara County, California, in the early days of the Covid outbreak. Testing was limited and seemed highly variable from place to place. Hence, we had very little confidence in our ability to know how prevalent the disease was, which was unfortunate because knowing the prevalence by geographic area could help us target policies to slow the spread while also helping us understand the contagiousness and lethality of the virus.

Researchers in Santa Clara acted quickly to conduct a study of Covid prevalence in their community (Bendavid et al. 2020). They recruited participants with geographically targeted Facebook ads, producing an impressive sample of 3,330 people who were tested for Covid. The sample composition was less impressive: 63 percent of the respondents were female (compared to 50 percent of the population in the county), and 8 percent of the respondents were Hispanic (compared to 26 percent of the county population) (Bendavid et al. 2020, 5).

The researchers argued that weighting would be sufficient to enable them to make conclusions about the county population. Their weights were large – not surprising given how unrepresentative the sample was – and the consequences of weighting were substantial. Of those tested, 1.5 percent had Covid. After applying their weights, the researchers reported the prevalence in the county was 2.8 percent, almost double the sample average. This is an important difference, for doubling the estimated prevalence would essentially halve the estimated death rate for those who contract the disease and would suggest a more rapid path to herd immunity.

For weighting to be valid, the nonresponse needs to be ignorable. That is, once we account for different response rates depending on measured variables,

Nonignorable Nonresponse 105

the distribution of disease in the sample is the same as in the population. This is a general statistical concept that manifests itself in a simple conceptual test. For any given group, are the people in the sample a random sample of the population? That is, are the Hispanic respondents in the Santa Clara County data a random sample of all Hispanics in the county? If this is true for all groups, then weighting will produce an unbiased estimate of county prevalence.

However, as pointed out by many commentators on the article, the Santa Clara sample may have differed from the underlying population not only in terms of observable characteristics such as age, race, gender, and zip code, but also in terms of unobserved characteristics such as health status. It is quite possible, for example, that those more likely to be sick were more likely to respond to the Facebook ads. If that were true, the proportion of sick people in the sample would be an overestimate, not an underestimate as the researchers argued.

BEHAVIORAL AND ORGANIZATIONAL SURVEYS The specter of nonignorable nonresponse looms in other contexts as well. Mercer (2020) compared results related to civic engagement from 10 nonprobability polls to Census-reported baselines. He found that a "large majority" of the bias was due to nonignorable nonresponse rather than imbalances in demographics.

Many organizations wish to assess how satisfied stakeholders are with what the organization is doing. Universities, for example, care deeply about the satisfaction of students and alumni. The problem is the type of people who respond to surveys by the university may be skewed in problematic ways. Kreuter, Presser, and Tourangeau (2008) found that alumni who experienced academic problems in college were less likely to respond to polls about university life, making it very hard for universities to appreciate, let alone respond to, concerns among former students who may have the most insight about where the university was going wrong. And among current students, the student response rates for teaching evaluations are notoriously low and potentially fickle as many wonder whether satisfaction surveys overrepresent students who are very pleased or very displeased with their instructors.

ECONOMIC ANALYSIS Labor economists are deeply interested in what kind of job training best helps unemployed people find jobs. Behaghel, Crepon, Gurgand, and Le Barbanchon (2015) assessed a French job training experiment in which unemployed people were randomly assigned to an intensive job program. Because they had official administrative data, researchers could assess the program directly. They also wanted to know job quality and other views and experiences of participants so they also conducted a phone survey. This produced an excellent opportunity for assessing possible nonresponse bias because the truth on the key question of whether someone got a job was known. The survey had a 57 percent response rate (that the authors characterized as "low"!). Nonrespondents were more than 10 percentage points more likely to have gotten a job. Apparently, people who got a job were too busy to answer the survey. In other words, willingness to respond and getting a job were correlated, meaning nonignorable nonresponse clouded the ability of the phone survey to accurately characterize employment outcomes.

What's more, there was evidence that the effect of the program was higher among the respondents. That is, when using the phone survey to compare those who had been randomly given more intensive job training and those who received the standard fare, the results suggested the intensive effort boosted employment by 13.6 percentage points. But since they had administrative data, they knew that in the whole population, the intensive training boosted employment by 9.6 percent. In other words, nonresponse bias meant not only that decision-makers using the survey would think that more people were getting jobs than they actually were, they would also think that their program worked better than it did. Maybe that's good news – but only if you don't care that it's wrong.

Nonignorable nonresponse can produce other distortions. Pollster Ann Selzer, famous for her accurate polling in Iowa, was tasked with assessing how many people were familiar with transcendental meditation; here's what she found (Leonhardt 2020):

> "There's a self-selection in people's willingness to talk to polls," she said. She recalled conducting a 45-minute-long survey for a private client years ago about Transcendental Meditation. "Our finding was that about half the people we talked to had an experience with Transcendental Meditation," she said. "Do you think that's true?"

Surveys to identify the number of gun owners have the opposite problem: Survey questions about gun ownership are extremely off-putting to gun owners, many of who own guns in part because of a distrust of outsiders (Urbatsch 2018).

Nonignorable nonresponse is likely even more severe in environments in which the self-selection is stronger than in surveys. The famous Kinsey Reports of the 1950s were based on thousands of interviews with people about their sex lives. Shockingly for the staid fifties, the reports suggested, Americans were not-so-staid behind closed doors. The reports were good fodder for conversation, but have not held up as social science because they were based on voluntary opt-in surveys. It's far from crazy to wonder if the type of people willing to talk about their sex lives were a bit friskier than nonrespondents.[1]

More recently, many researchers are intrigued about the possibility of using Twitter (rebranded as "X") to gauge public opinion. But the risks are clear: No one thinks Twitter "is real life," as the people on Twitter are unrepresentative both demographically and ideationally (Mellon and Prosser 2017). Any effort to try to distill any meaningful information from Twitter content will need first and foremost to address the nonignorability of the selection process into posting on Twitter.

---

[1] It didn't help the representativeness of the sample that they sought respondents among prisoners and male prostitutes.

5.2 NONIGNORABLE NONRESPONSE: INTUITION

There is little doubt, then, that nonignorable nonresponse is possible in many contexts and more possible as we move away from random sampling. But what exactly is the problem? Before moving to formal statement of the problem, we will begin with a contrived example in which nonignorable nonresponse is clear and the problems it causes are unmistakable. We will then revisit that example in more relevant contexts, showing that the logic carries over directly.

Here's our contrived example: Suppose we want to estimate the points people would score in the NBA. That is, we want to predict how you or your friends or your neighbors or anyone in the country would do as a professional basketball player. We'll start by thinking of the sample that we observe in the NBA. We can roughly characterize the odds someone is in the sample as a function of height, something that is easily observable, and athleticism, something that is not.[2]

We observe, of course, only a limited sample: Those who actually play in the NBA. Can we generalize from this sample to the entire population? We all know the answer: Of course we can't. But why is that the case? Figure 5.1 shows a schematic. Height is on the horizontal axis, and athleticism is on the vertical axis. The shaded area represents range where people are (relatively) likely to make it into the NBA; the nonshaded area indicates a range where people are unlikely to make it into the NBA.

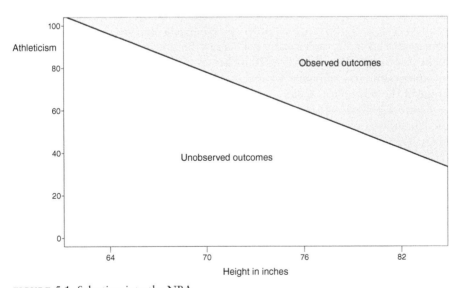

FIGURE 5.1 Selection into the NBA

---

[2] Or, more accurately, we might say that athleticism can be observed, but is difficult to quantify and therefore is seldom available as a variable in analyses.

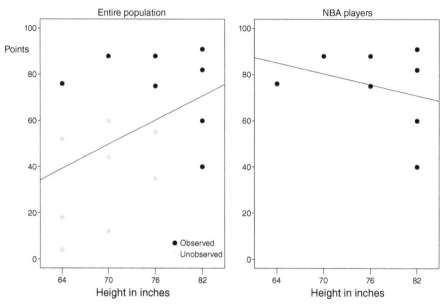

FIGURE 5.2 Height and performance in the NBA among those who made it and did not

On the far right of the figure, we see that very tall people are reasonably likely to make it to the NBA, whatever their athleticism. As we move left and people get shorter, the range of athleticism that gets one into the NBA narrows. Someone who is 76 inches tall (6′4″) must be above average athleticism to make it into the NBA. Someone 70 inches (5′10″) must be well above average in athleticism, and someone 64 inches (5′4″) needs to be in the very highest range of the athleticism scale.[3]

Figure 5.2 illustrates the outcome from this selection process. The panel on the left shows outcomes we would observe if everyone played a season in the NBA. This is the "truth," the behavior of some population about which we are trying to understand. The dark shaded dots are for people who actually made it into the NBA, and the gray dots are for those who did not. The players who made it had the combination of height and athleticism discussed earlier and tended to score a lot of points. The people who did not make it tended would be neither tall nor athletic and would not have scored much (and we're being generous to say they would score at all!). We see a clear relationship between height and points.

The figure on the right shows only those people who made it into our selected NBA sample; as we argued earlier, they were tall and/or athletic

---

[3] This may seem a bit far-fetched, but recall that all 5′3″ of Mugsy Bogues played productively in the NBA for years. It is safe to say he was extraordinarily athletic, probably more athletic than the 7′7″ Manute Bol, who also had a productive career in the NBA.

Nonignorable Nonresponse   109

enough to make it to the NBA. Can we generalize from the sample observed on the right to the "truth" in the panel on the left? Clearly not, in two different senses. First note that the average points in the panel on the right are 75, which is much higher than 55, the average of points in the whole population. Such a disparity is not at all surprising if people are selected into the NBA based on their ability to score points. Note also that the relationship between height and points is very different in our selected sample; there is a negative relationship. Here again, the reason is clear: The short people selected into the NBA were extraordinarily athletic, while the tall people included some klutzes.

This example is a bit silly. So now let's use the logic from this example in more realistic examples. First, suppose that we are looking at the relationship between high school GPA and college GPA. Suppose, as is often the case, that selection into college depends on high school GPA, which is observable to the university selection committee, and personal qualities such as diligence and desire to do good, which are observable to the admission committee in recommendation letters, essays, and descriptions of activities, but are hard to quantify and therefore may not typically make their way into university data. The situation would resemble Figure 5.1, with the difference being that the horizontal axis would be high school GPA and the vertical axis would reflect the applicant's character. Applicants with very high GPAs might be likely to get in regardless of what their letters say, while applicants with low GPAs would only be admitted if their letters and other materials suggested extraordinary character.

This would then lead to a situation resembling Figure 5.2, but now the horizontal axis is high school GPA and the vertical axis is college GPA. If everyone were admitted, we might observe a clear relationship between X and Y, as in the figure. However, among those who were actually admitted, we would observe patterns similar to Figure 5.2: (a) The students admitted to college would have higher grades than those who were not admitted would have had, and (b) there would be no relationship between high school GPA and college GPA because the applicants with high GPAs in high school who were admitted included some students who really were not that diligent or studious while the applicants with low high school GPAs who were admitted were limited to only those applicants who showed signs of extraordinary character.

We can extend the logic to surveys. Figure 5.3 shows a case in which people select into surveys based on two factors, education (which is easily observable) and social trust (which is not). It's the same as a figure we saw earlier, just with the axes relabeled. Figure 5.4 then shows the measured opinions from people who answered the survey; unobserved outcomes are the opinions of people who did not respond to the survey. On the left, we see the entire population. This is the truth that we are trying to approximate with our survey respondents. The average feeling thermometer of the Democratic Party for this population of 16 individuals is 55, and there is a clear relationship between education and warm feelings toward the Democratic Party.

110   Part II: Framework for Modern Polling

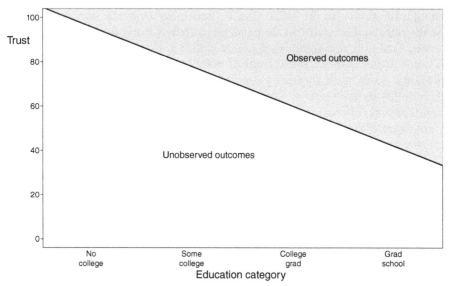

FIGURE 5.3 Selection into a political survey

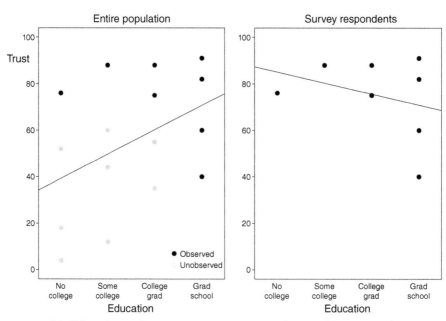

FIGURE 5.4 Education and trust among survey respondents and nonrespondents

However, given the sampling mechanism depicted in the previous figure, we only observe the eight dark shaded dots in the panel on the right. This group runs much warmer toward Democrats than the population, with an average

Nonignorable Nonresponse

feeling thermometer of 75, much higher than the average feeling thermometer toward Democrats in the population. Also, the relationship between education and feelings toward the Democratic Party is actually negative in the observed sample. Because the data in this figure are identical to Figure 5.2, the source of problems is the same: Response is nonignorable in that one of the factors driving nonresponse is unobserved and causally related to the outcome we are trying to measure. This means that respondents run warmer and that the people with less education will be particularly warm relative to their educational peers as a relatively high degree of trust was needed for them to overcome the extent to which low levels of education depressed the likelihood of responding.

These three stories are, by design, identical with regard to the underlying data. In each case, the existence of nonrandom selection inhibited our ability to learn accurately about the population from our sample. The point is not that we have characterized the magnitudes: Surely, the differences between the population and the observed sample in the NBA example are muted relative to reality and the effects in the political example are exaggerated. The point is to highlight the mechanism: It is the same in each example.

The influence of this nonignorable nonresponse is not easily solved. Figure 5.5 weights our survey data following the procedures outlined in Chapter 3. The size of the circle for each observation is proportional to its weight. For the lower education levels, the weights equal 2 as people in each of these groups constitute one-quarter of the population but only one eighth of the observed

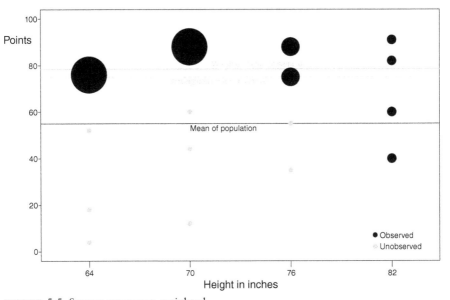

FIGURE 5.5 Survey responses, weighted

sample. For the highest education group, weights are 0.5 as these types of people constitute only one-quarter of the population but one half of the observed sample.

Weighting does little to improve the situation. The population average is 55. The unweighted sample average is 75, which vastly overstates the population average. The weighted average is even *worse* as it goes to 78. The regression line connecting height and points continues to be negatively sloped. And, perhaps the biggest risk is if we were to try to characterize subgroups as we would dramatically overstate the feeling thermometers among people with lower levels of education.

5.3 A GENERAL MODEL OF NONRESPONSE

Our task now is to move from illustrating the problem to providing a framework that helps us characterize the problem in general terms. Key to this task is to develop the concept of correlation between the decision to respond and the response itself. This concept has come up repeatedly, and here we define it graphically and mathematically.

In each of the illustrations in Section 5.2, there was some unmeasured factor that affected both whether an individual was observed in the data. For the NBA case, this factor was athleticism. For the college case, the factor was character. For the survey case, the factor was social trust. These are very specific examples and illustrative examples, and now we will generalize them into a variable we will label R^*, with the letter R indicating the variable relates to response and the $*$ indicating that we do not directly observe this variable. We'll refer to this variable as the response propensity. People with high values of R^* really want to answer surveys. People with low values of R^* really don't. Think of a classroom in which a teacher asks a question. People with high values of R^* are raising their hands as high as they can, just barely restraining themselves from blurting out the answer. People with low values of R^* are looking down, probably at the phones. They would rather eat a slug than answer the question.

The central question in determining whether nonresponse is ignorable or nonignorable is determining whether R^* is related to Y, the variable we are trying to estimate for a population. The top panel of Figure 5.6 shows an example in which R^* is not related to Y. Each dot is a person. The x-axis shows the value of R^* for each individual; the y-axis reflects the value of Y for each individual. We'll use figures that look like this quite often going forward. We are not saying that the distribution of people actually looks like this, only that it provides a useful reference point in which there are more people in the middle of both R^* and Y than at either extreme. It looks kind of like a fish and, in this case, the fish is flat, which means that there is no relationship between R^* and Y.

To confirm this, look up from any given value of R^*: The average Y value of the dots for this value of R^* is always 50. In other words, the kids raising

Nonignorable Nonresponse

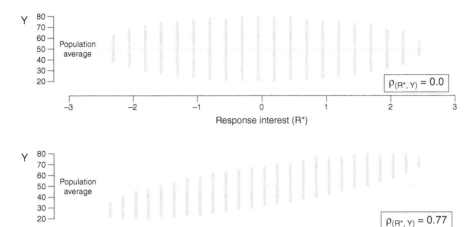

FIGURE 5.6 Hypothetical distributions of response propensities and Y in a population

their hands so hard as to dislocate their shoulders (the dots on the right of the figure) have the same average value of Y as the kids with their heads buried in their phones (the dots on the left of the figure). This is an instance of ignorable nonresponse as the propensity to respond is unrelated to Y. We could get a sample of only a few people on the right (the eager beavers), or we could get a sample of everyone: Either way, the average would be expected to be 50.

The bottom panel of Figure 5.6 shows an example in which R^* is related to Y. Each dot is still a person, and axes represent the same characteristics. The difference is that the fish is tilted, which means that there is a relationship between R^* and Y. The people on the right who are eager to respond have high values of Y. The people on the left who are reluctant to respond have low values of Y. Nonresponse is nonignorable in this case because the propensity to respond is related to Y. If we ask only a few people, we'll get a selection of the eager beavers and they'll be high Y types. If we ask a larger sample, we'll get more people in the middle of the R^* range and we'll observe a lower average value of Y. The danger of tilted fishism (meaning nonignorable nonresponse, of course) is that in a world with very low response rates, we'll get just a few people on the right and their views of Y may be far from the true population average.

The figures illustrate the difference between ignorable nonresponse in the top panel and nonignorable nonresponse in the bottom panel. We move to formalize this distinction by introducing a parameter that characterizes the relationship between R^* and Y. This parameter is $\rho_{R^*,Y}$, which is the Greek letter *rho* with subscripts R^* and Y. This parameter measures the correlation between the propensity to respond, R^*, and Y. If $\rho_{R^*,Y} = 0$, the correlation is zero and nonresponse is ignorable as it is in the top panel of

Figure 5.6. If $\rho_{R*,Y} \neq 0$ the correlation is nonzero and nonresponse is nonignorable as it is in the bottom panel of Figure 5.6. (The figure shows a positive correlation between response propensity and Y. For a negative correlation, the fish would tilt downward.)

We're going to introduce an additional type of correlation, one that is closely related to what we have just seen. So far we have been thinking about the correlation of Y with the latent (meaning unobserved) propensity to respond, which we denote as $\rho_{R*,Y}$ (note the asterisk). We can also think about the correlation of Y and whether someone actually responds or not, a quantity we denote as $\rho_{R,Y}$ (note the lack of an asterisk). This quantity is something we can directly calculate if we observe R and Y. We will focus on this measure of the association between response and outcome for the rest of the chapter. Conceptually, it connects naturally to our discussion. In practice, there are some nuances, nuances we discuss in the online appendix.

To formalize these ideas into a relatively simple framework we follow Meng's (2018, 689) to characterize survey error with a single equation. It is one of the rare social scientific contributions that is simple, yet comprehensive and powerful (see also Bethlehem 2002; Tourangeau and Plewes 2013).

We focus on the sample mean of a variable of interest, Y, from a sample of n observations drawn from a population of size N. (The logic extends to other statistical quantities such as regression coefficients.) We indicate responsiveness as $R_i = 1$ if individual i responds and 0 otherwise. This R differs from R^*. R equals 0 or 1 and is something we observe R. R^* is the unobserved ("latent") propensity to respond; in our example, it ranges from -3 to $+3$.

Our goal is to calculate sampling error, which is simply how far our estimate of the sample mean is from the true population mean. At this point, we are not doing any statistical modeling; we are simply calculating the difference between the average value of Y for people with $R = 1$ and the average value of Y for the entire sample. This is essentially an accounting identity. Although the equation we present could be used to simplify calculations, we will use it to re-write sampling error in a way that decomposes the error into three theoretically interesting quantities.

We'll denote the observed sample mean among respondents as $\overline{Y}_n$ where the lower-case n subscript indicates the number of people in the sample (i.e., people for whom $R = 1$). The quantity we care about is the difference between the mean of Y in the $R = 1$ group and the entire population, which we write as $\overline{Y}_n - \overline{Y}_N$. The appendix to this chapter uses algebra and the statistical definitions of covariance and correlation to rewrite this quantity as

$$\overline{Y}_n - \overline{Y}_N = \underbrace{\rho_{R,Y}}_{\text{data quality}} \underbrace{\sqrt{\frac{N-n}{n}}}_{\text{data quantity}} \underbrace{\sigma_Y}_{\text{data difficulty}} \tag{5.1}$$

Nonignorable Nonresponse 115

The derivation of this equation did not model randomness or add other traditional statistical steps. It is literally just a way to rewrite $\overline{Y}_n - \overline{Y}_N$ in a way that is always true, for any selection process. In other words, for any sample from a population, Equation 5.1 is exact. The beauty of this identity is that it parses sources of error into three interesting categories, each of which tells us something important about what we can learn from survey samples.

DATA QUALITY ($\rho_{R,Y}$) The first term in Equation 5.1 is $\rho_{R,Y}$, the correlation in the population between R and Y. This quantity can be taken to reflect quality of data with regard to sampling. Bradley et al. (2021) refer to this quantity as the "data defect correlation."

Because Equation 5.1 is an accounting identity, we know that if $\rho_{R,Y} = 0$, then the mean of the sample will literally equal the mean of the population. This fact points to central insight of random sampling: If R is based on a truly random process, then $\rho_{R,Y}$ will be expected to be quite close to zero. Remember, though, that Equation 5.1 is an accounting identity so even when a sample is randomly chosen, it is unlikely that the correlation of R and Y will literally equal zero; hence, there will be sampling variation, a factor we incorporate below.

When $\rho_{R,Y} \neq 0$, the sampled mean ($\overline{Y}_n$) will not equal the population mean ($\overline{Y}_N$) unless $n = N$ (meaning the sample is the entire population) or $\sigma_Y = 0$ (meaning the value of Y is the same for everyone in the population), neither of which are interesting polling contexts. Hence, the quality of all polling in our post-random sampling world hinges directly on this quantity. The larger $\rho_{R,Y}$, the larger the sampling error, the exact magnitude of which will interact with the other terms in ways that we explore below.

DATA QUANTITY The second term in Equation 5.1, $\sqrt{\frac{N-n}{n}}$, relates to the size of the population (capital N) and the size of the sample (lower case n). Two consequences emerge from this term. First, as long as $\rho_{R,Y} \neq 0$ and $\sigma_Y \neq 0$, the actual error will fall as the sample size n increases.[4]

This effect of sample size will not surprise many contemporary pollsters, but we should note that the effect is quite different than the effect of sample size in random sampling. Recall from Section 2.3 that the expected mean from a random sample is the true value *no matter what the sample size is*. The power of a larger sample in random sampling is to reduce the sampling variance of the mean. In Meng's equation (Equation 5.1), a larger sample is associated with smaller error. Roughly speaking, Meng's equation says that *all else equal*, the polling bias diminishes as the sample size gets larger.

There is a deeper, more counterintuitive aspect of the data quantity term in Equation 5.1: Sampling error depends on the size of the population, N.

---

[4] That point may not jump out of the equation. To confirm, note that the term inside the square root will get smaller as n gets larger. Mathematically, we can show that the derivative of the error equation with respect to n is negative, meaning that the sampling error declines as n, the sample size, increases.

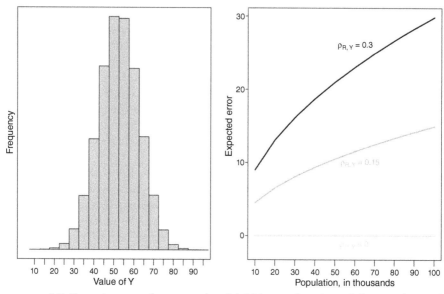

FIGURE 5.7 Error in mean from sample of 1,000 as a function of data quality and population

This result is shocking to modern polling sensibilities. Recall that one of the incredible properties of random sampling was that it unlinks the size of the population from the properties of the estimator. A (truly) random sample of 1,000, for example, will be equally accurate for any target population, be it a small state in the United States or the entire country of India.

In Equation 5.1, however, the target *population* size (N) matters for any nonzero $\rho_{R,Y}$. The bigger the target population, the more error there will be for a given sample size and nonzero $\rho_{R,Y}$ and σ_Y. Figure 5.7 illustrates the relationship between population size and expected error by showing the sampling error when estimating the mean of Y from a sample of size 1,000. The left panel shows the distribution of the true data: Y has a mean of 50 and standard deviation of 10. Honestly, we don't really need to see the left panel, but we include it here to put the magnitude of the errors that is displayed in the panel on the right in context. The line on the bottom of the panel on the right shows that if $\rho_{R,Y} = 0$, then the sampling error is zero, no matter what the population size. This is consistent with our intuition about random sampling. If $\rho_{R,Y} = 0.15$, however, we see error rising with the population size. That is, *for the same size sample*, error will grow as the target population grows. And it grows quickly: The error in our sample mean for a sample of 1,000 speeds past 10 for even a smallish population of 100,000. We don't even want to

Nonignorable Nonresponse

think about what happens for a country of 300 million.[5] The error grows even more rapidly with population size in Figure 5.7 if $\rho_{R,Y} = 0.3$. Errors that are 10 or bigger are pretty dispiriting given the true distribution displayed in the panel on the left.

Because linking sampling error to population size is apostasy to people steeped in the random sampling paradigm, it is worth unpacking this result. One way to think about how the population matters is to think of sampling as a process like queuing for concert tickets where the first n people in line get tickets. If we are pulling from a huge population, the first 1,000 people in line will be very hard-core fans of the band. That is, if we are looking at the 14 million people living in Tokyo, it is easy to imagine that the first 1,000 people in line will be bonkers for the band. If we're looking at the 100,000 people in Peoria, Illinois, the first 1,000 people in line will be fans, to be sure, but will include less fanatical people; there simply aren't that many hard-core fans in a smaller city.

Figure 5.8 illustrates the effect of population size by using a tilted fish figure to show samples of 20 from relatively large and small populations. As before, each dot is a person. On the x-axis is the person's interest in responding; the higher this is, the more likely a person responds. On the y-axis is Y, which is the value of interest. In this case, Y is a feeling thermometer with an average of 50 and a standard deviation of 10. The figure illustrates a case in which $\rho_{R,Y} > 0$, meaning the response is nonignorable.

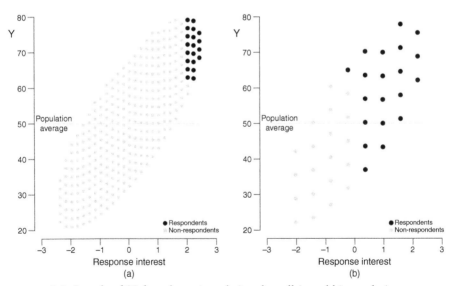

FIGURE 5.8 Sample of 20 from large (panel a) and small (panel b) populations

---

[5] Meng (2018) assesses such an example; it's not pretty.

The dark shaded dots are the people who responded. Because of the nonignorable nonresponse, they are not a random sample of the entire population. In the large population panel (a) on the left, there are 328 people, 20 of whom respond. The respondents are quite unrepresentative. Every one of them has a value of Y above 60, and their average value of Y is 71, which is much higher than the population average of 50.

In the small population panel (b) on the right, there are 40 people of whom 20 responded. The respondents are also unrepresentative due to the nonignorable nonresponse, but the magnitude of the unrepresentativeness is much smaller because the pollster had to go deeper into the pool to get 20 responses. This means that less unrepresentative people made their way into the sample, leading us to see values of Y as low as 35 and an average value of Y among respondents equal to 60, which is higher than the population average of 50, but not as far off as for the large population example.

In actual surveys, this dynamic could lead error to increase with population size. If we sample 1,000 people from Tokyo, we may well be getting the people with highest propensity to respond who also have distinctive views. If we sample 1,000 people from Peoria, we're going lower down the chain in terms of response propensity and hence reaching people with less of a connection between response propensity and opinions. We discuss how to de-link population size and sampling error in Chapter 6.

One of the things that the Meng equation clarifies is that we cannot think of nonresponse in isolation. Nonresponse will lower n. This is a problem *only if $\rho_{R,Y}$ is not zero*. If $\rho_{R,Y}$ is zero or very small, we will have a small amount of bias, even with substantial nonresponse (Groves, Fowler et al. 2009, 190). One implication is that trying to cure polling by increasing response rates is likely inefficient and possibly ineffectual. Low sample sizes are a problem when response and Y are correlated and this continues to be the case even as the sample size gets very large. A better conceptual starting point is to focus on $\rho_{R,Y}$. If it is zero, then low response rates are less worrisome. If it is not zero, then one should focus on either lowering it or using methods that account for nonzero values of $\rho_{R,Y}$.

DATA DIFFICULTY The final term in Equation 5.1 is σ_Y, the standard deviation of Y.[6] Meng (2018) refers to this quantity as data difficulty in the sense that errors will be smaller if Y varies only a little in the population. If we imagine an extreme case where the value of Y is the same for everyone in a population, $\sigma_Y = 0$ and our estimate will be fine even if theoretically there were nonignorable nonresponse.[7] Or, more realistically, if the value of Y is the same for all but a few people in the population, the error will be modest even

---

[6] Note that this is a population quantity so we need to use N in the denominator when calculating the variance of Y, not $N-1$ as is typical in a sampling context.

[7] The correlation of a binary R and Y is a surprisingly subtle relationship. If Y were the same for everyone in the population, the correlation of R and Y would have to be zero, for example. See Meng (2018, 697) for more discussion of this point.

Nonignorable Nonresponse 119

if there is nonignorable nonresponse. Generally, this aspect of expected polling error is taken as a given, although later when we add covariates we can think about reducing the unexplained error in Y, which will, all else equal, reduce the sampling error when $\rho_{R,Y} \neq 0$.

5.4 HETEROGENEITY IN ρ

It is hard to talk about politics for long without discussing opinion in subgroups. Trump's victory in 2016 was widely attributed to his success among noncollege Whites in crucial battleground states. His relatively strong performance in 2020 was attributed by some to relative improvements among Hispanics and African-Americans. Similar interests in subgroups are common for researchers in marketing, health, and other areas for which specific groups are particularly interesting.

Pollsters working from the random sampling paradigm know to be cautious about subgroup analyses for the simple reason that the numbers can be small, sometimes very small. The averages for these subgroups will be unbiased (meaning they will not be systematically high or low), but they will be quite imprecise for the reasons we discussed in Chapter 2 if the subgroup sample is small, something that is typically the case. This is one of the remarkable features of random sampling: If we want to characterize the views of all 150 million voters in the US within 3 percent, we need a sample of 1,000. If we want to characterize the views of the White noncollege voters in Michigan within 3 percent, we also need a sample of 1,000. In fact, a national poll would only produce a handful of White noncollege voters in Michigan and we cannot, therefore, say anything meaningful about such a targeted group. This is one of those concepts that pollsters understand in their bones, but nonpollsters sometimes find surprising.

From the random sampling perspective, we are not helpless to discuss subgroups of course. Some polls target subgroups to get sample sizes needed for group-specific analyses. Or if we merge results across polls, we often patch together sufficient subgroup samples.

The Meng framework makes it easy to see a further complication: The patterns of nonignorable nonresponse may vary by group. So far we have articulated the model in terms of a single $\rho_{R,Y}$ parameter for the entire population, but that is likely a simplification in many instances. We know that nonresponse varies across groups (Peytchev 2013; Groves and Peytcheva 2008). We also have evidence that bias can vary across groups. For example, Mercer (2016) found that in the nine nonprobability polls they compared to known benchmarks, the results for Hispanics and African-Americans were off by more than 10 percentage points.

It is therefore possible – and probably likely – that the extent to which R and Y are related varies across groups, including the possibility that the direction of the bias is different for different subgroups (Peress 2010, 1429; Lin and Schaeffer 1995; Voigt, Koepsell, and Daling 2003). Sometimes, the biases could offset each other. In Part IV of this book, for example, we find strong evidence that response is nonignorable for Democrats and Republicans, but that the direction of bias in the parties is opposite: Democratic respondents are more liberal on average than typical Democrats in the population while Republican respondents are more conservative on average than typical Republicans in the population. If we are trying to characterize the full population, these two biases mostly offset each other. But other times these biases may not sufficiently offset each other. In the 2016 state-level polls, there were likely offsetting ρ parameters across groups to some degree, but on balance, it seems highly plausible that the overall ρ in the population was far enough from zero to skew poll results toward Hillary Clinton.

The more general point is that we need to be constantly vigilant about the possibility that nonignorable nonresponse biases our findings. When we are interested in subgroups, we cannot lean on the hope that the differences balance each other out. For example, if we are trying to assess the opinions of Democrats or Republicans or Hispanics or any other group, we need to be alert to the possibility that there is a group-specific value of ρ. For example, many pollsters have noted a leftward shift among White liberals on race. This could, of course, reflect a shift in opinion, but we should not ignore the possibility that Democratic respondents are more liberal on race than Democrats in general. Similarly, a Republican politician interested in their "base" may observe results that are skewed to the right, perhaps leading them to justify more extreme position-taking.

And these patterns likely change over time (Berinsky 2004, 139) and could even be different depending on whether the questions are about income, politics, or health. So just as the random sampling paradigm pushes us to make sure we have adequate sample sizes for subgroups, the nonignorable nonresponse framework encourages us to build in assessments for nonignorability in every survey and for every subgroup that we would like to characterize.

5.5 CONCLUSION

Nonignorable nonresponse has long been important in survey research. In the *Literary Digest* and mid-century quota-sampling eras, nonignorable nonresponse likely had devastating results. In the glory days of random sampling, however, nonignorable nonresponse was held at bay because random sampling with perfect response severed the connection between factors that affect the decision to respond and factors that affect the response itself.

Unfortunately, as nonresponse rose, the door was opened for nonignorable nonresponse to affect randomly sampled surveys Now that nonresponse has reached alarming levels, the door is wide open. With the increasing reliance on opt-in surveys, we can wonder if the door has been blasted off its hinges.

Nonignorable Nonresponse

This chapter presented a model for polling that incorporates nonignorable nonresponse based on Meng's (2018) general formulation of sampling error. Central to Meng's formulation is the correlation of response and outcome. If the correlation is zero in a given population for a given response pattern, there is no sampling error. Random sampling will typically not produce literally zero correlation between R and Y so there will typically be some error, but its magnitude will be small and in proportion to the low correlation between R and Y. When sampling is not random, however, the expected and observed values of the correlation between R and Y may be larger and, when that happens, the damage is not simply proportional to ρ but is proportional to the *population* size, meaning the wheels can come off a national poll pretty quickly when there is even relatively minor correlation between response and Y.

Thinking about the Meng equation helps us appreciate the metaphorical crossroads facing the polling community. One option is to stay the course. Pollsters can assume away ρ and continue to try to weight their way out of nonresponse. When ρ is very small or zero, these approaches will produce good results. However, those who stay the course cannot forget the possibility that their assumption that ρ is zero may not always be true. When this happens, the status quo approaches can fail – and do so proportionately to *population* size, an unnerving prospect to say the least.

The other way forward embraces the Meng equation and builds a concern about ρ into the science of polling. A first insight is what we have covered here: The stakes can be high given the damage a small ρ can do in a large population. This highlights the perilous state of contemporary polling where sampling frames are increasingly based on opt-in behavior. This approach is not simply cautionary, however; once we embrace the possibility of nonzero ρ, we can build a tool kit of prescriptive insights as well, insights that we will need not only when characterizing populations, but also when characterizing subgroups. Chapter 6 therefore uses the Meng equation to develop specific ideas about the kinds of surveys that give us the best chance to contain the damage from nonignorable nonresponse in a low-response world.

APPENDIX: DERIVATION OF MENG EQUATION

Begin by rewriting the sample average on terms of R:

$$\overline{Y}_n = \frac{\sum_{i=1}^N R_i Y_i}{n} = \frac{\sum_{i=1}^N R_i Y_i}{\sum_{i=1}^N R_i} = \frac{\frac{\sum_{i=1}^N R_i Y_i}{N}}{\frac{\sum_{i=1}^N R_i}{N}} = \frac{\overline{RY}}{\overline{R}} \tag{5.2}$$

where $\overline{RY}$ and $\overline{R}$ are the population averages of $R \times Y$ and R, respectively.

The mean in the whole population (the "truth") is $\overline{Y}_N$ where the capital N subscript indicates the population size rather than the sample size.

The difference between the mean of Y in the $R = 1$ group and the entire population is $\overline{Y}_n - \overline{Y}_N$:

$$\overline{Y}_n - \overline{Y}_N = \frac{\overline{RY}}{\overline{R}} - \overline{Y}_N$$

$$= \frac{\overline{RY} - \overline{Y}_N \overline{R}}{\overline{R}}$$

$$= \frac{covar(R, Y)}{\overline{R}} \qquad (5.3)$$

where $covar(R, Y)$ is the covariance of R and Y.

Next we convert the covariance to correlation. Covariance is a statistical measure of association with no fixed range. Correlation is a more intuitive measure of association that ranges from -1 to 1. When the correlation of two variables is $+1$, they move perfectly together (if X goes up, Y goes up by corresponding amount, although perhaps on different scales). When the correlation of two variables is -1, they move in opposite directions (if X goes up, Y goes down). When the correlation of two variables is zero, they have no relation, meaning that X_i has no linear predictive power with regard to the value of Y_i.

We denote correlation with the Greek letter ρ. Correlation is the covariance divided by the product of the standard deviations of the two variables (σ_R and σ_Y, respectively). This means that $covar(R, Y) = \rho_{R,Y}\sigma_R\sigma_Y$ where $\rho_{R,Y}$ is the population correlation of R and Y. Substituting into Equation 5.3

$$\overline{Y}_n - \overline{Y}_N = \frac{\rho_{R,Y}\sigma_R\sigma_Y}{\overline{R}}$$

$$= \rho_{R,Y}\frac{\sigma_R}{\overline{R}}\sigma_Y$$

Because R is binary, its standard deviation is $\sigma_R = \sqrt{p(1-p)} = \sqrt{\frac{n}{N}\left(1 - \frac{n}{N}\right)}$. In addition, $\overline{R} = \frac{n}{N}$. Substituting for σ_R and $\overline{R}$ and doing some algebra yields Equation 5.1:

$$\overline{Y}_n - \overline{Y}_N = \underbrace{\rho_{R,Y}}_{\text{data quality}} \underbrace{\sqrt{\frac{N-n}{n}}}_{\text{data quantity}} \underbrace{\sigma_Y}_{\text{data difficulty}}$$

6

Contemporary Polling and Nonignorable Nonresponse

> Even seemingly small defects in quality can almost completely wipe out the statistical information in our data, regardless of how large it is.
>
> Bradley et al. (2021)

Chapter 5 sought to explain how and why nonignorable nonresponse is a problem. What should we do with that knowledge? That is, how can we use our understanding of nonignorable nonresponse to inform our polling? This chapter offers a first step in answering this question by exploring some of the implications of the Meng equation, allowing us to highlight the strengths and weaknesses of major types of polling.

Broadly speaking, modern pollsters use either probability or nonprobability samples. The probability samplers attempt to approximate random sampling by randomly contacting people until the desired number of people responds. The nonprobability samplers figure out ways to cost effectively get as much data as they can. Both groups use weighting or another ignorable nonresponse-oriented technique to patch up their samples to offset observable patterns in who responds.

Each of these approaches is tempting. Modern probability samplers ground their approach in the theoretical virtues of random sampling. The nonprobability sampling approach offers larger samples and lower costs. Sometimes, their samples are impressively large and it's hard not to wonder if maybe these huge nonrandom data sets will be more useful than the smaller random (or random-ish, given nonresponse) data sets of the probability samples. And pretty much everybody loves weighting because it can erase demographic and possibly other differences between the survey sample and population.

However, as is widely recognized, each of these approaches has weaknesses. Our task in this chapter is to think about their flaws relative to each other in light of the potential for nonignorable nonresponse. Nonprobability polling approach comes off poorly for reasons that harken back to the *Literary Digest* fiasco. The random sampling approach is far from perfect, but here we rename it the random contact approach – because what is random is who they contact, *not* who responds once contacted – and show that using random contact shifts error from being proportional to the population size – which can be catastrophic – to being proportional to response rates – which is not great, but better.

This chapter proceeds as follows. Section 1 assesses the big data approach by introducing the idea of effective sample size, a concept that allows us to compare potentially large nonrandom samples to their random sampling equivalents. The results are often not pretty for nonrandom big data, even when the nonignorability of nonresponse is quite modest. Section 2 assesses the random contact approach that has become the last refuge of those clinging to the random sampling paradigm. The approach does not eliminate sampling error but contains it in a useful way. Section 3 decomposes sampling error into elements associated with choosing whom to contact and elements associated with individual choices given that they are contacted. This section helps clarify where the biggest threats are throughout the survey process.

6.1 EFFECTIVE SAMPLE SIZE

Big data is alluring, especially in an era where online social interactions vastly expand our ability to scale up certain data collection strategies at relatively low cost. In this section, we will develop the concept of effective sample size to help us compare potentially very large nonrandom samples to random samples. We will use the Meng equation to assess the sample size of random samples that would produce an equally precise estimate for any given nonrandom sample.

We work with the concept of mean-squared error (MSE), which is the squared value of the error expected from any given estimator. We're squaring the error so that a too-high estimate of a given magnitude will be considered equally problematic as a too-low estimate of the same magnitude. Mean-squared error is a useful concept because of a potential trade-off between bias and precision. Figure 6.1 shows distributions for two hypothetical 'ways to estimate $\overline{Y}$, the average of Y in some population. The true value in the population is 50. The estimator indicated with the thick line is unbiased, meaning that on average $\hat{\overline{Y}} = \overline{Y}$. It is also rather imprecise meaning that the probabilities of observing $\hat{\overline{Y}}$ far from $\overline{Y}$ are reasonably high. The estimator indicated with the taller thin line is biased, meaning that we can expect it to generally produce values of $\hat{\overline{Y}}$ that are lower than the true value. It is relatively precise, however, with most of the distribution relatively close to $\overline{Y}$. These two distributions have the same mean-squared error: The unbiased estimator does this by being correct on average but producing some estimates that are rather far from the true value. The biased estimator produces the same level of mean-squared error by producing estimates that are more closely clustered together even as the estimates tend to underestimate the population average.

Contemporary Polling and Nonignorable Nonresponse

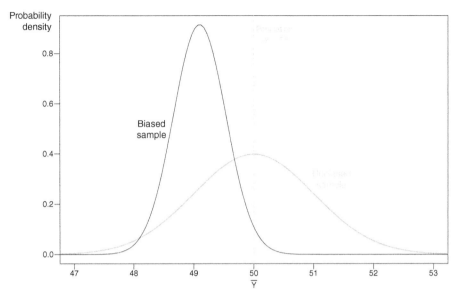

FIGURE 6.1 Two sampling distributions with the same mean-squared error

Figure 6.1 suggests a potential logic for comparing samples with different properties. A large nonrandom sample may be biased, but if it is only a bit biased and is much more precise, we may be equally well off as having the unbiased but less precise estimate we get from a smaller random sample. In order to make such a comparison more concrete, we will calculate the effective sample size, n_{eff}, which is the size of a truly random sample that would produce the same mean-squared error as a nonrandom sample of size n from a population of size N with correlation of R and Y equal to ρ. We should, at least in mean-squared terms, be equally well off with our nonrandom sample or with a random sample of size n_{eff}.

Note that this calculation is generous toward the nonrandom sample because even with similar values of mean-squared error, the nonrandom sample will be biased and we know that polling errors are not only problematic due to the absolute value of error but the direction of the error. The problems with surveys for presidential elections in 1936, 1948, 2016, and 2020, for example, were as much related to the direction of their bias as to the absolute value of their inaccuracy.

The online appendix derives an approximation of n_{eff} when n is large but still far from N.[1] It is

$$n_{\text{eff}} \sim \frac{n}{\rho^2(N-n)+1} \tag{6.1}$$

---

[1] Meng (2018, 698) derives an approximation for the upper bound of the effective sample size, which is used by Bradley et al. (2021, 19) in their calculations. See the online appendix for more details.

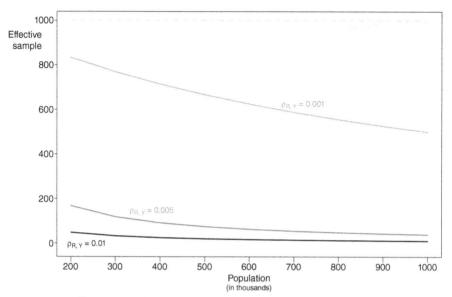

FIGURE 6.2 Effective sample sizes for sample of 1,000 as a function of population size and data quality

If $\rho^2 = 0$, the effective sample size is approximately the observed sample size. As ρ^2 moves away from zero, n_{eff} decreases more or less in proportion to $N - n$, meaning that the effective sample size gets small rapidly for a large population. In other words, for large populations with nonignorable nonresponse, small random samples will provide roughly the same information as a massive nonrandom sample.

Figure 6.2 provides a sense of the magnitudes by showing examples based on Equation 6.1 for an observed sample of 1,000. If $\rho = 0$ then there is no nonignorable nonresponse and the effective sample is 1,000 whatever the population is. If there is very modest correlation of $\rho = 0.001$, the effective sample size is around 800 when the population is 200,000 and drops to 500 when the population is 1 million. If $\rho = 0.005$, which is roughly the magnitude Meng (2018) estimated for the 2016 presidential election, the effective sample size is below 200 even for a population of 200,000 and falls rapidly from there, reaching around 40 for a population of 1 million. The drop-off in information is more severe for higher values of ρ. Effective sample sizes only get smaller for the $\rho \neq 0$ cases and populations larger than 1 million.

Several real-world examples highlight how severe the information loss can be when nonresponse is nonignorable in large population surveys. Meng (2018, 707) merges all polls from major pollsters in the final weeks of the 2016 election and compares results to state-level results to estimate that ρ was on the order of 0.005, a seemingly small degree of nonignorability. Recall, however, that the *total population* size is in the denominator of the effective

Contemporary Polling and Nonignorable Nonresponse

sample size calculation so even this modest correlation led to a dramatic loss of accuracy. Specifically, Meng calculated that the effective sample size of the 2.3 million observations in the merged poll of polls to be only around 400. In other words, a truly random sample with 100 percent response of 400 people would have produced an estimate with the same mean-squared error as the nonignorably nonrandom sample of 2.3 million people produced by merging all the polls in the last weeks of the campaign. Bradley et al. (2021, 8) undertook a similar exercise when assessing a Facebook survey of vaccination rates that had more than 250,000 respondents. They calculated that a truly random sample with merely 10 respondents would have produced an estimate with the same mean-squared error.

6.2 THE POWER OF RANDOM CONTACT

We've seen that many pollsters, especially those with more resources, stick to the random sampling as much as possible by interviewing only randomly selected people. We refer to this approach as the random contact approach. The good news for this approach is pollsters often have a decent sampling frame from which to pull their contact list. The bad news is that they can't force people to respond, though, and therefore end up with a response pool that may be infected by nonignorable nonresponse.

A natural question arises: Is it worth it? Random contact approaches require huge investments in acquiring a good sample frame and then contacting thousands of people who do not respond. Given the corrupting influence of nonignorability outlined so far, maybe pollsters should give up on probability sampling and simply move to convenience samples. The results would still be bad, but at least they would be cheap, right?

Happily for probability samplers, such logic is incorrect. The Meng equation can help us understand why. Random contact will not eliminate expected sampling error, but it will convert the error from interacting with population size to interacting with response rates. Low response rates remain a problem, but nonetheless the scale of the problem shrinks dramatically. In other words, probability samplers can say to themselves "we're not perfect, but we're better than the nonprobability folks."

To show this, we proceed in two steps. First, we show intuitively how randomly choosing whom to contact unlinks the connection between sampling error and population size. After that, we revisit Equation 5.1 to reconsider how nonignorable nonresponse affects error when contact (but not response) is randomized.

Figure 6.3 starts with the "large" population in panel (a) of Figure 5.8. Each dot represents a person with their value of Y (e.g., a feeling thermometer for a politician) on the y-axis and their propensity to respond on the x-axis. The population looks like a "tilted fish" because there is a positive relationship between propensity to respond and Y. The filled-in gray dots are randomly

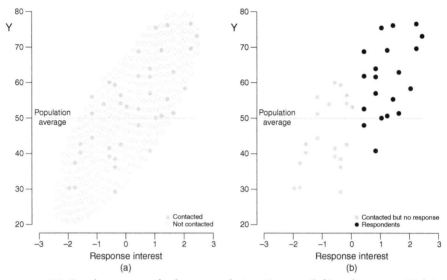

FIGURE 6.3 Random contact for large population: Contact (left) and response (right)

selected individuals contacted by the pollster. The open circles are people the pollster does not contact.

Random contact does not imply that those who respond are a random sample. After all, people choose to pick up the phone or respond to an email and this process could very well be influenced by many nonrandom factors, including factors correlated with Y, the feature we are trying to estimate in the population. Panel (b) on the right of Figure 6.3 shows who responds among those randomly sampled. This sample continues to be unrepresentative.

Here's the key though: While the sample from the random contact survey is unrepresentative, it is not as unrepresentative as the pool of respondents we saw from the large population in panel (a) of Figure 5.8. The random contact has essentially converted the large population into a smaller one. This is hugely important as we no longer get the n most responsive people in the whole population (which is wildly unrepresentative for a large population), but instead hear from the n most responsive people in a smaller representative sample. The respondents in the random contact case depicted in panel (b) of Figure 6.3 have an average value of Y of 56, which is larger than the population average, but not as bad as the sample average of 71 that emerged from the no random contact case depicted in panel (a) of Figure 5.8.

The important intuition that emerges from Figure 6.3 is that random contact essentially converts a large population to a small one. In other words, random contact decouples sampling error from *population* size. Random contact does not eliminate error, but it makes it much more manageable, which is a huge victory.

Contemporary Polling and Nonignorable Nonresponse 129

As detailed in the online appendix to this chapter, sampling error with random contact is

$$\overline{Y}_n - \overline{Y}_N \quad = \quad \underbrace{\rho_{R,Y}}_{\text{data quality}} \underbrace{\sqrt{\frac{1 - p_r}{p_r}}}_{\text{response rate}} \underbrace{\sigma_Y}_{\text{data difficulty}} \tag{6.2}$$

This equation looks broadly similar to the Meng equation on page 114 with one crucial difference: In the random contact case, the error depends not on the total population, but on the response rate, p_r. So even though randomly contacting potential respondents does not eliminate error when $\rho_{R,Y} \neq 0$, it delinks sampling error from the population size. Since populations can be very large, this can be incredibly useful.

Equation 6.2 contains other important insights as well. First, although it is a bit hard to see immediately, the equation shows that higher response rates push down error. (Formally, the derivative of the sampling error with respect to response rate is negative.) This means that if $\rho_{R,Y} \neq 0$, sampling error goes down as response rates rise. Conversely, when $\rho_{R,Y} \neq 0$, sampling error increases as response rates decline.

Second, the effects of response rates and nonignorability interact. This was true, of course, in the nonrandom contact world as we saw in Figure 5.7 in Chapter 5. When dealing with large populations, even a large survey without random contact could easily become useless with even a small amount of nonignorability. The interaction persists in the random contact case, but things are nevertheless better. Given random contact, the nonignorability interacts with response rates rather than total population meaning that things can still go wrong, but at least they'll to do so more slowly.

Figure 6.4 illustrates how polling problems interact by plotting error in the random contact model using Equation 6.2. The outcome variable is a feeling thermometer that ranges from 0 to 100, with a mean of 50 and a standard deviation of 10. The left panel of Figure 6.4 plots a histogram of such data. The panel on the right of Figure 6.4 shows the sampling error for random contact with various combinations of nonresponse rates and $\rho_{R,Y}$. The line at the bottom shows error when $\rho = 0$. In other words, nonresponse is not a problem when there is no nonignorable nonresponse.

The story changes as $\rho_{R,Y}$ rises. The second line from the bottom is for the case when $\rho_{R,Y} = 0.15$. We see that the sampling error now rises with nonresponse and explodes as nonresponse gets very high. For ease of exposition, we highlight several points. When nonresponse is around 40 percent (a reasonable standard in the glory days of random sampling), our sampled mean will be about 1 point higher than the true mean. Not great, but definitely something we could live with. When nonresponse is around 60 percent, the sampled mean will run about 2 percentage points higher than the true mean. As nonresponse hits 95 percent, the error rises to 6 points. When nonresponse hits 99 percent,

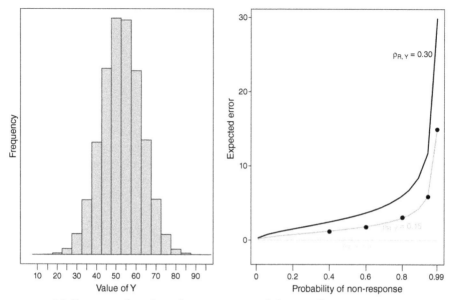

FIGURE 6.4 Error as a function of nonresponse and data quality

the error is about 15 points, rendering the results essentially useless. The top line shows expected error when $\rho_{R,Y}$ is 0.30; error rises even more explosively with nonresponse.

Appreciating the interaction of nonignorability and nonresponse sheds light on several aspects of the contemporary polling environment. First, nonresponse is not sufficient to cause problems. Groves and Peytcheva (2008) analyzed a series of mostly random contact surveys in which the population averages were known, allowing them to assess the relationship between response rates and bias. They found no relation. Instead of taking this to mean that response rates do not matter, Equation 6.2 suggests that response rates matter only when nonignorability is substantial. It is possible that in some surveys there was bias with low nonresponse (corresponding, e.g., to a high ρ and low nonresponse rate in Figure 6.4) and in other surveys there was no bias with a high nonresponse rate (corresponding, e.g., to a low ρ and high nonresponse rate situation).

In addition, the interaction of polling weaknesses helps us think about different polling circumstances. A weakness in one aspect can be offset by strength in another. For example, if $\rho_{R,Y}$ is high, the damage will be mitigated for a random contact poll if p_r is close to 1. If the response rate, p_r, is very low, we will not be too concerned if $\rho_{R,Y}$ is very low. In the Golden Age of polling, random digit dialing kept $\rho_{R,Y}$ low and social norms kept response rates relatively high, keeping the overall error relatively low.

At the same time, weakness in one aspect of polling exacerbates weakness in another. This means that levels of $\rho_{R,Y}$ that were tolerable in the era of

Contemporary Polling and Nonignorable Nonresponse 131

decent response rates have become dangerous now. Thirty years ago, response rates were often around 60 percent and even when $\rho_{R,Y}$ was not zero, error was manageable. The same $\rho_{R,Y}$ now is more threatening when response rates often run below 2 percent (see, also Tourangeau, Conrad, and Couper 2013, 17). For example, in Figure 6.4 the error from $\rho_{R,Y} = 0.15$ with a nonresponse rate of 0.4 was under 3; if nonresponse rates rise to 0.99, the sampling error rises to well above 10.

It is also possible that polling response, like so much in life, has become politicized in ways that it was not before, thereby pushing up $\rho_{R,Y}$. In an era with high response rates, this would be an annoyance, but perhaps not much more. But with low response rates, higher values of $\rho_{R,Y}$ are disturbing. At 95 percent nonresponse, for example, an increase in $\rho_{R,Y}$ from 0.15 to 0.3 drives up sampling error from around 5 to around 20.

These results also reinforce the idea that more data are not necessarily better (Lohr 1999, 257). Someone looking to survey a large organization may think, reasonably enough, that sending an email to everyone in the organization is the best way to get the most accurate result as it would maximize the number of responses. The random contact model points in a different direction: Results may be more accurate by first randomly selecting a subset of people to query for responses. The resulting data set may be smaller, but it will be less likely to suffer from the negative effects of population size on sampling error. In this case, as so often in polling, small and good is better than big and bad.

6.3 SOURCES OF ERROR AT DIFFERENT STAGES OF SURVEY PROCESS

Data size, response rates, and nonignorability interact in potentially complicated ways. In this section, we break down the Meng equation to highlight how these various terms interact at different stages of the polling process to help us identity which aspects of polling error are most problematic. Doing so helps us think about how best to design surveys in the face of potential nonignorable nonresponse.

We will divide survey research into two stages. In the first stage, a pollster identifies a group of people to contact. The process of identifying a sampling frame and a set of contacted individuals is under the control of the pollster. In the second stage, the people contacted decide whether or not to respond, a process largely beyond the control of pollster.

Our goal is to decompose sampling error across these two stages in order to help us appreciate the relative magnitudes of error across stages. We'll see that a very small amount of nonignorability in the sampling frame can be devastating as it interacts with population size; nonignorability in the response stage continues to be problematic, but is more bounded as it will interact with response rates. These ideas were developed in Bradley et al. (2021) and Meng (2021).

Our interest is using a survey to estimate $\overline{Y}_N$, the population mean in a target population for a variable Y that has a variance σ_N^2. In the first stage, a pollster contacts n_{con} people. This stage depends first on the *coverage* of the sampling frame, a concept that indicates how well the sampling frame covers the population of interest.

When polling a large target population such as adults in the United States, some coverage gaps are inevitable. Even the Census Bureau struggles to develop a list of all adults in the country, and as a practical matter, any sampling frame will be imperfect. During the Golden Age of surveys, sampling frames were thought to be decent as telephones were nearly universal and telephone number-based sampling was quite feasible.

Some contemporary sampling frames raise more serious coverage concerns. For example, if we sample from Facebook users, it is quite possible that coverage will be affected by the fact that there are systematic differences in who is on Facebook (let alone who is active on Facebook). Sampling frames comprised of people who have opted into an online panel are also likely suspect; for example, White working-class people who have lower levels of trust in institutions may be less likely to join an online panel.

The contact stage also depends on whom the pollster decides to contact. Contact may be based on random selection or through some kind of weighted or stratified random process. For this section, we merge the sampling frame and contact stages into a single contact stage, producing a conceptual set of variables that characterize the population of people given an opportunity to respond to a poll. We indicate the contacted people with the variable $R_i^{(1)}$, which equals 1 if person i is contacted and 0 if not. Important parameters at this stage include $\rho_{R^{(1)},Y}$, which is the correlation of $R^{(1)}$ and Y, and σ_{con}^2, which is the variance of Y in the contacted sample.

The observed survey data are finalized in a second stage in which the contacted individuals decide whether to respond or not. In concrete terms, do the contacted people answer the phone or click on the link? Clearly, nonignorable nonresponse can enter this stage as well; picture the phone ringing for a survivalist in his bunker compared to an email coming into the Red Cross volunteer in her apartment. This second stage produces an observed sample of $n_{\text{obs}} \leq n_{\text{con}}$ for whom $R_i^{(2|1)} = 1$. Key parameters in this second stage are σ_{obs}^2, which is the variance of Y in the observed sample, and $\rho_{R^{(2|1)},Y}$, which is the correlation of $R^{(2|1)}$ and Y for the people contacted.

To highlight how different characteristics of the polling process affect error, we divide sampling error into two sources: One part captures the difference between the observed mean and the contacted mean, and the other part captures the difference between the contacted mean and the population mean (Meng 2021, 11). Sampling error in this formulation is

$$\overline{Y}_{\text{obs}} - \overline{Y}_N = [\overline{Y}_{\text{obs}} - \overline{Y}_{\text{con}}] + [\overline{Y}_{\text{con}} - \overline{Y}_N] \tag{6.3}$$

Contemporary Polling and Nonignorable Nonresponse 133

Applying the logic used to create the Meng equation, the error can be represented as

$$\overline{Y}_{\text{obs}} - \overline{Y}_N = \rho_{R(2|1),Y}\sqrt{\frac{1-p_r}{p_r}}\sigma_{\text{con}} + \rho_{R(1),Y}\sqrt{\frac{N-n_{\text{con}}}{n_{\text{con}}}}\sigma_N \qquad (6.4)$$

where p_r is the response rate among the contacted.[2]

Equation 6.4 is a bit busy, but contains several important insights. The first element depends on $\rho_{R(2|1),Y}$ and is proportional to the response rate among those contacted. The lower the response rate, the larger this term is, which is not great. The second term in Equation 6.4 is where catastrophe lives. It depends on $\rho_{R(1),Y}$ and is proportional to the population size. That is trouble when the population is over 300 million. We saw in Figure 5.7 that errors get large quickly in a large population when there is nonignorable nonresponse.

The implication of this result is foundational for understanding modern polling. A smallish randomly contacted sample with a low response rate from a good sampling frame may have less error than even a very large randomly contacted sample with a good response rate from a problematic sampling frame. In other words, we should probably believe a one percent response rate from a good sampling frame like a voter file more than a 50 percent response rate from a dodgy sampling from a sample of Facebook users. We've seen already that Bradley et al. (2021) found that a small survey based on a carefully constructed sampling frame predicted Covid vaccination rates better than massive data sets based on less rigorously curated sampling frames.

6.4 CONCLUSION

Meng (2021) likens sampling to tasting soup. If the soup is well stirred, any spoonful will be like any other and will provide a good idea of how the soup tastes. That is, if $\rho = 0$, even a small sample can represent the whole. If the soup is not well stirred, though, a single taste is less informative. The risk of getting an unrepresentative taste is somewhat true if we make a cup of soup, truer if we make a pot of soup, and really true if (weirdly) we make a soup the size of the Pacific Ocean.

This metaphor and the framework undergirding it help us assess some of the major approaches modern pollsters use to combat nonresponse. Nonprobabilistic, big data approaches are like having a really big spoon. It seems like a good idea, but if the soup is the size of a metaphorical ocean and poorly

---

[2] We use the fact that $\frac{n_{\text{con}}-n_{\text{obs}}}{n_{\text{obs}}} = \frac{1-p_r}{p_r}$ where $p_r = \frac{n_{\text{obs}}}{n_{\text{con}}}$. We could also write $\sqrt{\frac{N-n_{\text{con}}}{n_{\text{con}}}}$ as $\frac{N-n_{\text{con}}}{n_{\text{con}}} = \frac{1-p_{\text{con}}}{p_{\text{con}}}$ where $p_{\text{con}} = \frac{n_{\text{con}}}{N}$. We write these terms differently to highlight the critical elements of each term. The number of contacts will typically be much smaller than the target population, meaning that N dominates error associated with the contact stage. Among those contacted, the relative size of the respondents to the set of people contacted is most often how we think of the observed sample relative to the contacted sample.

stirred, even a huge spoon will not do much good. Random contact is attractive because it puts a well-stirred sample in our cup which then may settle a bit so that our spoon doesn't get a perfectly representative sample of what is in the cup but at least we're starting with a more reasonable selection than someone dipping a big spoon into an ocean-sized soup.

Two themes emerge (see Meng 2021). The first is that data quality is more important than data quantity. When the outcome of interest directly affects whether we observe someone in the sample, the error gets worse with population size. Increasing sample size is almost powerless in the face of such a daunting source of bias. This means we must resist the siren song of several seemingly intuitive claims. More data are not necessarily better if it comes from sources where response is correlated with Y. In fact, large data sets can often be less informative than small samples that are random or at least derived from random contact. And getting more data by increasing response rates is no panacea, especially when the response process is nonignorable.

The second theme is that certain design features are valuable in the face of potential nonignorability. A random sample is, as always, incredibly powerful. But even when nonresponse at the individual levels makes a truly random sample impossible, random contact shifts error from being proportional to the population size to being proportional to the response rates. In an era of very low response rates, this is cold comfort but is comfort nonetheless: Error in proportion to response rates is often orders of magnitude less threatening than error proportional to population size.

These are important principles to guide polling, but taken in isolation do not provide us with many tools to directly attack nonignorable nonresponse. Can we do more? That is, once we've randomly contacted people from the best sampling frame we can muster, what more can we do to combat nonignorable nonresponse that inevitably arises due to coverage leakage in our sampling frame and potentially substantial nonresponse due to individual choice?

The answer is that we can do quite a bit. The literature on nonignorable nonresponse has developed substantially in recent years and provides many tools to diagnose and potentially counteract nonignorable nonresponse. The tools are varied and not mutually exclusive but can broadly be divided into two categories: Tools that help us model nonignorable nonresponse and tools that help us gather the type of information that make these models work better. Chapters 7–10 therefore develop the logic of selection models that account for nonignorable nonresponse and then discuss their parametric flexibility and data demands.

PART III

FIGHTING NONIGNORABLE NONRESPONSE

7

Bounding Damage from Nonignorable Nonresponse

> The plausibility of [ignorable nonresponse] has been questioned sharply.
>
> Manski (1989)

Nonignorable nonresponse is widely acknowledged as a potential problem. But, as we have seen, the word on the street among pollsters is that it's something we cannot do anything about other than finding the best weights possible and hoping for the best.

The theme of this book is that we can do better. The goal of this part of the book is to provide tools that will help us take on nonignorable nonresponse more directly. We begin this process by presenting methods that help us appreciate the potential scale of the problem. These methods do not diagnose or correct for nonignorable nonresponse – we'll get to that soon enough – but they help us appreciate what might be at stake as we think about nonignorable nonresponse for our data.

Section 1 of this chapter describes how to calculate bounds that define the range of possible values of population values that are consistent with the observed data. These calculations require virtually no assumptions and are robust to nonignorable nonresponse (Manski 1990). They are simple, yet elegant. The bounds tend to cover large ranges of possible population values, highlighting just how much could go wrong when we observe only a small subset of the population. In fact, the span of the bounds is often so large as to be uninformative. In short, when nonresponse is substantial, bounds models tell us that we cannot be certain about much other than we cannot be certain about much.

Section 2 gets more granular with our bounds. The idea is to sidestep trying to estimate nonignorability and to instead postulate possible levels of nonignorability and assess how results would change (Hartman and Huang 2023). In other words, these tools allow us to ask "I don't know if there is nonignorable nonresponse, but what if we missed a really important weighting

138   *Part III: Fighting Nonignorable Nonresponse*

variable?" If these hypothetical levels of nonignorable nonresponse would change our conclusions about who is ahead in a race or whether there is majority support for a given policy, then we should be transparent about this vulnerability and, ideally, move onto to the methods we discuss in the following chapters to undo the effects of nonignorable nonresponse. If, however, our conclusions are the same even if nonignorable nonresponse were quite large, we can be more confident that our conclusions are robust to nonignorability and can be more confident in using weighting and related tools that are appropriate for ignorable nonresponse.

7.1 BOUNDS

We start with bounding methods that make essentially no assumptions about the data-generating process (Manski 1990). These methods simply explore the logical range of possibilities consistent with an observed sample. Suppose, for example, we are measuring support for the president and observe a sample of 500 people in which 300 people support the president ($Y = 1$) and 200 people do not support the president ($Y = 0$).

To appreciate the range of population values logically consistent with this sample, we explore two extreme ("bounding") cases: One in which *all* the nonrespondents were supporters of the president and one in which *all* the nonrespondents did not support the president. The lower bound of support for the president in the population simply takes the observed support in the sample and divides by the population; that is, we simply assume that the 300 supporters of the president we observe in the sample were the *only* supporters of the president in the entire population; everyone else in this extreme scenario opposes the president, an extreme version of nonignorable nonresponse in which ρ is positive because the president's supporters are more likely to respond. The upper bound of possible support for the president comes from assuming that there are only 200 *non*supporters of the president in the entire population and they all responded. Everyone else in this extreme scenario supports the president, an extreme version of nonignorable nonresponse in which ρ is negative because the president's supporters are less likely to respond.

The calculations for such bounds depend on the response rate. Table 7.1 provides calculations for 3 scenarios. In the scenario at the top of the table, the population consists of 625 people and the response rate is 90 percent given that 500 of the 625 people in the population responded.[1] The observed proportion of Y is 0.6. For the lower bound estimate, we assume that we observed every supporter of the president, meaning that everyone who did not respond did not support the president. In case, the proportion for the contacted population

---

[1] We could also assume that the "population" contacted is representative of the entire population, severing the link between population size and error in a manner similar to what we saw in Chapter 6. If we include the full population of the United States, for example, the bounds would essentially go from 0 to 1 for all the cases shown in the table.

Bounding Damage from Nonignorable Nonresponse 139

TABLE 7.1 *Population bounds for multiple response-rate scenarios*

Case	Response rate	Population	Observed Y 0	1	Unobserved Y 0	1	$\overline{Y}$
Scenario 1: High response rate							
(a) Sample	0.8	625	200	300	–	–	0.6
(b) Lower bound	0.8	625	200	300	125	0	$\frac{300}{625} = 0.48$
(c) Upper bound	0.8	625	200	300	0	125	$\frac{425}{625} = 0.68$
Scenario 2: Medium response rate							
(a) Sample	0.5	1,000	200	300	–	–	0.6
(b) Lower bound	0.5	1,000	200	300	500	0	$\frac{300}{1,000} = 0.30$
(c) Upper bound	0.5	1,000	200	300	0	500	$\frac{800}{1,000} = 0.80$
Scenario 3: Low response rate							
(a) Sample	0.05	10,000	200	300	–	–	0.6
(b) Lower bound	0.05	10,000	200	300	9,500	0	$\frac{300}{10,000} = 0.03$
(c) Upper bound	0.05	10,000	200	300	0	9,500	$\frac{9,800}{1,000} = 0.98$

would be $\frac{300}{625} = 0.48$. For the upper bound estimate, we assume we observed everyone who did not respond did support the president. In this case, the proportion of supporters of the president in the contacted population would be $\frac{425}{625} = 0.68$. In other words, the true support for the president among the 625 people in the contacted population *must* be between 48 and 68 percent. That's reasonably wide range but nonetheless gives us some information about the true distribution of presidential support.

In the next scenario, the response rate is 50 percent: 500 of the 1,000 people contacted actually responded. The observed proportion of Y is still 0.6. If everyone who did not respond did not support the president, then the proportion for contacted population would be $\frac{300}{1,000} = 0.30$. If everyone who did not respond did support the president, then the proportion for contacted population would be $\frac{800}{1,000} = 0.80$. In other words, the true support for the president among the 1,000 people in the contacted population *must* be between 30 and 80 percent. That range is getting pretty large and may not be useful for many applications. And, ominously, the response rate here in this scenario is actually much higher than many polls actually achieve.

The third scenario at the bottom of the table is based on a more realistic response rate of 5 percent: 500 of the 10,000 people contacted actually responded. The observed proportion of Y is still 0.6. If everyone who did not respond did not support the president, the contacted population proportion would be $\frac{300}{10,000} = 0.03$. If everyone who did not respond did support the president, the contacted population proportion would be $\frac{9,800}{10,000} = 0.98$. In other words, when nonresponse is high, the true support for the president in the contacted population could be pretty much anything.

Bounds are both edifying and humbling. They usefully allow us to explore possibilities based on minimal assumptions. If nonresponse is not very high, the bounds may be informative. But more often than not, bounds humble us: For realistic levels of nonresponse the observed data do little to pin down the possible true proportions in the contacted population. In these cases, the contribution of bounds is not so much to help us understand the contacted population as to make it clear that we have more work ahead of us if we are to extract information about the contacted population in an environment in which nonresponse can be nonignorable.

7.2 ROBUSTNESS DIAGNOSTICS

Another direction for dealing with nonignorable nonresponse is to assess whether results are vulnerable to it. In this approach, the analyst does not try to measure nonignorable nonresponse, but instead posits plausible scenarios in which nonignorable nonresponse occurs and assesses whether conclusions would change in these scenarios as compared to the baseline approach that assumes away nonignorable nonresponse. That is, sensitivity analysis allows us to ask for any survey result whether the results would change if nonignorable nonresponse were a serious problem. If no, great – we'll have one less thing to worry about. If yes, however, then it makes sense to be more cautious about the results and, ideally, to take steps to more directly measure and account for nonignorable nonresponse.

Hartman and Huang (2023) provide an excellent example of this type of research (see also Siddique and Belin 2008; Bailey, Hopkins, and Rogers 2016). Their approach involves assessing how two types of confounding variables could create nonignorable nonresponse bias that would be unaddressed in conventional weights.

- **Partially observed variable:** A potential weighting variable for which we observe the values only for individuals in the survey sample. These variables are often answers to a survey question – we know what the respondents answered but do not know the distribution of answers that would be given by the whole population.
- **Fully unobserved response variable:** A potential weighting variable for which we do not observe the values for anyone. Often these are variables that relate to concepts such as trust or religiosity that may not have appeared in a given survey.

Bounding Damage from Nonignorable Nonresponse 141

We can observe the relationship of a partially observed variable to Y in the sample, but we do not know whether it predicts response because we do not know its population distribution. The political interest variable that we discussed in Chapter 1 is an example of a partially observed variable: It strongly predicted presidential vote choice in the 2020 ANES survey, but we cannot use it in a weighting scheme because we do not know the distribution of political interest among nonrespondents.

Hartman and Huang deal with partially observed variables by positing certain values in the population and weighting toward those. For political interest, one could look at the sample and see that the sample average was two on a four-point scale (with high values indicating more interest). What if the population average was 1.5? If we knew that, we could use raking tools discussed in Chapter 3 to yield a weighted sample with that average of political interest. Because the sample average is higher, this would mean that respondents with high values of political interest would get small weights and respondents with low political interest would get large weights. We could then repeat the exercise across a range of possible averages of political interest in the population.

A researcher then asks if their interpretations of the survey results change across plausible distributions in the population. If the estimates change only a little, then one could conclude that the results are not sensitive to omitting political interest from the weights. On the other hand, if the results change a lot, the researcher would want to note this and, ideally, work with some of the models described below to counter nonignorable nonresponse.

The second type of confounder that Hartman and Huang assess is fully unobserved. These types of variables are common in the discussions about polling. For example, we often hear speculation that Republican-leaning voters are less trustful of others and that this distrust makes them wary of responding to polls. Trust is often a fully unobserved variable because most polls do not ask questions about it. What are the consequences of omitting trust from weights?.

To assess this, Hartman and Huang develop a model in which there is an unobserved confounder, U, that affects Y and R and should therefore be in the optimal weights. They then derive the bias inherent in the weighted results we would get if we excluded U from the weights. This bias depends on two unobserved parameters, one that captures how far the actual weights are from the optimal weights and another that captures how much nonignorability there is in the population data. For any given result, one can posit values of these two parameters and assess how much bias there is.

Since the bias depends on two parameters, it not easy to characterize how much influence a confounder has. Therefore, Hartman and Huang provide reference points based on observable variables. That is, they calculate how much bias one would see if one excluded something like age or education from the model. One can then create a plot that shows how much survey results change due to the omission of the confounder as a function of these two variables, with the observable values for known variables such as age and education noted on the plot. If the results wouldn't change unless the unobserved confounder had a lot more effect on R and Y than something like education, we may be inclined to believe that the results are robust to exclusion of the unobserved confounder. On the other hand, if the results would change if the unobserved confounder had similar effects as something with a modest effect on weights and outcomes, then we would be right to worry that the results are sensitive to exclusion of such a confounder and should therefore be treated with more caution.

Reporting these types of analyses may be as useful as reporting margins of error. We know from random sampling theory the magnitude of error that can occur due to randomness. From Hartman and Huang, we can also know the magnitude of error that can emerge due to nonignorable nonresponse. For example, if a pollster finds the Democratic candidate is leading by 3 percent, the pollster could also report that the results would change to a Republican lead if the confounder had, say, three times the effect of omitting education. If we believe education is a big deal and that unobserved variables like trust are unlikely to have triple the effect of education, then we would feel confident in the results. In another case, a pollster might find that their conclusions change if an unobserved variable had half the effect of education, in which case we would be more skeptical, in a manner roughly analogous to the way we would treat a poll with a large margin of error.

7.3 CONCLUSION

The goal of this book is to understand and then respond to possible nonignorable nonresponse bias. In this chapter, we lay the groundwork for our response by discussing bounding methods that characterize the potential magnitude of the problem. At an general level, Manski bounds describe the range of possible population values given the observed data. These bounds are based on extreme scenarios. What if *all* of the supporters of the president in the entire country ended up in our survey sample? The true value of support would be much lower than in the sample, of course. Or, conversely, what if *all* of the nonsupporters of the president in the entire country ended up in our survey sample? The true value of support would be much higher than in the sample.

These logically possible, but empirically unlikely scenarios, provide worst-case scenario bounds. When response rates are high, these bounds can be small enough and give us insight about the population from our sample. Unfortunately, for realistic response rates, these bounds are incredibly wide – often effectively spanning the range of possible values of Y. In this case, the Manski bounds highlight how little we can be absolutely sure about based on our observed sample.

Bounding Damage from Nonignorable Nonresponse 143

We can, however, still get a sense of how susceptible our results are to nonignorable nonresponse. Sensitivity analysis such as offered by Hartman and Huang can tell us how vulnerable our results are to nonignorable nonresponse. Just as magnitude of error helps us calibrate how confident we should be in the face of uncertainties due to random sampling, the sensitivities calculated using Hartman and Huang's method can help us calibrate how confident we should be in the face of uncertainties due to possible nonignorable nonresponse.

If we are going to learn more from our data, we will need a model.[2] The model will inevitably involve assumptions, and we will focus in Chapter 8 on articulating these in a clear way. With a model in hand, we can see the mechanism underlying how selection models work, shedding light on how different they are from weighting models and providing a foundation for estimation strategies that will directly account for nonignorable nonresponse.

---

[2] Needing a model is not particular to nonignorable nonresponse modeling. After all, weighting is deeply model-dependent.

8

Selection Models for Nonignorable Nonresponse

> A better understanding of the sources of and solutions to selection bias
> ... requires a framework that places the assumptions front and center and puts
> the focus on assessing the degree to which those assumptions are justified.
>
> Andrew Mercer (2020)

Polling is hard and getting harder. As people became increasingly unlikely to respond to traditional probabilistic surveys, it becomes harder to justify these surveys based on random sampling theory. Nonprobability surveys have even less grounding in theory. They work fine – until they don't. Given that nonignorable nonresponse occurs when unmeasured factors affect both the probability of response and the content of response, a bit of fatalism may be natural. After all, if unobserved variables are at the core of the problem, how can we address the problem using data we observe? Perhaps the best we can do is to lower expectations. Chapter 7 showed that when nonresponse is substantial we can only be perfectly sure that we cannot be perfectly sure. So perhaps our "pollsters and the media [should] emphasize – and Americans [should] recognize – that polling can be misleading" (Leonhardt 2020).

The point of this part of the book is that we need not be so pessimistic. In fact, we can be proactive even in the face of possible nonignorable nonresponse. The literature on nonresponse provides a broad range of selection models that empower us to fight back against nonignorable nonresponse. These tools require new thinking and depend on assumptions, some of which are easier to stomach than others. But, as we shall see in this and subsequent chapters, these assumptions are seldom as stark as the assumption that dominates current polling practice: The assumption that nonignorable nonresponse does not exist.

The goal of this chapter is to introduce selection models in a way that highlights important intuition about how they work. Section 1 formalizes the implicit model we've been working with already: First respondents decide to

Selection Models for Nonignorable Nonresponse 145

respond, and second, we observe the data of interest for those who respond. Section 2 uses the model to highlight a bad news, good news story. The bad news is that statistical estimation of a two-equation model like this will be challenging. The good news is that the model helps us recognize the traces nonignorable nonresponse leaves in observable data. Understanding these traces will be essential to dealing with nonignorable nonresponse. Section 3 introduces perhaps the most famous selection model of all, the Heckman selection model. Section 4 uses the Heckman model to highlight the starkly different way that selection and weighting approaches use information. This is a fundamental point: Selection models and weighting models use similar information, but use it in almost opposite ways. In some perfectly reasonable scenarios, selection models will effectively lower the weight on observations that conventional models weight heavily. The Heckman model is far from perfect, however, as Section 5 explains.

This chapter contains a mix of intuitive and technical content. Sections 1 and 2 should be of interest to everyone. There are some equations, but the general ideas are intuitive and help us appreciate how selection models are constructed and why they are difficult but not impossible to estimate statistically. Sections 3, 4, and 5 are more technical. Some readers may prefer to skim them for the general ideas.

8.1 A GENERAL SELECTION MODEL

Our goal is to develop statistical models that can handle nonignorable nonresponse. We begin with a two-stage model that builds on our discussion in Chapter 5. In the first step, an individual responds to a survey question, a process we model in terms of the latent propensity to respond, R_i^*, as we introduced in Chapter 5. A latent variable is an unobserved variable that underlies an observed variable. In this case, the latent variable R_i^* is a continuous variable that captures the unobserved eagerness of person i to respond. The variable R_i (notice there is no asterisk) is the observed response. R_i equals 1 if person i responded and 0 if person i did not respond. The higher the value of R_i^* (the latent variable with the asterisk), the higher the probability that $R_i = 1$.

We model the latent propensity to respond as a function of a covariate Z that is only in the response equation and a covariate X that is in both the response and outcome equations. The error term is τ. The equation is

$$R_i^* = \gamma_0 + \gamma_Z Z_i + \gamma_X X_i + \tau_i \tag{8.1}$$

We observe i's response if $R_i^* > 0$; in other words, $R_i = 1$ if $R_i^* > 0$.

The outcome of interest, Y, is a survey response, such as support for the president or views on a policy issue. We model Y as a function of an intercept

146   *Part III: Fighting Nonignorable Nonresponse*

β_0, a covariate X, and an error term, ϵ, which we assume (as is standard) to have an average value of zero.[1]

$$Y_i = \beta_0 + \beta_X X_i + \epsilon_i \tag{8.2}$$

The errors in the selection equation (Equation 8.1) and the outcome equation (Equation 8.2) may be correlated. That is, we allow for the possibility that people who are more keen to respond than we would predict based on covariates (meaning $\tau_i > 0$) are also more likely to have higher values of Y ($\epsilon_i > 0$). The easiest way to think about how this correlation can arise is to consider a case in which there is an unobserved variable (such as social trust) that affects R and Y. Because it is not observed, it is in the error terms of Equations 8.1 and 8.2, leading them to be correlated.[2]

We denote the correlation of τ and ϵ with ρ where $-1 < \rho < 1$. This correlation plays a vital role in many selection models. For now we treat ρ as fixed across the entire population; in the empirical analyses, it will become important to allow ρ to vary across subgroups. This ρ is closely related to the $\rho_{R*,Y}$ discussed in Part II. It differs from the $\rho_{R,Y}$ (notice R does not have an asterisk) in the Meng equation, which is the correlation of the actual response (which equals zero or one) and Y. I discuss these differences in the online appendix for this book. The distinction across the types of error is less important when trying to understand the structure and functioning of selection models, but can become important when simulating data or predicting error.

We only observe the value of Y for people who respond to the survey. We denote this as $Y_i|_{R_i=1}$, where the vertical line stands for "conditional on." The expected value of observed responses is

$$E[Y_i|_{R_i=1}] = \beta_0 + \beta_X E[X|_{R_i=1}] + E[\epsilon_i|_{R_i=1}] \tag{8.3}$$

where $E[\epsilon_i|_{R_i=1}]$ is the expected value of the error term given that person i responded.

For simplicity, we will work with an outcome equation in which there is no X variable. In this case, the β_0 coefficient will simply reflect the population average, which is often a quantity of interest. The average of the observed sample will not necessarily reflect the true population average, however. It is

$$E[Y_i|_{Y_i \text{ observed}}] = \beta_0 + E[\epsilon_i|_{R_i=1}] \tag{8.4}$$

Equation 8.4 says that the expected value of Y for an individual who responded is a function of the true population average (β_0) and the expected

---

[1] The models can be multivariate if the coefficients γ_Z, γ_X, and β_X and covariates Z and X are vectors.

[2] It is also possible for the error terms in the two equations to be correlated if Y directly affects the probability of response. In this case, we can add $\gamma_Y Y_i$ into Equation 8.1 and substitute for the value of Y_i using Equation 8.2. There will be an ϵ term in the response equation, which will induce correlation with the ϵ error term in the outcome equation. We will explore this second pathway in Section 9.3 where we create weights for a model in which R response depends directly on the value of Y.

Selection Models for Nonignorable Nonresponse

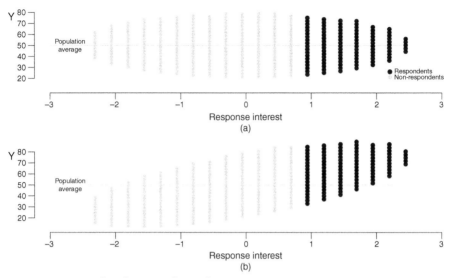

FIGURE 8.1 Two distributions of Y and response propensity

value of the error given that someone responded. The equation offers a straightforward way to characterize nonignorable nonresponse. Suppose Y measures the evaluation of a liberal politician in a *New York Times* poll. If liberals are more likely to respond to *New York Times* pollsters, then the average of responses will be higher than the true average because $E[\epsilon_i|R_i=1] > 0$. This would be a classic example of nonignorable nonresponse. On the other hand, even though the 1 percent response rate for the *New York Times* poll implies that the sample will consist of people who are more eager to respond, it is possible that these people are not systematically different with respect to their values of Y, which means that $E[\epsilon_i|R_i=1] = 0$ and nonresponse will be ignorable.

Using the approach we used in Figures 5.6 and 5.9, Figure 8.1 illustrates Equation 8.4. In it, each dot is a person. Values of Y are the vertical axis, and values of R^* are on the horizontal axis. People who responded are indicated with dark shaded dots. For each observation, ϵ_i is simply the vertical distance from the dot to the line, representing how far above or below Y_i is compared to the population average of Y. In panel (a) on top, the ϵ values for the people who responded are balanced above and below zero, meaning $E[\epsilon_i|R_i=1] = 0$ (the expected value of the error term given response is zero). In contrast, the ϵ values for the people who responded in panel (b) on the bottom are mostly positive and clearly average above zero, suggesting that $E[\epsilon_i|R_i=1]$ is greater than zero in the case of nonignorable nonresponse. When nonresponse is nonignorable like this, $E[\epsilon_i|R_i=1]$ will be nonzero for any possible level of response.

148   *Part III: Fighting Nonignorable Nonresponse*

Before we turn to what works when identifying nonignorable nonresponse, we can use Figure 8.1 to see limits to focusing on increasing response rates. Many pollsters view boosting response rates as an important defense against nonignorable nonresponse. In a limited sense, they are on to something because the bias of the sample average of Y decreases as a sample gets larger. In terms of Figure 8.1, we see that if we increased the sample size (by extending the dark shaded dots to the left), the sample average will move toward the population average. But notice the limitation. Increasing response rates does not eliminate bias until we get perfect response. And, higher response rates themselves do nothing to help us diagnose nonignorable nonresponse. That is, the higher response rates increase the number of dark shaded dots, but do not tell us whether the top or bottom panel is correct and that is the key piece of information we need to understand the presence and magnitude of nonignorable nonresponse.[3]

8.2 IDENTIFYING NONIGNORABLE NONRESPONSE: INTUITION

This simple framework sheds light on the challenges and opportunities of working with selection models. First the challenge: Selection models may be hard to identify. Identification in the statistical sense refers to making sure that only one set of parameter values can explain observed data. We've probably all seen an identification problem in junior high math such as $X + Y = 7$. This model is not identified because $X = 3$ and $Y = 4$ satisfy the equation, as does $X = 1$ and $Y = 6$.

In the selection model context, the problem is that a single observed outcome can be explained in multiple ways.[4] In the case of survey research, it is common that multiple combinations of unknown parameters could produce the results we observe. For example, suppose that we run a survey and find that 55 percent of respondents support the president. What should we believe about support for the president in the population?

Figure 8.2 illustrates the problem. A natural interpretation is that 55 percent of the population supports the president (we'll set aside issues related to the sampling distribution of the estimate for the moment). But note that this interpretation requires us to believe that $\rho_{R,Y} = 0$, as we highlight with point A in the figure. We could also observe the *same* observed 55 percent support rate if $\rho_{R,Y} = 0.1$ and the actual support in the population was 45 percent, as

---

[3] Trying to increase response rates has other issues as well. Yeager et al. (2011) found that survey estimates were *less* accurate as response rates went up across 14 probabilistic telephone and internet surveys. Peytchev (2013, 91) discusses how efforts to increase response rates (such as paying people to respond) could induce a stronger relationship between response and outcome.

[4] More formally, a model is statistically identified if only one set of parameter values can characterize the observed data. If two or more sets of differing parameter values produce the same statistical likelihood, the model is not identified. Miao, Ding, and Geng (2017) provide a general discussion of identification of selection models.

Selection Models for Nonignorable Nonresponse

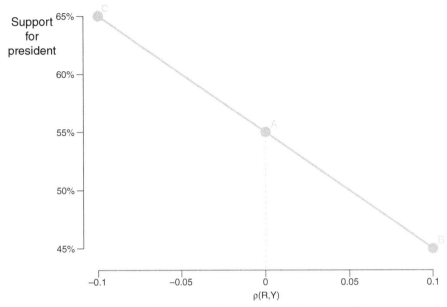

FIGURE 8.2 Statistical identification problem for survey that shows 55 percent support for the president

indicated by point B in the figure. In this scenario, the supporters of the president were more likely to respond, producing a sample average that was higher than the true average.

And, of course, the nonignorable nonresponse could have gone the other way. Point C in Figure 8.2 shows that we could also observe 55 percent support for the president in a survey if the support in the population were 65 percent and $\rho_{R,Y} = -0.1$. In this case, the supporters of the president were less likely to respond, producing a sample that had lower support for the president than there actually is in the population. In other words, the combination of true population average and $\rho_{R,Y}$ is not identified by simply observing a sample average. The typical way out of this problem is to assume $\rho_{R,Y} = 0$, but that is not very satisfying; much of the rest of this book will try to switch from assuming such a state of affairs to testing whether it is true.

The news is not all bad, however. We can use the two-equation framework to isolate traces of nonignorable nonresponse in observed data. At this point, we'll do this with a heuristic example. We'll add statistical details in Section 8.3 and Chapter 9, but honestly, the intuition is the most important thing.

Figure 8.3 shows response interest and Y for several cases. The two panels on the left are examples in which there nonresponse is ignorable. They are "flatfish" because there is no relation between response interest and response. The two panels on the right are examples in which there nonresponse is nonignorable. They are "tilted fish" because Y rises as response interest rises. The

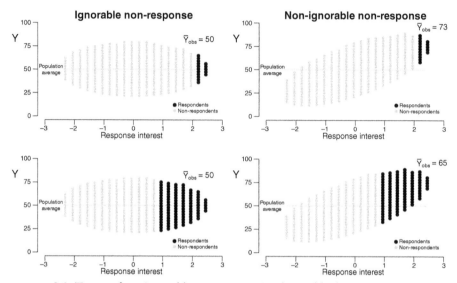

FIGURE 8.3 Traces of nonignorable nonresponse in observable data

panels on the top are cases in which the response rate is around 5 percent. The panels on the bottom are cases in which the response rate is higher, around 25 percent.

The key characteristic of the ignorable nonresponse cases on the left is that for any given value of response interest, there are an equal number of people with values of Y above and below the population average of Y. This means that for any slice of respondents, we will, in expectation, observe a sample average equal to the population average. In each of the two panels, for example, the average value of Y among those sampled is 50, even though the response rates differ quite a bit.

The situation is different for the nonignorable nonresponse cases on the right. In those cases, the average of the observed sample changes depending on the response rate. In the top panel on the right, the small response rate produces a sample that is quite extreme, with a sample average of 73. In the bottom panel on the right, the sample continues to be unrepresentative of the population, but it is less extreme, with a sample average of 65.

We have found the Holy Grail of nonignorable nonresponse: Evidence of nonignorability from observed data. Suppose that we conduct a poll with different polling protocols: Half the people are contacted rather perfunctorily, and their response rate is 5 percent as in the top panels. The other half is contacted more aggressively, and their response rate is the 25 percent depicted in the bottom panels. If the observed averages across the two types of polling protocols are the same, the data are consistent with the ignorable nonresponse patterns on the left. If, however, the observed averages across the two types of

Selection Models for Nonignorable Nonresponse 151

polling protocols differ, the observed sample is consistent with the nonignorable nonresponse patterns on the right. In statistical terms, we could estimate a model predicting Y as a function of a variable indicating whether someone was in the high response group in the bottom panels. If the estimated coefficient on that variable is near zero, we have evidence response is ignorable; if the estimated coefficient on that variable is less than zero, we have evidence that the high response group has lower average values of Y, as in the right-hand panels of Figure 8.3.

These figures illustrate the foundational logic of selection models: While it is true that nonignorable nonresponse depends on the correlation of unobserved variables, it is not true that nonignorable nonresponse leaves no trace. When nonresponse is nonignorable, survey averages will vary as response rates vary; when nonresponse is ignorable, survey averages will not change as response rates vary. Going forward, we will present statistical models that incorporate nonignorable nonresponse. There will be many ways to do this, but this intuition is at their heart.

We will come back multiple times to this logic. To get a sense of how it works in practice, consider the work of Schoenmueller, Netzer, and Stahl (2020) on online reviews. Online reviews skew positive, and they provide evidence that the people who write reviews are more positive, suggesting a relationship with "response" and outcome. In one set of experiments, they provided incentives for people to respond to songs and compared those responses to the numerical ratings of songs on Amazon. Nonincentivized respondents correspond to the top panel, and incentivized respondents correspond to the bottom panel. They found that incentivized respondents were less positive, consistent with nonignorable nonresponse in Figure 8.3. What's more, they found that their measures of consumer response to song from people less subject to nonignorable nonresponse were better able to predict sales than reviews actually left online.

8.3 THE HECKMAN MODEL

In order to build a toolkit of ways to estimate statistical models based on the above intuition, we'll begin with perhaps the most famous selection model, the Heckman selection model that helped James Heckman win the Nobel Prize in Economics in 2000. The model has been used to study political surveys as well (e.g., Brehm 1993; Berinsky 2004). The attraction of the model is that it allows us to be more precise about Equation 8.4. We'll address the disadvantages of the Heckman model later in this chapter and in Chapters 9 and 10.

Heckman's trick is to assume that the errors in the selection and outcome equation follow a bivariate normal distribution with correlation ρ. The mean of the distributions for each error term is zero, and the marginal distribution of each variable is normal. The interesting action is in the correlation. If $\rho = 0$,

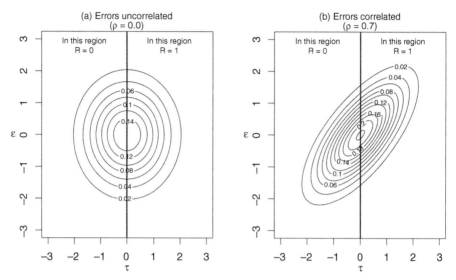

FIGURE 8.4 Contour maps for two examples of bivariate normal error terms

the expected values of τ and ϵ are unrelated to each other. If $\rho \neq 0$, then the expected value of one error term for any given individual will not be zero.

Figure 8.4 shows two examples of bivariate normal distributions. Panel (a) on the left shows the contour plots of a bivariate normal distribution when $\rho = 0$. Contour plots are like maps of mountainous geography. Each of the lines represents an elevation, in this case the height of the probability density. The higher the number indicated on the line, the more likely we are to see observations on that line. The circle in the middle indicates possible combinations of τ and ϵ with relatively high probability, while the outermost circle represents combinations of τ and ϵ with relatively low probability. Panel (a) on the left corresponds to the flatfish cases depicted on the left side of Figure 8.3.

The figure depicts a simple case in which $\tau_i > 0$ means $R_i^* > 0$ and therefore $R_i = 1$. Hence, the area to the right of the vertical line in the middle indicates the region in which the values of Y will be observed. Notice that in that area, the probabilities for ϵ are balanced above and below zero. In other words, the expected value of ϵ is zero for people who respond.

Panel (b) on the right side of Figure 8.4 shows an example of a bivariate normal distribution when $\rho > 0$. Similar to what we saw in the bottom panel of Figure 8.1, the distribution is tilted indicating that when $\tau > 0$ we're getting higher probabilities that ϵ is above zero as well. In this case, when $\tau_i > 0$, $R_i = 1$ and we are likely to also observe values of $\epsilon > 0$. In other words, in panel (b) the expected value of ϵ is greater than zero for people who respond.

The idea of correlated errors is a bit abstract. To make it more concrete, we can link the concept of correlated errors to a common scenario people think of when they worry about nonignorable nonresponse. In this scenario,

Selection Models for Nonignorable Nonresponse 153

there is some unobserved variable such as trust of strangers that affects the propensity to respond and is correlated with political opinions. Such a variable can create nonignorable nonresponse because we won't hear from the people who don't trust people they don't know and these people will, for example, disproportionately support Donald Trump. If we label the unobserved variable U, the following model is consistent with this scenario:

$$R^* = \gamma_0^* + \gamma_Z^* Z + \gamma_U^* U + \tau^*$$
$$Y^* = \beta_0^* + \beta_U^* U + \epsilon^*$$

Because we only observe Z, the unobserved error term in the response equation is $\gamma_U^* U + \tau^*$. The unobserved error term in the outcome equation is $\beta_U^* U + \epsilon^*$. For this scenario, we assume τ^* and ϵ^* are uncorrelated, meaning that the source of possible correlation is the fact that the unobserved variable U may affect both response and the outcome. As derived in the online appendix, the correlation between these error terms will be

$$= \frac{\beta_U \gamma_U \sigma_U^2}{\sigma_{e_Y} \sigma_{e_R}} \tag{8.5}$$

Equation 8.5 conveys that the correlation of errors – and hence the degree of bias in observed data – is a function of the *product* of β_U and γ_U, which means that the omitted variable needs to affect both R and Y. If U only affects one equation (either response or outcome), there is no correlation of errors between the two equations and hence U will not cause nonignorable nonresponse bias.

At first glance, there is a resonance between Equation 8.5 and conventional weighting. As we saw in Section 3.4, a good weighting variable affects both R and Y. In this sense, U would be a great variable to include in the weighting calculation. However, U cannot be a weighting variable because it is unobserved. Hence, its influence on both equations will cause conventional weighting estimates to be biased. Selection models, however, will estimate – and therefore control for – the correlation of errors caused by the existence of this U variable that affects both R and Y. In other words, the existence of U *undermines* conventional weighting models while it *justifies* selection models.

The payoff from the Heckman model is that we can calculate the expected values of one error term given another when they both come from a bivariate normal distribution. To keep things simple, we'll work with a response model with only Z. Applying a bit of algebra to Equation 8.1 shows that $R_i = 1$ when $\tau_i > -\gamma_0 - \gamma_Z Z_i$. Heckman's insight was to use the statistical properties of a bivariate normal equation to specify the following function for the expected error in the observed outcome equation:

$$E[\epsilon_i | R_i=1] = E[\epsilon_i |_{\tau_i > -\gamma_0 - \gamma_Z Z_i}]$$
$$= \rho \sigma_\epsilon \frac{\phi(\gamma_0 + \gamma_Z Z_i)}{\Phi(\gamma_0 + \gamma_Z Z_i)} \tag{8.6}$$

where

154   *Part III: Fighting Nonignorable Nonresponse*

- σ_ϵ is the standard deviation of ϵ
- $\phi()$ is the normal probability density function
- $\Phi()$ is the normal cumulative density function, which is equivalent to the fitted probability of response from a first-stage probit model of response.[5]

The fraction on the right-hand side of Equation 8.6 is referred to as the inverse Mills ratio.

Equation 8.6 has a lot going on. First, we can clearly see that the expected value of the error term for observed individuals is zero when $\rho = 0$, suggesting that we can test for ignorable nonresponse by testing whether $\rho = 0$. Second, the denominator of the inverse Mills ratio is particularly interesting because $\Phi(\gamma_0 + \gamma_Z Z_i)$ equals p_i, which is the probability that person i responded, a key variable when thinking about nonresponse. This means that the expected value of ϵ_i is inversely related to p_i. In other words, when ρ is positive, the observed values of Y from people who had a low probability of responding (people with low values of p_i) are the ones with the higher expected error terms for the outcome equation.[6]

Weighting and Heckman models use the *same* information in *different* ways. Weighting models divide all variables by p_i, the probability of response for an individual. Heckman models include M_i, which depends on p_i, albeit a complicated manner. The key insight is that p_i is in the denominator of M_i, so this means that while weighting models multiply Y and other variables by a function of $\frac{1}{p_i}$, selection models include a function of $\frac{1}{p_i}$ as a covariate.

Practically, having an equation for the expected value of the error term allows us to estimate the Heckman model in two steps. Building from Equations 8.4 and 8.6 and assuming for simplicity that $\sigma_\epsilon = 1$,[7] the expected value of Y for the observations can be rewritten as follows.

$$
\begin{aligned}
E[Y_i|_{Y_i \text{ observed}}] &= \beta_0 + E[\epsilon_i|_{R_i=1}] \\
&= \beta_0 + E[\epsilon_i|_{\tau_i > -\gamma_0 - \gamma_Z Z_i}] \\
&= \beta_0 + \rho\sigma_\epsilon \frac{\phi(\gamma_0 + \gamma_Z Z_i)}{\Phi(\gamma_0 + \gamma_Z Z_i)} \\
&= \beta_0 + \rho M_i
\end{aligned}
\tag{8.7}
$$

---

[5] Achen (1986) uses a linear probability model to estimate the response equation, an approach that requires stronger parametric assumptions than Heckman's model, but is easier to work with. Wooldridge (2002, 563) shows that the Heckman model works with weaker assumptions: τ is normally distributed and $E[\epsilon|\tau] = \delta\tau$. A probit model is a statistical model used when the dependent variable takes on only values of 0 and 1. In this case, the dependent variable is 0 for nonrespondents and 1 for respondents. Readers unfamiliar with probit models may wish to refer to Chapter 12 of Bailey (2021).

[6] The numerator of M_i is also a function of p_i. To see this, note that $\Phi^{-1}(\gamma_0 + \gamma_Z Z_i) = \gamma_0 + \gamma_Z Z_i$, meaning that the numerator of M_i can be rewritten as $\phi(\Phi^{-1}(p_i))$. If one plots M_i as a function of p_i, the p_i in the denominator explains most of the variation.

[7] In practice, of course, $\sigma_\epsilon \neq 1$ and we would adjust estimated coefficients accordingly. This quantity is the standard error of the regression in the outcome equation.

Selection Models for Nonignorable Nonresponse 155

where M_i is the inverse Mills ratio.

The Heckman model can be estimated in two steps. The first step involves estimating the γ parameters via a probit model in which the dependent variable is R, which equals 1 for respondents and 0 for nonrespondents. With these estimates in hand, we can calculate M_i for every observation. The second step involves estimating Equation 8.7 using these calculated values of M_i for each observation.[8] If the estimated ρ parameter is significantly different from zero, we have evidence of nonignorable nonresponse. Otherwise, the data are consistent with ignorable nonresponse and weighting and related adjustments are appropriate.

It may not be immediately apparent in the equations, but the Heckman model relies on the intuition we developed earlier based on Figure 8.3. First, recall that M_i is a function of p_i. In other words, as the probability of response varies, so too does M_i. Think of high values of M_i as analogous to the top panels in Figure 8.3 (since p_i is in the denominator of M_i values of p_i close to zero will correspond to high values for M_i). Think of low values of M_i as analogous to the bottom panels in Figure 8.3 (values of p_i close to one will correspond to relatively low values for M_i). This means that in essence a Heckman model is testing whether Y varies by response rate. A positive coefficient on M_i would indicate that the people with high M_i (and low p_i) have higher values of Y than people with low M_i (and high p_i), consistent with the panels on the right of Figure 8.3. A zero coefficient on M_i indicates that there is no difference in Y as a function of M_i (which, in turn, depends on p_i), consistent with the panels on the left of Figure 8.3.

8.4 CONTRASTING WEIGHTING MODELS AND SELECTION MODELS

While the Heckman selection model obviously differs mathematically from weighting, the conceptual importance of these differences is hard to see. In fact, though, selection and weighting models use data very differently: If ρ is nonzero, a Heckman model effectively gives less weight to low propensity observations which is the opposite of how weighting models give more weight to such observations.

This section illustrates this point by comparing properties of the estimates produced by several approaches. Table 8.1 displays the models, their parameters of interest and additional information. In each model, we seek to estimate the population mean β_0, as expressed in the simple model defined by Equation 8.2. The simple average approach simply involves estimating the population mean with the sample mean. The weighted average uses the tools described in Chapter 3 to estimate the sample average via a weighted average of the

---

[8] The Heckman model can also be estimated directly with full information maximum likelihood (FIML). The two-step approach is conceptually useful because it reformulates the selection problem as an omitted variable problem (Greene 2003, 782), but the FIML approach typically performs better (Galimard, Chevret, Curis, and Resche-Rigon 2018).

TABLE 8.1 *Marginal effects of Y_i on $\hat{\beta}_0$ in different approaches*

Approach	Model	Parameter	Estimate	$\dfrac{\partial \textit{Estimate}}{\partial Y_i}$
Simple average	$Y_i = \beta_0 + \epsilon_i$	β_0	$\hat{\beta}_0 = \overline{Y} = \dfrac{\sum Y_i}{n}$	$\dfrac{1}{n}$
Weighting	$w_i Y_i = w_i \beta_0 + w_i \epsilon_i$	β_0	$\hat{\beta}_0 = \dfrac{\sum w_i^2 Y_i}{\sum w_i^2}$	$\dfrac{w_i^2}{\sum w_i^2}$
Heckman	$Y_i = \beta_0 + \rho M_i + \epsilon_i$	ρ	$\hat{\rho} = \dfrac{\sum (M_i - \overline{M})(Y_i - \overline{Y})}{\sum (M_i - \overline{M})^2}$	$\dfrac{\dfrac{n-1}{n}(M_i - \overline{M})}{\sum (M_i - \overline{M})^2}$
		β_0	$\hat{\beta}_0 = \overline{Y} - \overline{M}\hat{\rho}$	$\dfrac{1}{n} - \overline{M}\dfrac{\partial \hat{\rho}}{\partial Y_i}$

Selection Models for Nonignorable Nonresponse

observed sample. The Heckman approach uses Equation 8.7 as applied to the observed values of Y to estimate β_0 in Equation 8.2 for the reasons described in Section 8.3.[9]

A simple average of observed data provides a good baseline. It is simply the average of Y in the observed sample. No adjustment for nonresponse is made. Increasing the value of Y_i by one for one observation in a sample of n observations will therefore increase the estimated average by $\frac{1}{n}$, as indicated in the right-most column of Table 8.1.

As discussed in Chapter 3, analysts using weights multiply each observation by $w_i = \frac{1}{p_i}$ where p_i is the probability that $R_i = 1$. The model is

$$w_i Y_i = \beta_0 w_i + w_i \epsilon_i \tag{8.8}$$

The marginal effect of increasing a single observation of Y_i by 1 on the weighting estimate depends on the weight placed on that observation. The larger the weight, the larger the effect. And since weights are larger for observations with low probabilities, this means that observations from people who represent groups that are less likely to respond are going to be given more weight in the weighted average. This is intuitive: After all, the point of weighting is to give extra weight to low probability observations.

Analysts using a two-step Heckman model will estimate Equation 8.7, which is a bivariate regression model where the covariate is M_i. As discussed in Section 8.3, M_i is calculated based on parameters from a first-stage equation predicting R_i based on Z_i.

Understanding the influence of a single observation Y_i on the parameters in the Heckman model involves two steps. First, the effect of increasing Y_i on ρ depends on p_i. If p_i is low, then $M_i > \overline{M}$ (because p_i is in the denominator of M_i) and the effect of increasing Y_i on $\hat{\rho}$ is positive. That is, seeing high values of Y_i for low p_i observations will increase our estimate of ρ. This takes a bit of noodling, but makes sense: Low propensity respondents have large values of M_i. If they also have larger than average values of Y_i, then $\hat{\rho}$ must be greater than zero, as high values of M_i go with high values of Y_i.

The effect of Y_i on β_0 is what we really care about. Recall that β_0 is our estimate of the population average. If we increase Y_i by 1, our β_0 estimate average goes up by $\frac{1}{n}$ *minus* the effect of Y_i on ρ. We just saw that for low p_i observations, higher values of Y_i will increase the estimate of ρ. The effect of Y_i on ρ enters negatively in the equation for the effect of Y_i on β_0 meaning that the net effect of increasing the value of Y_i by one for a low p_i observation may be to *decrease* our estimate of the average value of Y in the population.

---

[9] See Bailey (2021) for more details on the statistical models in Table 8.1. Chapter 6 of Bailey (2021) shows that the simple average can be estimated with OLS. The weighting model is a bivariate regression model with no intercept; Chapter 13 of Bailey (2021) derives the estimator for such a model. The Heckman model is a standard bivariate regression model with an intercept and covariate (M_i). Chapter 3 presents the calculations for such a model.

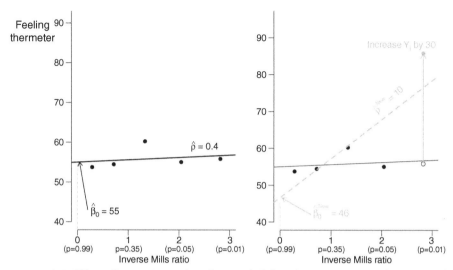

FIGURE 8.5 Effect of increasing Y_i for a low probability observation in Heckman model

This is a lot to keep track of. Therefore, Figure 8.5 shows how a Heckman model can convert higher observed values of Y into *lower* estimates of the population average. The example is hypothetical and a bit extreme; the point is to show how a Heckman model operates. The panel on the left shows a scatterplot of feeling thermometer ratings toward a politician and M_i values for five people. M_i is the inverse Mills ratio, which we have noted tracks the inverse of the probability of response. The response probabilities correspond to each value of M_i to highlight that a very low probability responder is on the right of this plot. The solid dark line indicates the fitted line from a Heckman model for these five observations. The slope of this line is 0.4, indicating modest relation between M_i and Y_i. The estimate of β_0 is simply where the fitted line crosses the point at which $M_i = 0$. Here, it is 55, which is quite close to the sample average.

The panel on the right of Figure 8.5 shows the same data with one change: We suppose that the person with the lowest probability of responding (the dot on the right) rated the politician 30 points higher on the feeling thermometer than they did in the panel on the left. This shifts the sample average of Y to 62 and shifts the weighted average of Y even higher to 81. (The weighted average shifts so much because observations with low probability have large weights.) It might seem natural to expect that the population estimate in a Heckman model would also shift higher.

This is not what happens. The higher value for the observation on the right pushes the slope of the new line estimated by the Heckman model to become much steeper. This makes sense because we now have evidence that the low probability observations tend to have high values of Y. The slope in this panel

Selection Models for Nonignorable Nonresponse 159

is 10. Because the slope is so much steeper, the intercept has shifted downward and our estimate of the population mean is $\hat{\beta}_0 = 46$.

The reason this happens is because data in a Heckman model are informative about not only Y, but also ρ. In this case, the low probability observation on the right in the panel is telling us that ρ is quite large. A large ρ suggests that our sample suffers from nonignorable nonresponse bias. Once we think that, we want to adjust how we infer population values from the sample accordingly. In this case, the positive slope in the panel on the right tells us there is positive nonignorable nonresponse bias implying that our sample is overly favorable toward the politician. In other words, the evidence suggests that the population is not as warm toward the politicians as the sample and therefore our population estimate should be lower than the sample average. The Heckman model provides the specific mathematical foundation for making this adjustment; in this case, it leads us to estimate the population average as 46, which is the intercept in the line estimated by the Heckman model.

The key distinction between the Heckman and other models is that data in the Heckman model are simultaneously informative about the correlation of errors and about the relationship between the independent and dependent variables. In some cases, a low probability observation will indicate that there is correlation in the error terms, rather than directly providing information about the average of Y in the population. In other cases, a Heckman model may surface no sign of nonignorable nonresponse (as in the panel on the left of Figure 8.5) and observations will be more or less directly informative about the population average. In weighted models, in contrast, observations are always taken to be directly informative about the average of Y, with low probability observations taken to be particularly informative.

Recognizing that the approaches treat low probability observations very differently raises the obvious question of which method is better. The answer we've been pointing to all along is, of course, that if nonresponse is nonignorable, then weighting is biased. A Heckman selection model accounts for the nonignorable nonresponse, producing different answers when $\rho \neq 0$.

Figure 8.6 shows bias from simulations for the three estimation approaches as a function of the correlation of ϵ (the error in the outcome equation) and τ (the error in the selection equation). The OLS model is a generalization of simply calculating the sample mean. All three methods are unbiased when the correlation of errors is zero, but the expected coefficients from OLS and weighting get steadily further from the true value as the magnitude of the correlation of errors gets larger. This makes sense because OLS and weighting assume $\rho = 0$. Interestingly, we see that nonignorable nonresponse has more malign effects on weighting than OLS: The magnitude of the bias for weighting is larger than for OLS when $\rho \neq 0$. These simulation results track Goldstein's experience discussed in Chapter 5 on page 55 because when there is nonignorable nonresponse, the low p_i observations are particularly problematic and weighting places great emphasis on these observations unlike OLS that treats

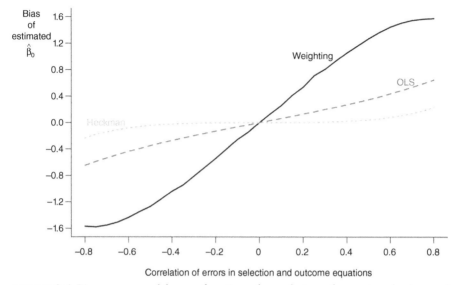

FIGURE 8.6 Bias across models as a function of correlation of error in selection and outcome equations

them with equal weight as high p_i observations. The Heckman model shows little sign of bias until the absolute values of ρ get quite large and the estimates of ρ break down.

These simulations are friendly toward the Heckman model because we assume the errors are bivariate normally distributed, as in the Heckman model. It is plausible that another functional form connecting the two error terms may produce less favorable results for the Heckman model. Chapter 9 extends selection models to cases in which errors are not jointly normal.

8.5 LIMITATIONS OF THE HECKMAN MODEL

The Heckman model converts a complex system defined by two equations into a relatively simple model. Amazing as that is, many scholars also suspect it is nonetheless not very useful. Channeling the findings of many others, Copas and Li (1997, 59) report that the Heckman models "does not always give sensible answers and is now no longer regarded as the panacea for all data selection problems."

CHALLENGE 1: FUNCTIONAL FORM A common critique of the Heckman model is that it makes a strong functional form assumption by assuming that the errors in the response and outcome equations follow a bivariate normal distribution (see, e.g., Winship and Mare 1992, 341). Put simply, many scholars worry that it may not be true that the errors come from this very specific joint distribution. As Tourangeau and Plewes (2013, 55) put it, many survey

Selection Models for Nonignorable Nonresponse 161

researchers have viewed selection models like Heckman's "with skepticism, mainly because most selection models make strong assumptions about the nonresponse mechanism that may not hold in practice."

Before we wade into the responses to this critique, we should note its irony – and even audacity. Often, critiques of the Heckman model's parametric assumption are presented as part of the justification for using weights rather than a Heckman model. But it's not like weighting models do not make strong assumptions: They require that response is ignorable. It is as if describe a mole on your arm to your doctor as oval-shaped and the doctor responds "That's not an oval. Listen to you with your strong assumptions!" When you follow up to ask the doctor how she would describe the mole she says "Easy – it does not exist!"

Concerns about functional form are, nonetheless, valid. There are three lines of response to such concerns. First, parametric assumptions are not always problematic. Certainly, many maximum likelihood models, including probit and logit models, have proven quite useful despite their specific parametric assumptions. And the parametric assumption here may well be reasonable: The bivariate normal assumption says, loosely, large absolute values of τ and ϵ are less likely than small absolute values and that the degree of correlation can range from -1 to 1. A joint distribution with these characteristics may well approximate many plausible real-world associations between the error terms. We'll see simulation examples in Chapter 9 from Peress (2010) and of cases in which the normality assumption is wrong, but produces reasonable results as long as the first-stage instrument was good. Second, multiple articles in the literature have found that data weaknesses are more of a problem than functional form. We elaborate on this issue in Chapter 10. Third, and perhaps most directly, the literature has made great strides in formulating selection models with few or flexible assumptions about functional form. Selection models will always present real challenges, but the days are long past when they were limited to assumptions of bivariate normality. We cover these advances in Chapter 9.

CHALLENGE 2: DATA REQUIREMENTS One reason the Heckman model is not widely used in survey research is that real-world data may simply not be up to the demands of the model. First, the model requires data on nonrespondents, which may not always be feasible. After all, they did not respond! This problem is not insurmountable. Section 10.5 will show how to deal with this situation with the right survey design. In general, if one has enough information to create weights, one has enough information to implement a Heckman model.

A more fundamental weakness for many applications is that the Heckman model performs poorly unless there is at least one variable that explains response quite well and is not included in the outcome equation (Gomes, Radice, Camarena Brenes, and Marra 2019; Bushway, Johnson, and Slocum 2007; Puhani 2000; Coppock, Gerber, Green, and Kern 2017; Galimard

162   *Part III: Fighting Nonignorable Nonresponse*

et al. 2018). To see this, we will work from a form of the Heckman model that generalizes from Equation 8.7 to include a covariate (and could easily be expanded to include multiple covariates):

$$E[Y_i|_{Y_i \text{ observed}}] = \beta_0 + \beta_1 X_i + \rho M_i \tag{8.9}$$

Following standard OLS results (Bailey 2021), the variance of the $\hat{\rho}$ estimate in Equation 8.9 is

$$var(\hat{\rho}) = \frac{\hat{\sigma}^2}{Nvar(M)(1 - R_M^2)} \tag{8.10}$$

where $\hat{\sigma}^2$ is the variance of the regression, $var(M)$ is the variance of the inverse Mills ratio, and R_M^2 is the R^2 from a regression model explaining M as a function of X. Recall that the variance of $\hat{\rho}$ governs how accurately we are able to estimate ρ. If the variance of this estimate is very high, then we will have a poor estimate of ρ. Because the distinguishing feature of Heckman models is their estimation of ρ, an inability to accurately estimate this parameter severely undermines the benefits of the model.

The variance of $\hat{\rho}$ will be high or even infinite – and therefore the statistical power will be low or zero – in two common circumstances.

- **Heckman models fail if no Z is included in the response equation**
  In our simple setup, the response is a function only of Z. If Z does not do a good job explaining R, the $\hat{p}$ will not vary much which in turn means that the variance of M (a function of $\hat{p}$) will be low and the variance of the estimate for $\hat{\rho}$ will be high. In an extreme case in which γ_Z in the response equation (Equation 8.1) is equal to zero, $\hat{p}$ and in turn M_i will be a constant and $var(M) = 0$. Because $var(M)$ is in the denominator of Equation 8.10, the variance of $\hat{\rho}$ will be infinite, rendering the estimation of ρ impossible. If γ_Z is close to zero, we will have a very small variance of $\hat{p}$ and, in turn, M and a correspondingly high variance of $\hat{\rho}$.
- **Heckman models struggle if $Z = X$**
  The second circumstance leading to a high variance of $\hat{\rho}$ occurs when the variable in the response equation is the same as the variable in the outcome equation. In many survey contexts, the variables that are used to explain the response process are also the variables used to explain the outcome, creating a multicollinearity problem that renders the approach unreliable.
  Consider an example in which we have the same the dichotomous covariate in the response and outcome equations. We'll call it D_i; this means $Z_i = D_i$ in the response equation and $X_i = D_i$ in the outcome equation. Suppose, for example, that D is a dummy variable for men that we include in the response and outcome equations. The value of M_i will take on two values: One value when $D_i = 0$ and another value when $D_i = 1$. That means that when we put M_i in Equation 8.9, it will be perfectly correlated with D_i because its two values depend completely on the value of D_i. This

Selection Models for Nonignorable Nonresponse 163

implies that $R_M^2 = 1$ which means the variance of $\hat{\rho}$ will be infinite because $(1 - R_M^2)$ is in the denominator of Equation 8.10.

If the single variable across the two questions is a continuous variable, such as age, we will not have perfect multicollinearity between X and M due to the nonlinearity of the inverse Mills ratio function. Nonetheless, even in this case high multicollinearity is quite common, which will make $(1 - R_M^2)$ quite small and $var(\hat{\rho})$ quite high. The online appendix provides more detail.

This logic extends to a circumstance in which the same factors explain response propensity and outcome. This is a problem in many applied contexts because it is quite common that the factors we think might affect response propensity might also affect the outcome. In public opinion models, for example, income, education, age, and party identification plausibly affect both whether people respond to a pollster and the content of their opinions.

And even if we do find a Z variable that belongs in the response equation but not the outcome equation, we can still have problems if Z is highly correlated with X. Suppose that Z that equals 1 for people in noncomputer jobs and 0 for everyone else. Suppose also that we are willing to argue that people whose jobs require little or no work on the computer may be less likely to respond to internet polls but still have, on average, the same opinions as people who work on computers. Even putting aside the strong assumption that this variable has no bearing on Y, our Z that we include in first stage may be highly correlated with education, income, age, and other factors so that we still have high correlation between Z and X. (We discuss in Chapter 10 how to design surveys to produce Z variables that are uncorrelated with X, which is ideal.)

Therefore, anyone interested in using a Heckman model needs to first assess the suitability of their data. And how do we do that? Before presenting an answer, we can first reject the rule of thumb that it is necessary and possibly sufficient to have a variable that is statistically significant in the selection equation and excluded from the outcome equation. This logic is not as unreasonable because having such a variable helps break the connection between the inverse Mill's ratio and the variables included in the outcome equation. This rule of thumb is also appealing because it corresponds to the intuition in two-stage least squares models, where an exclusion condition is necessary.[10]

---

[10] Researchers familiar with two-stage least squares (2SLS) models will recall that 2SLS models require inclusion of a variable that is statistically informative in the first stage and is excluded from the second stage (Bailey 2021). If no such variable exists, a 2SLS model is literally unidentified because the fitted value of the endogenous variable is a linear function of the variables in the first stage. The argument for a Heckman model is similar: We need a variable that explains response quite well but that is excluded from the outcome equation. However, the nonlinear form of the inverse Mills ratio means that a Heckman model will not literally be unidentified in the absence of such a model, but it is often practically unidentified for the reasons discussed in this section.

164   *Part III: Fighting Nonignorable Nonresponse*

However, if the substantive effect of the first-stage variable is modest, M may be highly correlated with X and we may have highly unreliable estimates of ρ.

A better way to assess the sufficiency of data for a Heckman-type model is to assess directly the degree of multicollinearity in the outcome equation between the inverse Mill's ratio and the independent variables in the outcome equation. Multicollinearity can be measured via R^2_M, the R^2 produced in a regression of the inverse Mill's ratio on all the other variables in the outcome equation.[11] If the R^2_M is low enough that multicollinearity does not cause unworkably large standard errors on coefficients, then we can simply use the results from the Heckman model. If R^2_M is large, then we need to think about the statistical power of our tests. Analysts should report this (or a similar diagnostic) as a matter of course so that readers will know if it is even possible to know if there is nonignorable nonresponse.

8.6 CONCLUSION

It is commonly believed that it is impossible to fight back against nonignorable nonresponse. That is not true. Models that address nonignorable nonresponse have been around a long time and provide tools to diagnose and potentially counteract nonignorable nonresponse.

The goal of this chapter is to start us on the road to building a toolkit of such models. Our first step was to formulate a simple two-stage response model, a model that provides grounds for both caution and optimism. Our caution comes from statistical identification challenges inherent in the model: It is really hard to pull apart the response and outcome processes. Nonetheless, our discussion leaves room for optimism because we see that nonignorable nonresponse leaves tracks in observable data.

The famous Heckman model adds some assumptions to that simple model and produces tractable and intuitive results. Among other benefits, the Heckman model can help us see important differences in selection and weighting models. Weighting models *always* give extra weight to low response propensity observations, while Heckman models do not and, in fact, give less weight to low response propensity observations when there is evidence of nonignorable nonresponse.

The Heckman model is far from the last word, however. In Chapters 9 and 10, we discuss how the research literature has matured in ways that allow us to address the key concerns about the Heckman model. In Chapter 9, we present a series of models that allow us to be much more flexible with regard to how we model the interaction of response and outcome. In Chapter 10 after that, we discuss how to ensure that we will have the data needed to make these models work well.

---

[11] The condition number of the matrix of independent variables in the outcome equation provides a very similar, although perhaps less intuitive, diagnostic measure (see, e.g., Bushway, Johnson, and Slocum 2007; Puhani 2000).

9

Next-Generation Selection Models

> ... relaxing the parametric assumptions required for identification in selection models for binary outcomes should remove an impediment to wider use of selection models for dealing with missing data....
>
> McGovern, Canning, and Bärnighausen (2018)

Here's what we know so far. Nonignorable nonresponse is plausible for many polls, especially those relying on increasing popular nonprobability sampling methods. Weighting does not solve the problem, but other models might. The Heckman model, for example, offers an intuitive way to estimate the extent of nonignorability while also producing sample estimates that net out the effects of nonignorable nonresponse.

The problem with the Heckman model is that it is prone to producing unstable and fragile results and has failed to catch on among pollsters. But the Heckman model is not the final word on selection models, and the main theme of this chapter is that the literature has made vast progress since the original Heckman model.

In this chapter, we focus on next-generation selection models that allow us to expand on the Heckman model in useful ways. One of the most common critiques of the Heckman model centers on the central role a very specific statistical distribution plays in it. This need not be the case, and we show in this chapter how copula models allow us to estimate selection models for a large range of other statistical distributions. We can go even further and use control function models that estimate key parameters of the statistical distribution that generated the data, whatever its properties. Control functions are not for everyone, though, because they only estimate the effects of X on Y (the β coefficients in our terminology). Control function models do not estimate the levels of Y in the population, something that is often important for pollsters.

Next-generation selection pushes past the Heckman model in other ways as well. Many survey practitioners think in terms of re-weighting their sample in a way that offsets nonresponse bias. As we have seen, conventional weighting approaches require us to assume response is ignorable, which is a potentially incorrect assumption and which is untestable within the conventional weighting paradigm. However, building on the logic we have developed about selection models, the elusive ideal of creating weights that account for nonignorable nonresponse is in fact possible. This will seem a bit magical – or even fanciful – to some, but we'll show how it is possible to generate weights that account for nonignorable nonresponse (Sun, Liu, Miao, Wirth, Robins, and Tchetgen Tchetgen 2018). Not only do these weights increase the weight on demographic groups that respond with lower probabilities, but they also increase weights on people with opinions that may make them less inclined to respond. While the estimation algorithm will be unfamiliar for some, it is rooted in a simple two-equation selection model similar to what we have seen so far.

There are also models that can accommodate more kinds of data than the Heckman model. We saw in Hartman and Huang's work in Chapter 7 that potentially important variables in a selection model can sometimes be partially observed, meaning that we observe them only for the people in the sample. In Chapter 1, for example, we discussed the situation in which people who were interested in politics were more likely to support Democrats. It seemed like common sense that this fact was relevant for nonresponse bias, but because we only observed interest in politics for those in the sample, we could not use the variable in the construction of weights and – it turns out – we cannot use such a variable in a Heckman model either. But by slightly modifying the Heckman model, we can enable it to incorporate such partially observed variables, opening up the door to more extensive tests for and corrections of possible nonignorable nonresponse.

These models go a long way toward addressing the limitations of the first-generation Heckman selection model. We might be tempted to think of them as an easy fix for the challenge of nonignorable nonresponse, like a simple pill one could take to lose weight. It's not that easy, neither for nonresponse bias nor for weight loss. There is more hard work required, and in Chapter 10 we highlight how these models still require good data. If we're lucky, the kind of data these models need may already exist in our data; more likely though, we'll have to create such data with appropriately designed surveys. These are topics we'll fully explain in Chapter 10, but for now it is useful to be clear that these models are only the first step in the process of using selection models to account for nonignorable nonresponse.

This chapter proceeds as follows. Section 1 directly addresses concerns about the Heckman model's bivariate normality assumption by presenting copula models that allow us to assess a vast range of parametric assumptions. Section 2 introduces even more flexibility by presenting the control function approach to estimation of selection models. Section 3 shows how to create weights that incorporate nonignorable nonresponse. Section 4 shows how to modify a Heckman model to allow for estimation of a nonignorable

Next-Generation Selection Models 167

nonresponse selection model when we have a response-related variable that is available only for people in the survey sample. As with Chapter 8, this chapter contains a mix of intuitive and technical content. The tools covered in here are quite technical, but we focus on presenting them verbally and graphically.

9.1 COPULAS

The Heckman model assumes that the errors in the response and outcome equations follow a joint normal distribution. As we have noted, this assumption may not be true. For example, what if the distributions of the error terms were more spread out than in a normal distribution? Generations of statistics students have grappled with this kind of idea when they learned that t-statistics in OLS models follow t-distributions that have, ahem, "fat tails." That is, extreme values are more likely in a t-distribution than in a normal distribution. In a bivariate context, it is possible that extreme values are more likely than suggested by a joint normal distribution. Or, more generally, the shape of the joint distribution of the error terms could have a very different shape that implied by the bivariate normal, especially if the data are quite skewed (Gomes, Radice, Brenes, and Marra 2019). Since we do not observe the error terms, we cannot know for sure.[1]

Copula methods allow us assess distributions other than the bivariate normal distribution (Gomes, Radice, Brenes, and Marra 2019; McGovern, Canning, and Bärnighausen 2018). A copula is a mathematical formula that characterizes a joint distribution of two variables as a function of the marginal distribution of each and a link parameter or function that connects the marginal distributions. The bivariate normal density is an example of a copula in which the marginal distribution of Y given X is a normal distribution and the marginal distribution of R^* given Z is also a normal distribution. These two distributions are linked via the correlation parameter ρ. If ρ is zero, the joint distribution of Y and R^* is the product of the marginal distributions and looks like the left-hand panel of Figure 8.4; if $\rho \neq 0$, the joint distribution is the bivariate normal distribution and looks like right-hand panel of that figure.

With names like "Frank," "Gumbel," and "Joe" (really), copula distributions do not always sound like statistical distributions. But they are useful because they provide a broad range of parametric distributions that can be used to define statistical likelihoods for given observed data. This means that copula models can be estimated with standard maximum likelihood estimation (MLE) tools and will produce estimates that have the properties of MLE estimates

---

[1] While one cannot know the distribution, one can potentially reject the null hypothesis that the errors follow a bivariate normal. The marginal distributions of the errors will be normal for a bivariate normal, and one can use a Lagrange multiplier-type test to test for the normality assumption in a probit model predicting response (Bera, Jarque, and Lee 1984).

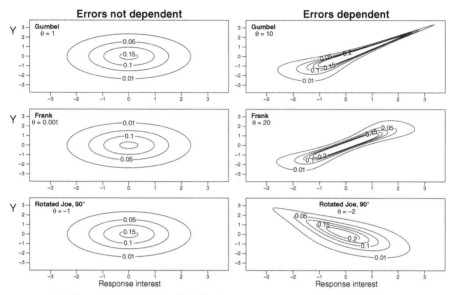

FIGURE 9.1 Examples of copula distributions

such as asymptotic normality (McGovern, Canning, and Bärnighausen 2018). Gomes, Radice, Brenes, and Marra (2019, 484) list examples.

The power of copulas comes from the range of possible distributions that they cover. Figure 9.1 shows contour plots for several copulas. Each plot shows relative probabilities for the joint distributions of R^* and Y. On the left-hand side are plots in which there is little or no dependence between the values of R^* and Y, akin to the contour plots of the normal distribution when $\rho = 0$ that we saw on the left-hand side of Figure 8.4. On the right-hand side are plots when there is clear dependence between R^* and Y, akin to the contour plots of the normal distribution when $\rho \neq 0$ that we saw on the right-hand side of Figure 8.4.

Each row shows illustrative examples for some non-normal copulas. For example, the top row shows the joint densities for the Gumbel distribution. When there is no dependence between the R^* and Y values, the contour plots are unremarkably symmetric. However, when there is a dependence, we get something like the tilted fish we have seen before, but for this Gumbel distribution the probability of two low values is much higher than for two high values. In other words, this copula distribution looks quite different than the bivariate normal with dependence across the error distributions. If we were estimating a copula model with a Gumbel distribution, the MLE process will find the value of θ that maximizes the observed likelihood.[2]

---

[2] The manner in which the θ parameter enters the likelihood varies across the copulas. Gomes, Radice, Brenes, and Marra (2019, 484) provide a table that shows the range of possible θ. For the unrotated Gumbel and Joe copulas, for example, θ ranges from 1 to ∞.

Next-Generation Selection Models 169

The second row of Figure 9.1 shows contour plots for two Frank copulas. The nondependence case on the left (which technically is a very low dependence case) is, again, a familiar looking symmetric distribution.[3] When the values of R^* and Y are interdependent, we get another tilted fish, but now with a keyhole shape, indicating that we are more likely to see two high values of the random variables or two low values of the random variable than we are to see two values around 0.

The third row of Figure 9.1 shows "Rotated Joe" copulas. Again, the no dependence case on the left is a familiar symmetric shape. The plot on the right shows the case with interdependence between R^* and Y, with a tilted fish again, but now with a negative slope, which is due to the rotation of a standard Joe copular. Similar to the Gumbel distribution, there is an asymmetry with high values of R^* and low values of Y being more likely than low values of R^* and high values of Y. The rotation essentially indicates where this distribution is pointed. Rotations of 90, 180, and 270 degrees are possible for copulas such as the Clayton, Gumbel, and Joe copulas.

For any given application, researchers typically estimate multiple copula models and focus on the model that best fits their data based on an Akaike or other information criterion (see, e.g., McGovern, Canning, and Bärnighausen 2018). Packages such as the GJRM package in R make this relatively painless (Marra and Radice 2017).

Copulas appear to provide the most distinctive results when data are weak. That is, we have suggested earlier that selection models perform best when we have a Z variable that strongly predicts response equation but can be excluded from the outcome equation. (We devote Chapter 10 to exploring this idea in more detail.) In many cases, though, we are not comfortable excluding any predictors of response from the outcome equation or, if we are comfortable excluding some Z from the Y equation, it may nonetheless do a poor job explaining R. In such cases, statistical identification depends closely on the parametric form, and copulas enable researchers to find the parametric form that most closely matches their data.

Gomes, Radice, Brenes, and Marra (2019) highlight the relationship between copulas and data quality by conducting simulations in which they vary the parametric form of the true data and the strength of the Z variable in predicting response. For non-normal true data, the copula models perform better than a Heckman model. When Z strongly predicts R, however, the copula models improve performance over the Heckman model only modestly.[4] When Z does a poor job predicting R, the copula models vastly

---

[3] For the Frank copula, θ cannot be zero, so our Frank copula plot on the left shows the density for a very low value of θ, which corresponds to very low levels of dependence.

[4] These results are consistent with Peress's (2010) simulation results that showed that his model that assumed bivariate normality performed fine when there was a good continuum of resistance variable even when the true joint error distribution was not normal.

170   *Part III: Fighting Nonignorable Nonresponse*

outperform Heckman models, which tend to be unreliable. These results suggest that researchers should prioritize identifying good Z variables and, once they've done the best they can on that front, move to assessing robustness via copula or other methods (Marra et al. 2017, 493).

The copula literature is large. For our purposes, two studies are particularly relevant because they explicitly dealt with a survey nonresponse problem. The context for both was efforts to assess HIV prevalence in Africa. Not everyone contacted responded, and the question was how informative the survey results were about the population in light of this nonresponse. Marra et al. (2017) looked at data from Swaziland, Zambia, and Zimbabwe from 2005 to 2007. Their data included between 4,000 and 8,000 observations in each country based on response rates that ranged from 78 to 92 percent. Despite the high response rates, the researchers were concerned that social norms and other incentives may have made some HIV-positive people reluctant to consenting to testing because they may not have wanted to risk the social or economic exclusion that could arise from testing positive (Marra et al. 2019, 491; McGovern, Canning, and Bärnighausen 2018, 4). Concerns about testing positive are well documented: One longitudinal study found that HIV-positive people were four times more likely to decline testing (McGovern, Canning, and Bärnighausen 2018, 12).

In addition to using copulas, two other methodological choices were important for Marra et al. (2019). First, they used interviewer identity as their response instrument, a variable that explained response but not HIV status. They argued, perfectly reasonably, that these variables belonged in the response but not outcome equation because reviewers differed substantially in their rates of getting people to consent to being tested and because interviewer identity should not in itself predict HIV status (Marra et al. 2019, 486, 493). Second, Marra and colleagues allowed the measure of dependence between the selection and outcome errors to vary by region (Marra et al. 2019, 486); we'll see in Chapter 12 other examples in which nonignorable nonresponse patterns vary quite clearly within a population.

Marra et al. (2019, 490) estimated their model using a series of copula models and chose the copula that best fit the data. For all country and gender pairs, the Joe copula rotated by 90 degrees fit best, an example of which we saw in the bottom right-hand panel of Figure 9.1. Figure 9.2 plots the results for each country and gender grouping the observed HIV positivity rates and the HIV positivity rates estimated via a "naive" estimator and via the rotated Joe copula model.[5] The figure includes 95 percent confidence intervals for both estimates. For men in Swaziland and Zambia and women in Swaziland, the copula model indicated that prevalence rates were substantially higher than

---

[5] The naive estimator is an imputation model-based that deals with missingness for covariates but does not address nonignorable nonresponse. It is, for all practical purposes, equal to the observed value of incidence in the sample (Marra et al. 2019, 490).

Next-Generation Selection Models

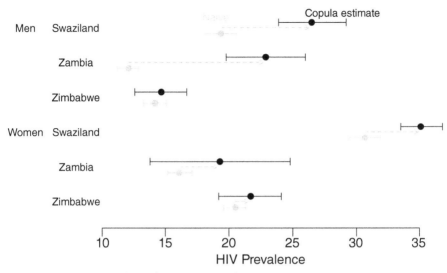

FIGURE 9.2 HIV prevalence from Marra et al. (2019)

the estimate based on the assumption that response was ignorable. And in all cases, the confidence intervals were larger for the copula estimates, which makes sense given that the indications of nonignorable nonresponse should naturally make us a bit more cautious about the informativeness of our data.

McGovern, Canning, and Bärnighausen (2018) undertook a similar study. They examined an HIV surveillance effort in rural South Africa in 2010. Response rates were lower than in the Marra at al. study, at about 45 percent for women and 33 percent for men. Prevalence of HIV in observed sample was 27 percent for women and 16 percent for men.

Motivated by similar concerns about nonignorable nonresponse, McGovern, Canning, and Bärnighausen (2018) estimated a series of copula models and reported the model that fit best. Their first-stage instrument was a variable that indicated whether contact was initiated in the last 10 weeks of the effort, a period in which potential respondents were given a food voucher. The voucher seemed to work, as the voucher period saw participation rates go from 42 percent to 58 percent for women and from 31 percent to 41 percent for men (McGovern, Canning, and Bärnighausen 2018, 5).[6]

The McGovern, Canning, and Bärnighausen (2018) study tracks quite closely to how we motivated nonignorable nonresponse models with Figure 8.3. The survey had two segments. In the first, corresponding to the figures in

---

[6] Note that they need to assume that prevalence did not change over the course of the study, a reasonable assumption given the relatively short time frame the surveillance was in the field. Otherwise, the time period dummy variable would need to be included in the outcome equation as well and would not qualify as a response stage instrument.

Part III: Fighting Nonignorable Nonresponse

the top panels, response rates were relatively low. In the second, corresponding to the figures in the bottom panels, response rates were relatively high. The question is: What happened to Y – the prevalence rate – as we moved from low to high response? If there was no difference in prevalence, the data would be consistent with the panels on the left in which nonresponse was ignorable. If, on the other hand, there was a difference in prevalence, the data would be consistent with the panels on the right in which nonresponse was nonignorable.

A change from Figure 8.3 is that the researchers expected ρ to be negative because they expected HIV-positive people to be less likely to consent to testing. This means that the "tilted fish" in the nonignorable nonresponse figures should tilt downward and that we would expect prevalence to be higher in the high response survey for the nonignorable nonresponse case.

As it happened, HIV prevalence in the sample went up when response rates did, consistent with a negative relationship between response interest and outcome. For women, HIV positivity rates were 9 percentage points higher in the high response period; for men, HIV positivity rates were 4 percentage points higher in the high response period.[7]

McGovern, Canning, and Bärnighausen (2018, 8) found that the Frank copula best fit the data, although their results using a normal copula were very similar. As with Marra et al. (2019), their results implied that population prevalence was higher than in the observed sample. For women, the authors estimated HIV prevalence was not the 27 percent observed in the sample, but 37 percent based on the copula model. There were differences for men as well, although they were not statistically significant.

Even though copula models vastly expand the range of parametric models we can assess, they are nonetheless limited to a list of specific possible parametric forms. In Section 9.2, we describe the control function approach that approximates the key parameters of the parametric form, whatever it is. They are even more flexible than copula models, but come with their own limitations.

9.2 CONTROL FUNCTIONS

The control function approach begins with Equation 8.4 that we presented in Chapter 7. It shows the expected value of Y for observations in the sample:

$$E[Y_i|_{Y_i \text{ observed}}] = \beta_0 + E[\epsilon_i|_{R_i=1}] \tag{9.1}$$

where we can write $E[\epsilon_i|_{R_i=1}] = E[\epsilon_i|_{\tau_i > -\gamma_0 - \gamma_Z Z_i}]$ as a control function $f(\gamma, Z)$ that characterizes the expected error as a function of parameters associated with the first-stage response function. The Heckman model can be thought of

---

[7] We will formalize a nonparametric test based on data like this in Chapter 10.

*Next-Generation Selection Models*173

as a very specific control function model because, given the model's assumptions, the control function is defined by the inverse Mills ratio weighted by ρ and the standard deviation of ϵ. Copulas also provide functions that characterize the expected value of ϵ for respondents.

The virtue of the control function approach is that it enables us to estimate parameters of the control function without specifying a parametric distribution ex ante. For example, Das, Newey, and Vella (2003) provide a semi-parametric selection model in which the control function is completely unknown and estimated from the data. They do this by using a polynomial expansion of the fitted response probability to approximate the expected value of the error term given response:

$$E[Y_i|_{Y_i \text{ observed}}] = \beta_0 + \beta_X X_i + \pi_1 p_i + \pi_2 p_i^2 + \ldots + \pi_k p_i^k$$

where p is the probability of response, $\Phi(\gamma_0 + \gamma_Z Z_i)$. This approach replaces the Heckman correction based on the inverse Mills ratio with a more flexible formulation of the conditional expectation of the error in the outcome equation given response is observed. To test for nonignorable nonresponse, we test the null hypothesis that all the π coefficients equal zero.

The literature on control functions is large and continues to grow. For example, Liu and Yu (2022) develop an estimator that requires only an assumption that the relationship between the error terms is monotonic. They can estimate parameters controlling for the control function in a very general way. Their Monte Carlo simulations show that their general method does a bit worse than parametric models when the parametric models are correct; that is, if the data are generated via a bivariate normal, their method will work fine, but not quite as well as a Heckman model that assumes bivariate normality. However, their approach performs substantially better than parametric models when the parametric model in the estimation is not same as the parametric model that generated the data. Since we cannot know ex ante the true (or even approximate) parametric model of the data generation process, their method is, therefore, better.

Control functions are best used when the researcher is interested in estimating β coefficients in an outcome equation. They are less appropriate when the researcher is interested in estimating the mean value of some value in a population. This is because of the identification problem we raised in Section 8.2. In Section 8.2, we noted that the average value of observed Y could reflect either the average in the population or the baseline level of the expected error term for respondents. Loosely speaking, for a simple model with no covariates in the outcome equation we cannot know where to put the intercept in the model: Does it go in β_0 – the average value of Y in the population – or does it go in γ_0 – the parameter that (more or less) governs the average of the error term given response. A parametric function helps resolve this question, but a control function cannot. Hence, the conventional approach is to assume that the intercept is zero for one or the other equations (see, e.g., Liu and Yu 2022, 7),

174   *Part III: Fighting Nonignorable Nonresponse*

an assumption that will not affect the estimation of coefficients on covariates, but which makes the estimates of average population levels not useful.

Liu and Yu (2022) provide an example that shows the potential benefit of the control function approach. They assess determinants of women's wages in 2013. The response mechanism is a bit different than a survey: Here, "nonresponse" occurs when women do not have wages to report because they are not working. The modeling considerations are similar to survey nonresponse, however, due to the possibility of nonignorable nonresponse because women with higher value in the job market may be more likely to get a job and hence be more likely to be observed in the data. Liu and Yu estimate a Heckman model and a series of control function models. They find that control function models produced similar results that differed from the Heckman results in interesting ways. For example, in the Heckman model there were nonlinear and increasing returns to experience while the control function models suggested diminishing returns to experience. In addition, the returns to some education categories were nontrivially different between the Heckman and control function approaches. Given the restrictive assumption inherent in the Heckman model, the control function results seem more robust and, therefore, more useful.

9.3 WEIGHTS FOR NONIGNORABLE NONRESPONSE

Sections 9.1 and 9.2 broaden the range of possible joint distributions for the errors in the response and outcome equations. In this section, we look at a selection model that allows us to create weights that directly account for nonignorable nonresponse. This is, at some level, a central dream of many survey researchers who feel comfortable with weights even as they recognize the potential for nonignorable nonresponse to be a problem.

Here, we look at Sun, Liu, Miao, Wirth, Robins, and Tchetgen Tchetgen's (2018) model. They specify the joint distribution of R and Y in general terms, allowing Y to directly affect R, which is slightly different than the selection models above where the relationship between R and Y occurs via correlation of errors in the two equations. We'll present a slightly simplified version in which the dependent variable Y is dichotomous, such as support for the president. The outcome in the full population depends on some covariate X but does not directly depend on R:

$$Pr(Y = 1|X) = p(\beta_0 + \beta_X X) \tag{9.2}$$

where p is some function such as a probit or logit function that returns a probability between 0 and 1.

Whether an individual responds depends on the covariate (X), a response instrument (Z) and Y itself. That is, whether someone responds depends in part on what their opinion is. We've seen this often in politics. Another illustration of this case is satisfaction with airlines: We're much more likely to hear about

Next-Generation Selection Models 175

someone's views when they are mad about a flight delay than when they are happy with an on-time flight. Here, we model response as

$$Pr(R = 1|X, Z, Y) = g(\gamma_0 + \gamma_Z Z + \gamma_X X + \gamma_Y Y) \tag{9.3}$$

where $g()$ is a function such as a probit or logit function that produces a probability between 0 and 1. The online appendix develops a two-step selection model in which nonignorable nonresponse can arise from unobserved variables (as we discussed in Section 8.3) or via the direct influence of Y on R (as here).

One might be tempted to approach this with a conventional weighting approach in which one estimates the probability of response and then weights data by the inverse of the probability of response. That will not work in this case because we do not observe Y for the $R = 0$ cases. In other words, we would only have data for Y for the people who responded, meaning that our data would be limited to a data set in which every value of R equals 1. If we know one thing about statistics, it is that we can't estimate models for variables that do not vary.

We can, however, model the data generation process as the simultaneous determination of Y for the $R = 1$ folks and R with the core equations being Equations 9.2 and 9.3. The estimation process is a bit trickier than typical statistical models; it uses a statistical technique called method of moments which is able to formulate a system of equations based on the model that can be solved for the values of the $\hat{\beta}$ and $\hat{\gamma}$ parameters. With the $\hat{\gamma}$ values in hand, we can then use Equation 9.3 to generate weights, weights we will refer to as nonignorable nonresponse weights – NINR weights, for short. The difference from conventional weights is, of course, that the value of Y is incorporated into these weights in way that accounts for nonignorable nonresponse.

The model can be used to diagnose nonresponse: If the coefficient on Y in the response equation is not significantly different from zero, we have evidence that nonresponse is nonignorable. In such a case, the $Y = 1$ observations would not generally be weighted up or down and the estimates would look very similar to those from a conventional approach to weighting based only on X. On the other hand, if the coefficient on Y in the response equation is significantly different from zero, we have evidence that nonresponse is nonignorable. In such a case, the $Y = 1$ observations would be weighted up or down and the estimates would differ from those produced by conventional weights.

To illustrate how NINR weights work, we step through a specific simulated example where Y is the support rate for the president. The data are generated by the following two equations:

$$Pr(Y = 1|X) = logit(-1.0 + 1.0X) \tag{9.4}$$
$$Pr(R = 1|X, Z, Y) = logit(-4.0 + 2.0Z + 2.0X + 2.0Y) \tag{9.5}$$

We run this simulation multiple times, producing on average populations in which 35 percent of the people support the president ($\overline{Y} = 0.35$). Figure 9.3

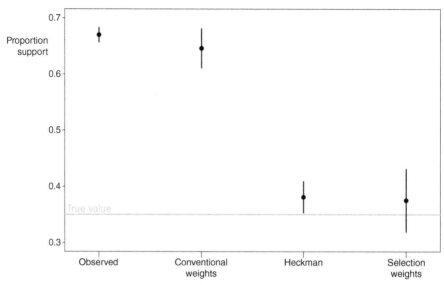

FIGURE 9.3 Various estimates of population support

displays the results for four estimates of $\overline{Y}$ based on the data in our simulations. We include standard error bars that reflect the 95 percent confidence intervals.

Because Y affects R in Equation 9.5, support among respondents is higher than in the population; in this instance, on average 67 percent of survey respondents support the president ($\overline{Y}|R = 1 = 0.67$), which is almost double the support in the full population. If we simply calculate the standard error on this estimate as if this were a simple mean from a random sample, we get very small confidence intervals, which would lead us to be confident in a very wrong result.

Figure 9.3 next shows the sample mean calculated using conventional weights. We do this by estimating a model in which R is a function of X and then calculating inverse propensity weights in the manner discussed in Chapter 3. In this example, X is a significant predictor of R and Y and therefore improves the estimate of $\overline{Y}$ somewhat. Because there is nonignorable nonresponse (due to the fact that Y is in the response equation), the estimate of 0.65 is still far from the truth. The confidence intervals are larger as we account for the variance-increasing effects of the weights, but even with the larger confidence interval, the results continue to suggest confidence in very wrong results.

Next is the average estimate based on a Heckman model. In this case, a Heckman model is modestly mis-specified because the data-generating process uses a logit function rather than the normal distribution assumed by the Heckman model. The estimated average by the Heckman models is 0.38, which is close to the truth. The standard error is relatively small, though, so on average

Next-Generation Selection Models 177

the confidence interval just barely covers the true value. In fact, even though these are perfectly good results, the confidence intervals from the Heckman model include the true value 70 percent of the time, which is less than the 95 percent of time that a correct confidence interval would produce.

Finally, as we discussed above, we use NINR weights based on Equations 9.4 and 9.5. On average, the mean estimate is 0.37 and the confidence intervals cover the true value in every simulation iteration.

At this point, we have kept things simple, with results from a single example with strong selection on the dependent variable. We'll explore how these weights perform under other conditions in Chapter 10. We can note now that as the effect of X on R and Y goes up, the conventional weights do a better job of undoing bias, but as long as Y affects R, they will be biased, potentially substantially. As the effect of Y on R goes down, so too does advantage of the nonignorable nonresponse weights. When Y has no effect on R, conventional weights and nonignorable nonresponse weights produce generally unbiased average results but the nonignorable nonresponse weights have large standard errors, suggesting that conventional weights are better in this circumstance.

Sun, Liu, Miao, Wirth, Robins, and Tchetgen Tchetgen (2018) work from a very general level. They begin by articulating if and when a fully nonparametric approach to estimating $Pr(Y = 1)$ is possible for nonignorable nonresponse. It turns out that a fully nonparametric model is not identified under all possible conditions (see also DiNardo, McCrary, and Sanbonmatsu 2006). The conditions under which the joint distribution of Y, Z, and R is identifiable are quite technical and not intuitive, but can be simplified to a sufficient condition that the model requires that there is no interaction of Z and Y in the response equation. While it would be great if there were no conditions on the model, this kind of thing is common in multi-equation models and is likely a weaker assumption than assuming away nonignorable nonresponse.

Estimating such a model is not trivial and is at the frontier of the literature. Sun, Liu, Miao, Wirth, Robins, and Tchetgen Tchetgen (2018) also present two other ways to estimate the model, including a so-called doubly robust estimator that will be consistent if one or both of Equations 9.2 and 9.3 are correctly specified. Bailey (2023) applies these models to the data discussed here.

Sun et al (2018) applied their model to a HIV seroprevalence survey in Botswana that asked 5,000 people to test for HIV. Although the response rate was quite high – around 80 percent – researchers were concerned that people with HIV would be less likely to participate, thereby biasing downward the prevalence in the observed sample. The raw percentage of HIV positives in the sample was 21.4 percent; conventional weighting changed the estimate very little. Using their inverse propensity weighting model that incorporates the effect of Y on response, they found a higher prevalence of 26.0 percent (which was similar to their doubly robust estimate of 25.8 percent). Given that the nonresponse rate was rather low, seeing a roughly 25 percent change in the estimate

178 *Part III: Fighting Nonignorable Nonresponse*

is striking. In addition, their model produced much higher standard errors. On the one hand, it is tempting to prefer estimates with lower standard errors, but in the case they argue convincingly that the uncertainty was much large than suggested by conventional weighting because such methods did not model or account for uncertainty about the extent of nonignorable nonresponse

9.4 MODELS FOR PARTIALLY OBSERVED RESPONSE INSTRUMENTS

The weights from the previous model are quite useful, but do have a practical limitation in that they require us to know the value of Z for everyone. In some circumstances, this may be fine, but in other circumstances this is a problem. For example, as we discussed in Chapter 1 and the introduction of this chapter, we may be attracted to a variable like political interest as it may predict response but not Y. We will know the value of that variable only for those who respond to the survey, which means we cannot implement the above models, whether conventional weights, copulas, Heckman, or nonignorable nonresponse weights. We could use Hartman and Huang's robustness approach that cleverly allows us to say, well, what if the level of political interest were A, B, or C in the full population, but we would still be speculating.

Peress (2010) offers a way to directly estimate a selection model even when we only observe our response instrument for respondents. It is an example of a "continuum of resistance" approach to survey nonresponse. In this approach, scholars model the eagerness of respondents to respond to a survey, which then enables them to extrapolate values of Y to nonrespondents based on the behavior of the low-propensity respondents. Later in Section 10.5, we'll show how to use randomized response instruments to allow us to use all selection models even when we only have data about respondents.

The key insight of continuum of resistance models is that nonresponse is not the only way that a disinclination to respond reveals itself. There are other ways in which respondents can show their interest in responding. For example, the number of calls needed to reach someone may reflect their willingness to respond (see also Chen, Li, and Qin 2018). After all, if you have to call someone 10 times before they answer, well, they're just not that into you. Traugott (1987) reported that for a poll in Michigan in 1984, 48 percent of those who answered on first call supported Reagan, which was much lower than the 59 percent support for Reagan among all survey respondents. Other observable variables work as well; Peress finds that the coding by interviewers of how cooperative the respondents were produces the most accurate predictions of verified turnout, results we discuss below.

The idea is that the most cooperative people have the highest values of R^* and the least cooperative people in the sample have the lowest value of R^*. If these groups differ in Y, then we have evidence that $\rho \neq 0$, which is the classic marker of nonignorable nonresponse. The idea is analogous to Figure 8.3 in

Next-Generation Selection Models

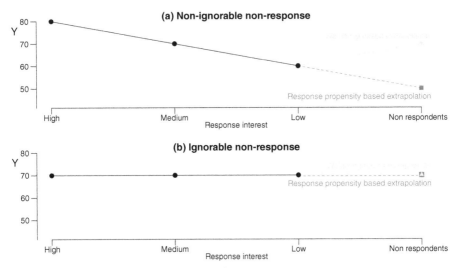

FIGURE 9.4 Extrapolations to nonrespondents

which we used differences in Y among different response propensity groups to diagnose nonignorable nonresponse.

With an estimate of the correlation of responsiveness and outcome, Peress (2010, 1421) extrapolates from the observed relationship between Y and response propensity to values of Y to nonrespondents. Figure 9.4 illustrates the process. In each panel, we plot the average values of Y for four groups of response propensity types. On the left in each panel are the high propensity types, followed by medium and then low-response propensity types. On the far-right in each panel are nonrespondents, the group with the lowest propensity to respond. The figure shows the average values of Y for the high, medium, and low propensity types from the data. In panel (a) on the top, $\rho > 0$: The high propensity types have the highest values of Y, and the medium and low propensity types have lower average values of Y. In panel (b) on the bottom, $\rho = 0$: There is no difference in the average values of Y across the various response propensity types.

The question is how to estimate the average values of Y for nonrespondents. Peress's extrapolations are based on the estimates produced when he maximizes the joint likelihood of Y and R given ρ and other parameters. If the observed sample shows signs of nonignorable nonresponse, $\rho \neq 0$ and the average Y values for nonrespondents will be extrapolated to a lower average value of Y as indicated by the square in panel (a) of Figure 9.4.[8] That is, if the

---

[8] We are depicting a simple case with no observable covariates. In actuality, Peress estimates fitted values of Y for multiple strata based on demographics and response propensity and then estimates the population average with a weighted average across these strata, akin to cell-weighting or MrP.

data indicate that among the respondents the people who are least interested in responding have low values of Y, the nonrespondents – who are even less interested in responding that the low-propensity respondents observed – will have even lower predicted average values of Y. If the observed sample shows no signs of nonignorable nonresponse, however, then the nonrespondents will be extrapolated as having the same average value of Y observed in the overall population as indicated by the square in the panel (b) of Figure 9.4.

Peress's approach differs markedly from the conventional weighting approach. Conventional weighting assumes that the unobserved observations have average values of Y equal to the observed values of Y.[9] The weighting extrapolation is indicated with a triangle and will extrapolate the average of observed Y to nonrespondents, as is shown in panels (a) and (b) of Figure 9.4. When nonresponse is nonignorable as in panel (a), estimating that nonrespondents have *higher* average values of Y than respondents with low propensity to respond is, in Peress's view, puzzling.

Plotting the extrapolation also highlights some limits of the approach. First, theoretically the values of Y for nonrespondents could be anywhere: Very high, very low, and anywhere in the middle. We simply do not observe them, and if we take the spirit of the Manski bounds from Chapter 7 to heart, the values of Y for the nonrespondents could really have any value, including ones that don't follow Peress's line of extrapolation.[10] Second, the extent of the drop-off in Y in the top panel as we move from the low-propensity responders in the sample to the nonrespondents will depend on the specific parametric assumptions. Perhaps with a different parametric assumption, the drop-off for nonrespondents is more or less severe.

To address such concerns, at least in an initial way, Peress presents a range of cases in which his predictions perform well even when his parametric assumption is wrong. He runs simulations in which he uses his model to estimate population quantities for five scenario cases in which the joint distributions of the errors are not the bivariate normal assumption of his model. In four scenarios, his model predicts population quantities quite well even though the parametric model in the MLE estimation is incorrect. It is only in an extreme case in which the performance of his model suffers. And even in that case, his model outperforms the weighting-based extrapolation. Peress's simulations have not, of course, exhaustively explored all possible deviations from normality. They have, however, shown that there exists a class of deviations from bivariate normality which do not cause serious problems for his bivariate normality-based model.

The payoff to the Peress model is its empirical performance. Peress (2010, 1424) analyzes National Election Study data from 1980, 1984, and 1988

---

[9] Note that in a weighting approach, this figure would apply for each distinctive demographic subgroup.

[10] We should be clear, though, that weighting does not elide this critique. It too extrapolates, it just happens to do so in a potentially questionable way, as in panel (a) of Figure 9.4.

Next-Generation Selection Models

and estimates his model using interviewer coding of cooperativeness as his response propensity indicator. He finds strong statistical evidence that $\rho \neq 0$ (with p-values < 0.01) and produces turnout estimates that are much closer to actual turnout than other measures. For example, in 1988 actual turnout was 50.3 percent. Simple reported turnout in the sample was 69.6 percent. Validated reported turnout was 59.8 percent, and weighted validated turnout was 57.7 percent. Peress's variable response propensity estimator was 50.9 percent, which was substantially closer to the truth.

Similar models are feasible in other fields. Burger and McLaren (2017) model tuberculosis testing as a nonignorable nonresponse problem because the patients sent to testing have higher risk of being positive. Using national policy changes that affected testing probabilities as their variables that affected response but not outcome, they estimated maximum likelihood and generalized method of moment models of tuberculosis prevalence which they validated against national surveillance testing based on random samples. They were the first to show that 25 percent of disease-resistant tuberculosis cases went undiagnosed in South Africa from 2004 to 2010.

Despite its conceptual and empirical appeal, models like these have not been widely adopted. One reason is complexity. The models' likelihoods are involved, and estimation of them is complicated by the fact that the likelihood contains integrals with no closed-form solution (Peress 2010, 1421). Second, the approaches require good data. For the Peress model, there needs to be a *multi*-category measure of respondent interest in responding, something that is not always available. The measure also needs to predict Y well. Peress shows that in his empirical applications callback measures did not lead to nearly as strong improvements in predicting turnout as did respondent cooperativeness. In addition, it is possible that observational measures of response propensity may be correlated with factors affecting outcome such as education, age, and race, which will impair the statistical power of these measures. In Chapter 10, we discuss approaches that generate randomized variables that could boost the performance of a Peress-type model.

9.5 CONCLUSION

By no means do we expect that nonignorable nonresponse corrupts every question on every survey. It is possible – and some would say likely – that response is ignorable, or nearly so, for many questions on many surveys, especially when the pollster has paid careful attention to identifying good weighting variables.

But nonignorable nonresponse is invidious. It is hard to rid ourselves of the thought that nonignorable nonresponse *might* be a problem. It is a bit like radon: It's not a problem in most houses, but failing to test could be exposing your family to serious danger. And if you live in an area where radon is common – akin to surveying sensitive topics where nonignorable nonresponse is plausible – then it becomes indefensible to fail to test.

Chapters 7, 8, and 9 argue that we should not be passive in the face of potential nonignorable nonresponse. The problem is important, and the academic literature provides a series of insights about how to deal with it. The first insight is that it is clear what *not* to do. Getting more data without regard to its provenance is a bad idea. More data are not necessarily better. We've known this at least since *The Literary Digest* fiasco in 1936.

The second insight is we can use selection models to see how nonignorable nonresponse can matter – and can be identified. The Heckman model is an example in which the equations clean up nicely when we assume a normal distribution generated errors in the response and outcome data. The Heckman model hasn't always performed particularly well, though, and this chapter presents a series of models that address the limitations of the Heckman model.

Many researchers have been concerned about the Heckman model's bivariate normality assumption. Sections 9.1 and 9.2 of this chapter show that the literature now provides a suite of models that accommodate other distributions. Copulas accommodate a long list of alternative parametric forms. Control functions go further and approximate the function that characterizes the potential nonignorable nonresponse function.

Further extensions have broadened the selection model toolkit. Sun, Liu, Miao, Wirth, Robins, and Tchetgen Tchetgen (2018) model the joint distribution of response and outcome in a way that allows Y to directly affect R. Their model enables us to produce weights that directly account for nonignorable nonresponse, weights that are manna from heaven for survey researchers who are comfortable working with weights even as they are uncomfortable with the conventional assumption that response is ignorable. Peress (2010) adapts the Heckman model to enable estimation of population parameters even when we only partially observe variables that affect response, a common situation in polling research.

As is common when trying to tackle challenging methodological problems, we are left with some good news and some less than good news. The good news is that critiques about the parametric inflexibility of the Heckman selection model have been largely addressed and that we can even generate weights that account for nonignorable nonresponse.

All is not rainbows and kittens though – at least not yet. These tools are powerful, but we cannot forget that they need powerful data as well. In many cases, conventional variables gathered in conventional ways will not provide enough information to unleash the potential of these models. Hence, we turn in Chapter 10 to addressing the second important challenge that lurks in selection models: How to find or, even better, create the data that will make nonignorable nonresponse selection models do their work.

10

Randomized Response Instruments

Design trumps analysis.

Donald Rubin (2008)

We concluded Chapter 8 by noting two problems with Heckman selection models: They assume a specific statistical distribution and demand a lot of data. Chapter 9 then presented a range of ways to deal with the first problem by implementing parametrically flexible models. These models are clever and useful, but that still leave us with the second challenge that selection models need good data. From a single set of data, we are trying to simultaneously estimate two interrelated processes. Without good data, we may end up with mush – even with a fancy statistical model.

Think of it like this. Chapter 9 allowed us to come home from the hardware store with seriously cool tools: Maybe a powerful drill, a router, and even something mysterious with lots of sharp things that spin. These tools won't build anything by themselves, though. We need materials – and the materials have to be of the right quantity and quality for us to build anything useful.

In other words, without the right data, the selection models may not work well, if at all. In general, we need a variable that is included in our response model and excluded from our outcome model. Sometimes we can find such variables. We saw several examples in Chapter 9, for example, where information on the interviewer or the respondent attitude seemed relevant for response but not outcome.

Finding these variables is hard and can be controversial. A better approach is *creating* them. The ideal data for selection models include a variable that affects R and is unquestionably unrelated to Y. We can create such a variable by creating a randomized response instrument, which is a variable we denote as Z that represents a randomly assigned treatment that affects the probability someone responds. If we have such a variable, we can build on the tilted fish logic of Figure 8.3 in which nonignorable nonresponse reveals itself in

184   *Part III: Fighting Nonignorable Nonresponse*

differences in Y that align with differences in response rates. In statistical terms, the Heckman, copula models and nonignorable nonresponse weights will have more statistical power when we have a randomized response instrument.

In the epigraph for this chapter, Donald Rubin tells us design trumps analysis. He means that a well-designed study analyzed with simple tools is more likely to be informative than a poorly designed study analyzed with complex tools. Applied to our current situation, the claim is that designing the survey study to produce good data is going to be as important, if not more important, than using sophisticated statistical methods. In particular, if we can produce a randomized response instrument, we will have information that can be analyzed in multiple ways, some of them quite simple. We're still going to use sophisticated models, but with good data, the results are more likely to be consistent across model choice.

In many polling contexts, it is easy to create randomized response instruments. The pollster simply needs to figure out some protocol that affects response rate and then randomize it. Perhaps the pollster contacts potential respondents a different number of times or in different ways. Perhaps the pollster offers people incentives to respond. Pollsters have long experimented with different approaches to generating response, and all that is required to harness the power of selection models is to randomly assign potential respondents to at least two of these approaches for a given survey.

This chapter proceeds as follows. Section 1 makes it clear that knowing the correct functional form is not enough to save a selection model. Section 2 shows the difficulty of using observational response instruments. Section 3 discusses how and why to create randomized response instruments. Section 4 shows how to use randomized response instruments in a simple test for diagnosing nonignorable nonresponse. The test is quite general but leans on a strong assumption, an assumption that our selection models do not require. Section 5 shows how randomized response instruments enable us to use the full suite of selection models even when we do not observe data for nonrespondents.

10.1 FUNCTIONAL FORM IS NOT ENOUGH

A major theme in this book is that conventional weights cannot account for nonignorable nonresponse. Even if we use the most advanced algorithms to identify the best conventional weights, weighting can fail if there are variables that affect Y and R that we do not observe in one or both of the sample and population. Whether this is common is unknown; what is known is that weighting can fail for any question on any survey.

Chapter 9 presented multiple models that directly model nonignorable nonresponse, often focused on increasing the parametric flexibility. We saw hints, though, that having good data may be more important than having the right functional form. In this section, we elaborate on this point by working through

Randomized Response Instruments 185

a case in which we know the correct functional form of the nonresponse, but do not have a response instrument. Shield your eyes; the results are not pretty.

These results are important because they explain, at least in part, the poor experiences many researchers have had in the past with selection models, especially Heckman models. They also reinforce the idea that these models become more reliable with good data, suggesting that we should devote as much or more attention to creating variables that make selection models work as we do to exploring the functional form.

We work with a model that modestly extends the model we presented in Section 8.1. The response model is

$$R_i^* = \gamma_0 + \gamma_Z Z_i + \gamma_X X_i + \tau_i \tag{10.1}$$

where Z_i is our response instrument that affects response but does not directly affect Y. For simplicity, we'll treat Z as a dummy variable, although it need not be.

The outcome equation is

$$Y_i = \beta_0 + \beta_X X_i + \epsilon_i \tag{10.2}$$

where X is the same as one of the variables in the response equation.

The key variable for our purposes is Z, which appears in the response equation but not the outcome equation. We'll consider the Z variable to be useful when γ_Z is far from zero, meaning that Z has predictive power for R. We'll discuss variables like Z more in Sections 10.3 and 10.4. For now, note that selection models do better when there is a variable in the response equation that is not in the outcome equation. The intuition is that a variable like Z can explain whether a respondent is in the top or bottom row of Figure 8.3, which is key to understanding if and how nonignorable nonresponse manifests itself.

Our goal in this section is to show that even if we know the correct functional form, our models may struggle if we do not have a variable like Z with a large γ_Z. We'll show this for a specific simulated case. Marra et al. (2017, 493) explored these issues and concluded that estimates were always biased when there was no response instrument, whether or not the model estimated was the same as the one that generated the data. When there was a response instrument, their copula models were able to extract estimates that were quite accurate. In other words, they found that parametrically flexible models do well with response instruments and struggle without them.

In our simulations, pollsters contact enough people to yield a sample of roughly 1,500 observations. The γ_Z is negative with a value implying individuals in the $Z_i = 1$ group are 50 percentage points less likely to respond. We allow X to affect response and outcome by setting $\gamma_X = 0.3$ and $\beta_X = 1$. We simulated 500 iterations for a range of values of ρ (the correlation of τ and ϵ) ranging from 0 to 0.8 in increments of 0.1.

Weighting in these simulations is based on the probability of response for each person using only X_i as a covariate in the response equation. This

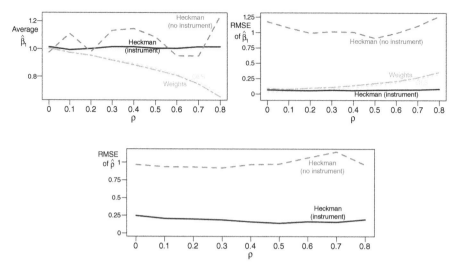

FIGURE 10.1 Simulation results

approach leads the model to place relatively more weight on observations that have a low probability of response. We also include an OLS model uses standard regression to estimate the model in Equation 10.2.

We estimate two selection models for each simulation iteration. First, the "conventional Heckman" model includes X as the only variable in the first- and second-stage models; this corresponds to the common situation in which the variables that affect selection also affect outcomes. Second, the response instrument model is a Heckman model that includes Z in the first-stage equation.

Figure 10.1 shows simulation results. The upper left panel shows the average value of $\hat{\beta}_X$ across 500 simulations for each value of ρ, the degree of correlation between the errors in the selection and outcome equations.[1] The OLS and weighting models exhibit very similar patterns, with the bias increasing as the correlation of errors increases. This is no surprise as it is well known that these models are biased in the face of nonignorable nonresponse.

The Heckman models appear to perform better, but with a major caveat. The solid line for the Heckman model with the randomized treatment variable indicates that the average estimate of $\hat{\beta}_X$ is quite close to the true value of 1 for all values of ρ. The dashed line for the conventional Heckman model that lacks Z is typically closer to the true value of one than the OLS and WLS models, but it is highly variable, which raises a red flag.

---

[1] The patterns are similar if we focus on $\hat{\beta}_0$ or the average of Y in the population for people with $X = 0$.

Randomized Response Instruments 187

The panel on the upper right sheds light on what is happening. It shows the square root of the mean-squared error (RMSE) of the β_X estimate for the various approaches. Roughly speaking, the RMSE shows how far off on average the estimates of $\hat{\beta}_X$ are from the true value. The lines for weighting and OLS tell a familiar story: The techniques do worse as ρ, the correlation of errors, increases.

The RMSE for the Heckman model with the response instrument Z is the solid line toward the bottom of the figure. This shows that the model produces results with low error, meaning they are close to the true value no matter the level of ρ, the nonignorability parameter. This strong result illustrates the benefit of having a first-stage variable that affects response and does not directly affect Y. This strong performance occurs even though the model with a response instrument has 25 percent *fewer* observations than the other models because half of the potential respondents were treated with a response-lowering protocol.

The ability of the Heckman model with Z to do more with less suggests that the informational quality of the observations in the model with a response instrument trumped the higher number of observations in the other approaches. We've seen small samples beat big ones before: Conventional random samples can be more useful than larger convenience sample because the random selection process produces more meaningful information.

In contrast, the RMSE of the conventional Heckman model is woefully large, despite the fact that the parametric assumption is correct. While the upper left panel indicated that the conventional Heckman model is less biased than weighting and OLS, the conventional Heckman model is, in fact, essentially useless because the RMSE dwarfs the RMSE in the other models. This result will not surprise those with experience with Heckman models as these models are prone to producing highly unstable and sometimes nonsensical results. The problem is that the inverse Mill's ratio from the first-stage model is highly correlated with the X variable in the outcome equation, making it very hard to identify both the effects of X and selection. This occurs even though the estimated effect of X in the first-stage probit model is highly statistically significant, with the z-statistics averaging over 10.

The bottom panel of Figure 10.1 provides a clue toward what is happening by displaying the RMSE for the estimate of ρ for the two Heckman models. The Heckman model with a response instrument performs much better than the conventional Heckman model. In fact, the conventional Heckman model has a RMSE for ρ of around one, which is pretty disastrous given that ρ is bounded to be between -1 and 1.

These simulations highlight two important points. First, selection models can perform poorly when there is no exclusion restriction even if the functional form assumption is correct. Their theoretical elegance and mathematical sophistication should not blind us to the fact that they need good data. Second,

188   *Part III: Fighting Nonignorable Nonresponse*

including a Z with good properties can enable selection models to outperform conventional models when there is nonignorable nonresponse.

10.2 THE PROBLEM WITH OBSERVATIONAL INSTRUMENTS

Many of the models we have presented so far are based on nonrandomized response instruments. These are variables that the researcher believes affected response but not the outcome in question. There are three challenges related to such variables.

1. They are simply hard to find. Surveys typically provide only a limited number of variables, and there may simply not be good candidate variables in the data.
2. The observational response instrument may be correlated with X, creating multicollinearity. Section 8.5 showed how correlation between X and Z could lead to high and potentially catastrophic levels of multicollinearity in Heckman models, a problem that carries over to other selection models.
3. The response instrument may actually affect Y. Consider political interest as a possible response instrument. It is not crazy to think political interest affects response but not political views, but it is possible that political interest directly affects some political opinions or that political interest is correlated with some other variable that affects Y. For example, suppose that recent news has been good for one political party. People with certain opinions may be more likely to report high political interest, creating a pathway from political interest to political opinions that makes that variable a poor response instrument.

The third point is particularly important. Claims that Z variables do not affect Y are routinely treated with skepticism. Virtually all of the standard demographic attributes for which we know national distributions – attributes such as age, race, gender, and region – could plausibly affect opinion. Survey responses are hard to definitively disentangle from each other. Coppock, Gerber, Green, and Kern (2017, 1) therefore conclude that exclusion assumptions "are often hard to defend on empirical or theoretical grounds" (see also Gomes et al. 2019; Bushway, Johnson, and Slocum 2007; Puhani 2000; Peress 2010, 1426).[2]

---

[2] Instruments are perhaps more familiar to experienced econometricians in the context of instrumental variable models such as two-stage least squares (see, e.g., Bailey 2021). Response instruments are characterized similarly in that they need to explain one variable (response for selection models, the endogenous variable for instrumental variable models) and not directly explain Y. The main difference is that instrumental variable models literally cannot be estimated if they are included in both equations due to perfect multicollinearity that arises if one tries to do that. Selection models such as the Heckman model are generally nonlinear such that one could as a practical matter estimate a model in which exact same variables are included in

Randomized Response Instruments 189

Some observational Z are promising. For example, if interviewers are randomly assigned to potential respondents, we may be comfortable using interviewer as our instrument if some interviewers are better able to induce response than others. (Of course, being honest requires us to note that this may not really be an observational response instrument because the interviewer assignment is a randomized treatment.)

In general, researchers rightly worry that observational response instruments affect Y. The consequences can be unpleasant. Consider first a possible observational response instrument that likely has a direct effect on Y, something like education. Education will typically predict response (which is good for response instrument), but will also typically affect Y (which is bad for a response instrument). Suppose that our dependent variable is favorability toward Democrats among US voters. In recent years, we would likely observe higher values of Y for highly educated people. If education is a response instrument, it is excluded from the outcome equation, meaning that selection models will attribute the love for Democrats among educated people to nonresponse rather than the truth, which is that educated people like Democrats more.

Now consider a more reasonable observational response instrument, something like the number of calls required to contact a person. While a connection between contactability and political (or other) opinions may not be obvious, it is possible. During Covid, many people speculated that liberals were more likely to stay home and, therefore, to answer surveys than conservatives who were less likely to let concerns about Covid keep them home. In this scenario, the number of calls would have a direct effect on Y, meaning that contactability would fail the second condition for a response instrument.

The consequences of Z affecting Y will vary across context, but the general implication is that a selection model in which Z is wrongly omitted from the outcome equation will be prone to finding a spurious relationship between Y and response propensity, which will suggest nonresponse is nonignorable even when it is not. This, in turn, can cause push estimated parameters and fitted values away from their true values.

Figure 10.2 illustrates the risks of an improper observational instrument by showing simulation results for simulations based on various parameter combinations. On the horizontal axis of each panel are parameter values that reflect the extent to which Y affects R. We show them in terms of the percentage point increase in the probability that R equals 1 for an increase of Y of one unit. The cases on the left in each panel reflect instances in which there is no nonignorable nonresponse because Y does not affect R; the cases on the right reflect cases in which Y has a relatively large effect on R. On the vertical axis in each panel are parameter values associated with the effect of Z on R. The

---

the response and outcome equations. However, as discussed in the online appendix for Chapter 8 one would likely see high levels of multicollinearity that would hamper accurate estimation. In the two-stage least squares literature, an instrument that is not wholly independent of Y is called a "quasi-instrument."

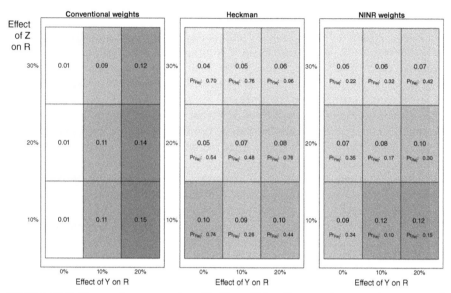

FIGURE 10.2 Comparing error when Z affects Y for direct pathway and non-normal errors (numbers indicate root mean-squared error; darker shades indicate higher error)

γ_Z values on the bottom indicate that Z increases the probability of response by 10 percentage points. The γ_Z values on the top indicate that Z increases the probability of response by 30 percentage points.

In each simulation Y a dummy variable based on the γ_Z and γ_Y parameters is indicated in the previous paragraph. In all simulations, Z directly affect Y as well, but we never include it in the outcome equation, consistent with our interest in knowing what happens when we use Z as a response instrument even though it affects Y. We also allow for X to affect response and outcome and use t-distributed errors.

The panel on the left is a heatmap depicting estimation accuracy from weighting models. The panel in the middle is for Heckman models, and the panel on the right is for the NINR-weighting model. The darker the shading, the larger the error. We measure estimation accuracy using the root mean-squared error (RMSE) of estimates, which is the square root of the average squared difference between the population average and estimated average. RMSE is a bit of mouthful for those not familiar with it; it is useful to think of it as the average distance of the estimate from the truth across the simulations.[3]

---

[3] We could also look at the bias of the estimates, which is how far the average of the estimates deviates from the truth. This is different from RMSE because a model that produces estimates is 10 units bigger than the truth half the time and 10 units less than the truth half the time will be unbiased, but will have a large RMSE. In general, the Heckman model has a small bias because on average it gets things right. However, as we saw in Section 10.1 the Heckman model can

Randomized Response Instruments 191

We also note the probability of rejecting the null hypothesis that response is ignorable for the Heckman and NINR-weighting models.

The panel on the left shows that weighting models do great when nonresponse is ignorable, which is when the effect of Y on R is 0. Weighting models become inaccurate as Y has a bigger effect on R.

The Heckman models depicted in the middle panel have different problems. When response is ignorable, they do worse than weighting models. Their RMSE is higher than the corresponding RMSE for weighting models. The Heckman model also is prone to incorrectly rejecting the null hypothesis of ignorable nonresponse, with the probabilities of rejecting the null ranging from 54 percent to 74 percent in the left-hand column of the Heckman panel. Using conventional statistical standards, the probability of rejecting the null hypothesis in this column should be 5 percent.

As discussed in our education and contactability examples above, the problem is that the Heckman model attributes the effect of Z on Y to nonresponse. In other words, these simulations show how selection models can lead us to see nonignorable nonresponse that isn't there when we use an observational response instrument that affects Y. The patterns for the NINR weights are similar in this regard, if perhaps a bit less extreme.

The news is not all bad for the Heckman and NINR weight models. In general, they perform better weighting when the nonresponse is ignorable (i.e., when the effect of Y on R is 10 percent or 20 percent), especially when the instrument is strong.

The specific RMSE values and rejection rates are sensitive to parameter choices. In this case, for example, the spurious nonignorable nonresponse induced by improperly omitting Z from the outcome equation is negative while the true nonignorable nonresponse that occurs when Y affects R is positive, inducing a complicated pattern. Hence, it is best to take the figure as illustrating two themes that emerge across a broader (undisplayed) range of parameter choices: (1) Selection models are prone to spuriously finding nonignorable nonresponse when they use observational Z variables that affect Y, and (2) even so, selection models can outperform weighting if the nonignorable is severe and Z has a strong effect on R.

10.3 RANDOMIZED RESPONSE INSTRUMENTS

Randomized response instruments avoid the problems of observational instruments because a randomized variable will in expectation be uncorrelated with all other variables, including X and Y. While creating randomized treatments can sometimes be challenging, doing so in survey contexts is not particularly hard. All survey researchers need to do is to design their survey protocols so

produce relatively large RMSE values because in some iterations it produces estimates that are quite high and in other iterations it produces values that are quite low. Using bias to measure accuracy will not capture such fluctuations, but RMSE will.

that a randomly selected group of potential respondents are contacted in a way that produces different levels of response (DiNardo, McCrary, and Sanbonmatsu 2006). The variable indicating membership in this treatment group will affect R, but not Y, and will be uncorrelated with X.[4]

Pollsters have many options to generate a randomized response treatment. For example, the pollster can devise two modes of contact for potential respondents. One is the standard mode already in use: Perhaps their policy is to send each potential respondent two emails asking them to respond. Respondents in the treatment group may receive, say, up to four emails asking them to respond. If the pollster randomizes potential respondents into these two groups, they have a promising randomized response instrument.

Such efforts will be familiar to experienced pollsters, as devising protocols that increase response propensity are a long-standing hobby horse in survey research (Singer and Ye 2013). The downside of such an approach, however, is that it will typically require more resources and can, if it involves persistent calls, degrade the quality of responses (Fricker and Tourangeau 2010).

It is also possible to implement a randomized response treatment that lowers response probability. Such an approach sends chills down the spines of many pollsters who are conditioned for abhor small samples. Lowering response rates is likely cheaper, though, a feature that practical pollsters may appreciate and which may enable them to put more resources in the other contact regimen. And the information content of low response probability observations may be higher. In a Heckman model, for example, the probability of response is in the denominator of the inverse Mills ratio. Decreasing probability of response by some amount will induce a larger shift in the inverse Mills ratio than increasing the probability of response by the same amount.[5]

Some pollsters may balk at messing with their response protocols. Increasing response rates for a subset of people may take more resources and could conceivably reduce the overall number of respondents. And, depending on how resources are allocated, treatments that decrease response rates may also decrease overall response numbers. But if we have learned anything from the *Literary Digest* and the Meng equation, it is that a large data set may be

---

[4] Technically speaking, every randomly sampled survey already creates a randomized variable that affects response because people who are not selected for contact have a zero probability of responding. This fact is not useful for Heckman or other selection models because observations with zero probability of response will have undefined or unvarying values for the variables needed. For example, the inverse Mills ratio in Heckman models is undefined for observations with $p_i = 0$.

[5] A high $\hat{p}_i$ person could have either a high or a low τ_i (the error in the response equation) and still be observed. A low $\hat{p}_i$ person, on the other hand, must have a high τ_i in order to be observed. Hence, observing either a high residual or low residual in the outcome equation for the low $\hat{p}_i$ person will give us information about a high τ observation, while a high residual or low residual in the outcome equation for a high $\hat{p}_i$ person will come with uncertainty about τ that will make it harder to estimate ρ, the correlation between τ and ϵ.

Randomized Response Instruments 193

no better – and could be substantially worse – than a smaller sample from a well-designed survey. In this context, having a lot of data, but not knowing if it suffers from nonignorable nonresponse may be worse than having a smaller sample size that includes information that enables us to assess whether nonresponse is nonignorable.

10.4 NONPARAMETRIC TESTS FOR NONIGNORABILITY

The main benefit of randomized response instruments is that they unlock the potential of the selection models we presented in Chapter 9. Those models are incredibly demanding of data, and randomization provides the independent information that is more likely to make them work.

With randomized response instruments, there are also additional tools available to us. In this section, we present two nonparametric tests for nonignorable nonresponse that are easy if we have a randomized response instrument. These tests formalize the intuition of Figure 8.3. For these discussions, we model nonignorability by allowing R to depend directly on Y as in Section 9.3. For simplicity, we focus on case in which the survey response of interest, Y, takes on values of 0 and 1. Our goal is to present a selection model in the most general terms possible. We consider the joint distribution of R, Y, Z, and X and then consider the implications of having a randomized response instrument in the presence and absence of nonignorable nonresponse. We are interested in estimating the population proportion, which we denote with P_Y.

First, we assume that we have a randomized response instrument Z that satisfies the two conditions

$$\text{Inclusion condition: } Pr(R = 1|_{Z=0,Y,X}) \neq Pr(R = 1|_{Z=1,Y,X}) \quad (10.3)$$

$$\text{Exclusion condition: } Pr(Y = 1|_{Z=0,X}) = Pr(Y = 1|_{Z=1,X}) = P_Y|_X \quad (10.4)$$

Equation 10.3 says that Z affects the propensity of responding for any given values of Y and X. Equation 10.4 says that Z does not affect the value of Y when we control for X.

We begin with simple model without any X covariates. If the R, Y and variables only depend on each other and Z is a randomized response instrument, we can test for nonignorable nonresponse with a simple difference of means test using the observed sample:

$$Y_i = \beta_0 + \beta_1 Z_i + \epsilon_i \quad (10.5)$$

We prove the theorem underlying this test in the online appendix. This nonparametric test formalizes the intuition we developed with Figure 8.3. When response is ignorable, the expected value of the observed values of Y will not differ according to the value of Z, consistent with what we observed in the left-hand side of Figure 8.3. When nonresponse is nonignorable, the expected

194 *Part III: Fighting Nonignorable Nonresponse*

values of the observed values of Y will depend on Z, consistent with what we observed in Figure 8.3.

The implication is that nonignorable nonresponse leaves traces that we can detect with a simple nonparametric test when there are no covariates. If we have a good response instrument, we can simply assess whether the values of Y in the observed sample differ according to the value of Z. If the values of Y do not differ according to Z, then we have evidence that response is ignorable and we can proceed with weighting or related tools confident that we have ruled out nonignorable nonresponse with evidence rather than by assertion. If the values of Y in the observed sample vary with Z, then we have evidence that nonresponse is nonignorable.

When we have covariates, the test is of the following form:

$$Y_i = \beta_0 + \beta_Z Z_i + \beta_X X_i + \epsilon_i \tag{10.6}$$

The two advantages of this test are that it is quite general and very simple. It is quite general because we are not specifying any statistical distributions for the error terms or variables. It is very simple because a simple linear regression is easy.

There is, however, an important caveat: The test requires that we observe *every* covariate that affects both R and Y.[6] This set of covariates is familiar to us because it is the set of X variables required for conventional weights as well, as discussed in Section 3.4.

There are two important things to note about the assumption about the X variables needed for this test. First, it is perfectly reasonable to be skeptical that we observe the full set of "true" weighting covariates. But let's be clear; if you don't like this assumption, you are *really* not going to like conventional weights, which make precisely this assumption. This test actually makes one less assumption than conventional weights: When using conventional weights, one assumes that the true weighting covariates are observed *and* that nonresponse is ignorable. Using Equation 10.6, we assume that the true weighting covariates are observed, but we do not assume nonresponse is ignorable. The approach *tests* for that possibility of nonignorable nonresponse rather than assuming it.

Second, if we are concerned about the possibility that there exist some variables that affect both R and Y, we have many other options. Chapter 11 will show how the Heckman model, copulas, control functions, and nonignorable nonresponse weights are robust to situations in which we do not observe the complete set of variables that affect both R and Y.

---

[6] To be clear, we need to observe all X such that the X variable affects both R and Y. We do not need to observe every X that affects R or every X that affects Y; we need only the subset of the X variables that affect R *and* Y.

Randomized Response Instruments 195

10.5 PARTIALLY OBSERVED NONRESPONDENT DATA

Randomized response instruments also allow us to implement selection models from Chapter 9 even when we do not observe X and Z for individual nonrespondents. This is a rather common situation: Nonrespondents did not respond so we may not know much about them. Weighting is fine in this situation, as long as the population distribution of X is known. Selection models, on the other hand, appear to be problematic because they require a first-stage model that predicts response. If we do not observe any attributes of the nonrespondents, such models will not work.

We know already that all is not lost for selection models in these situations. In Section 9.4, we discussed how to use a maximum likelihood approach to deal with situation in which we observed Z (and possibly X) only for respondents. However, that approach has limitations: It requires Z to have more than two levels and essentially extrapolates to nonrespondents from respondents with the values of the Z associated with the lowest probability of responding. As a maximum likelihood model, the approach also requires us to specify a parametric distribution for the errors.

In this section, we show that randomized response instruments open the door for us to estimate *all* the selection models as long as we have information about the distribution of the X variables in the population distribution, the identical requirement for weighting. In other words, when we have randomized response instruments, we can estimate selection models whenever weighting is possible. Because randomized response instruments are easy to create – pollsters experiment with such treatments all the time – this means that any pollster who weights can use selection models to test for nonignorable nonresponse.

There are two steps in running selection models in this context. First, we can generate a good estimate of X in the nonrespondent pool because we know the average of X in the population. We'll consider categorical variables as is standard in the weighting approach as well. Suppose we start with a pool of 5,000 people randomly selected from a population in which 50 percent of the people are women. This means that we expect 2,500 people in the pool to be women. If 1,000 people responded and 600 of them were women, then we know that 1,900 people in the nonrespondent pool were women, which is $\frac{1,900}{4,000} = 47.5$ percent of the 4,000 nonrespondents.[7] This logic applies to any weighting subgroup as well (e.g., Hispanic women with college degrees). The logic also applies to the response instrument Z because we know the proportion of potential respondents for whom $Z = 1$.[8]

---

[7] More generally, the proportion of the nonrespondent poll for whom $X = 1$ is $Pr(X|_{R=0}) = \frac{Pr(X)N - Pr(X|_{R=1})n}{N-n}$ where $Pr(X)$ is the probability, X equals one in the contact pool, N is the number of people contacted, and n is the number of people who responded.

[8] We'll treat Z as unobserved for nonrespondents in this discussion even as it may be observed in some cases as the pollster may know the outreach protocol used to contact each given potential respondent.

Second, we can generate the joint distribution of X and Z in the nonrespondent population because Z will be independent of X when it is a randomized response instrument. This means that the expected number of nonrespondents who had each possible combination of X and Z is simply the product of the probabilities for each variable. For example, the probability a nonrespondent has $X = 1$ and $Z = 1$ is $Pr(X|_{R=0}) \times Pr(Z|_{R=0})$. We can therefore create a pseudo- pool of nonrespondents with the expected number of each type of person.[9] This works even if X combines multiple demographic characteristics such that X is a categorical variable that indicates whether a person is in a group defined by multiple factors (such as ethnicity, gender, and education). With this group of pseudo-nonrespondents in hand, the Heckman, copula, control function and nonignorable nonresponse weighting models can proceed.

The randomization of Z is key. If the response instrument Z is observational, we will not know the joint distribution of Z and X among nonrespondents. We cannot use the observed distribution of Z and X for observational Z because the response process will create dependencies that may not exist among nonrespondents.

Implementing the pseudo-nonrespondent approach in our simulations is straightforward and produces results very similar what we saw in Sections 10.3 and 10.4. In Chapter 11, we present a series of simulations for multiple selection models. In the simulations we present, we use actual values of X and Z, but the results are very similar if we use pseudo-nonrespondents.

10.6 CONCLUSION

The theme of this chapter is that data beat models when fighting nonignorable nonresponse. As attractive as it is to have flexible ways to approximate the true functional form of the relationship between R and Y, selection models need good data. While researchers can sometimes find plausible Z variables in conventional survey data, often no such variables exist or not everyone is convinced by the Z proposed by a researcher.

This chapter therefore focuses on *creating* good respond instruments. Doing so is not hard: A pollster needs simply to randomize potential respondents into treatments that affect their propensity to respond. This approach is a natural extension of standard polling practice. Pollsters regularly randomly identify potential respondents in order to counter *Literary Digest*-type biases; with the randomized response instruments, pollsters also randomize contact protocols in order to generate data that will enable them to diagnose and, if need be, offset nonignorable nonresponse.

---

[9] In order to fully incorporate uncertainty, one could use multiple imputation after taking random draws of the number of nonrespondents in each group.

Randomized Response Instruments 197

Randomized response treatments enable several useful tools. We showed how to implement a simple test for nonignorability that makes no distributional assumptions. That test does assume – like weighting – that we observe all covariates that affect both R and Y. Hence, we may wish to stick with selection models, which do not make that assumption. Randomized instruments also enable us to estimate the full range of selection models even when we do not observe data for specific nonrespondents.

We have reached the climax of our story: Combining flexible statistical models and randomized response instruments allows us to fight the menace of nonignorable nonresponse. There are, however, a fair number of threads in the story, and we next turn to making sure we know how they relate. Hence, Chapter 11 revisits the Heckman, copula, control function and nonignorable nonresponse weighting models to compare how they operate in the face of various ways in which nonignorable nonresponse can express itself in the data. The payoff will be a decision tree that we can use when diagnosing and correcting for nonignorable nonresponse.

11

Putting It Together

What do we do now?

Robert Redford, *The Candidate*

In the 1972 movie *The Candidate*, Robert Redford plays a novice and not particularly serious candidate running for the US Senate. After some twists and turns, he wins. As shocked as anyone, he sneaks away from his election night party and famously asks his campaign manager "What do we do now?" The movie ends without an answer.

We're in a bit of a similar situation. Despite considerable interest in nonignorable nonresponse, we're new applying these tools because polls are rarely analyzed with models that directly measure and account for nonignorable nonresponse. But we'll try to do better than *The Candidate* by providing a path forward. This chapter does this by discussing specific ways that nonignorable nonresponse may manifest itself and how the various models perform across these contexts, including how they may fail.

In an idealized form, the path is

1. Create randomized instruments – and make 'em strong because selection models love powerful instruments.
2. Use the randomized instrument to diagnose nonignorable nonresponse.
3. If there is no evidence of nonignorable nonresponse, move to conventional weights.
4. If there is evidence of nonignorable nonresponse, use a model designed to deal with it, but remain cognizant of pitfalls.

This chapter proceeds as follows. Section 1 simulates and analyzes data across a range of scenarios. These simulations allow us to identify patterns that persist across data-generating processes. One important pattern is the conventional weighting is generally more accurate when nonresponse is ignorable.

198

Putting It Together 199

Hence, Section 2 discusses how to diagnose whether nonresponse is nonignorable. Section 3 integrates the approaches with a decision tree based on properties of the data. Section 4 discusses how selection models can fail.

11.1 SIMULATING NONIGNORABLE NONRESPONSE

Our goal in this chapter is to explain how the tools in the selection model repertoire fit together. We begin by exploring simulation models in which we examine the performance of multiple models across a variety of data generation scenarios. Doing so allows us to highlight important themes that persist throughout the discussion. We simulate two pathways for nonignorable nonresponse to arise:

- A **direct pathway** in which Y is in the R^* equation;
- An **indirect pathway** in which there is an unobserved variable U that affects both R^* and Y.

As we noted in Section 8.3, these pathways are closely related and both create correlation of errors across the selection and outcome equations. We simulate both direct and indirect pathways because they manifest different intuitions about how nonignorable nonresponse can arise. In addition, some models are explicitly derived based on one or the other.

For each simulation, we assess how close the estimates of average Y in each model are to the true population average of Y. In the initial simulations, Y and U are continuous variables and the errors come from a normal distribution. We produce three estimates for these initial simulations: The observed sample average, the weighted sample average, and the Heckman model-estimated average. In one sense, there isn't a lot of mystery as to what will happen at this point because we know from Chapter 3 that weighting estimates are biased when there is nonignorable nonresponse. This effort is useful, however, because it provides a sense of the relative performance of the Heckman model depending on the source and magnitude of nonignorable nonresponse and the strength of the response instrument.

Our first set of simulations uses direct pathway models, models in which nonignorable nonresponse arises because Y directly affects response propensity. We vary the strength of the influence of Y on response propensity and also the strength of the influence of Z on response propensity. We evaluate estimation accuracy using the root mean-squared error (RMSE), which is the square root of the average squared difference between the population average and estimated average. We discussed RMSE in Section 10.2.

Figure 11.1 shows the results. The darker the shading, the larger the error. The horizontal axis of each panel shows parameter values that reflect the extent to which Y affects R. We show them in terms of the percentage point increase in the probability that R equals 1 for an increase of Y of one unit. The cases on the left of each panel reflect instances in which there is no nonignorable

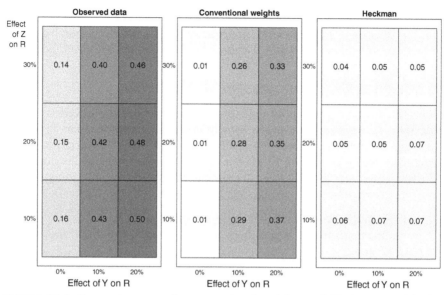

FIGURE 11.1 Comparing error for conventional weights and Heckman models for direct pathway

nonresponse because Y does not affect R; the cases on the right reflect cases in which Y has a relatively large effect on R. The vertical axis in each panel shows parameter values associated with the effect of Z on R. The γ_Z values on the bottom indicate that Z increases the probability of response by 10 percentage points. (We do not include simulations where $\gamma = 0$ because the Heckman model falls apart without a viable response instrument.) The γ_Z values on the top indicate that Z increases the probability of response by 30 percentage points.

The panel on the left of Figure 11.1 shows the error if we simply used the sample average. Due to both ignorable and nonignorable nonresponse, the sample is skewed and produces inaccurate estimates. The middle panel depicts error for conventional weights. The light shading for the left side of this panel indicates that weights do well when there is no nonignorable nonresponse. As Y has larger effects on R, however, conventional weighting estimates deviate far from the truth.

The panel on the right depicts the error for the Heckman model. The left-hand column of the panel shows that Heckman model performs worse than weighting when there is no nonignorable nonresponse. In all other scenarios, the Heckman model estimates are closer to the truth, often by a lot. The Heckman model's weakest performance is when Z has relatively small effect on R, as seen by the slightly darker shading in the bottom row of the Heckman panel. The implication is that, at least for this initial model, conventional weighting works great when there is no nonignorable nonresponse, but we'll do

Putting It Together

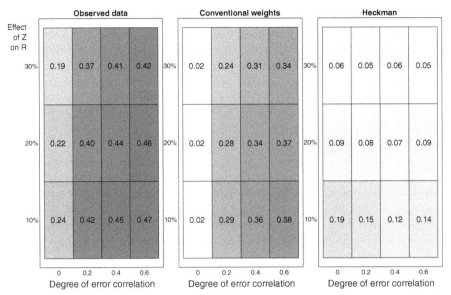

FIGURE 11.2 Comparing error for conventional weights and Heckman models for indirect pathway

much better if we use a Heckman selection model with a randomized response instrument when there is nonignorable nonresponse.[1]

Figure 11.2 conducts a similar exercise for indirect pathway models, models in which nonignorable nonresponse arises because an unobserved U variable affects response propensity and the outcome. We vary the strength of the influence of U on R^* and Y and also the strength of the influence of Z on R^*. The values on the horizontal axis reflect the correlation in the error terms caused by U. As in the previous figure, the values on the vertical axis reflect the extent to which Z affects R. The darker the shading, the larger the error.

The patterns are again clear. Conventional weighting does well when there is no nonignorable nonresponse. But as the correlation induced by U gets larger, conventional weighting performs worse. The Heckman model performs better when there is nonignorable nonresponse and particularly so when Z does a good job predicting response. As before, the implication is that when there is no nonignorable nonresponse, conventional weighting works great, while when there is nonignorable nonresponse, we'll do much better if we have a strong response instrument and use a Heckman selection model.

Although these simulations do not cover the full range of possible data generation scenarios, they nonetheless perform an important role in our

---

[1] This is, of course, a set of simulations with a specific set of parameter values. If the coefficients on X in the response and outcome equations are bigger, the differences between the weighting and Heckman models will be different. The general patterns that weighting does worse as the effect of Y on R increases never changes, however.

explication. Every serious polling analyst has considered at some point the possibility that there is some unobserved variable that they would love to have for their weights. Unlike conventional weighting approaches that need to assume away the existence of such variables, we have directly assumed – and modeled – such variables and shown that with a good response instrument we can generate good estimates even when we do not observe all the variables we would like for our weighting efforts. We'll allow more varied parametric relationships next, but at this point we have a proof of concept that we can defeat nonignorable nonresponse in plausible circumstances.

As we discussed in Chapters 8 and 9, many researchers are understandably nervous about the bivariate normality assumption in the Heckman model. We now therefore explore what happens when we have nonignorable nonresponse across in models in which the errors are not normally distributed. To keep things simple, we focus our discussion on the direct pathway to nonignorable nonresponse (meaning Y directly affects R); the patterns are similar for the indirect pathway.

We build from a similar setup as in Section 10.2. First, we look at models in which Y is dichotomous, such as in models predicting whether someone will vote for the Democratic candidate or approve the president. Second, we allow the errors to have non-normal distributions such as a t-distribution or a uniform distribution. In these distributions, errors that are relatively large in magnitude are more likely than in a model with bivariate normal errors. The results are similar across error distributions, so we present the model in which errors follow a t-distribution with three degrees of freedom.[2]

Our main interest will be the conventional weighting, Heckman and NINR weighting models. The NINR weighting models are designed to apply across more functional form contexts. Figure 11.3 shows the results. As before, weighting models do better when nonresponse is ignorable and the selection models do better when nonresponse is nonignorable. The selection models outperform conventional weighting whenever there is nonignorable nonresponse. And, even though there are several sources of non-normality in the data generation process, the Heckman model performs roughly as well as the NINR weighting model.

We observe similar patterns for different parameter values and for uniform errors as well. The implication is that we now have identified a range of data generation processes that selection models can handle much better than conventional weighting. We have not, of course, covered all possible data generation processes. We'll discuss processes for which selection models struggle later in this chapter.

---

[2] The fewer the degrees of freedom, the greater the difference between a t-distribution and a normal distribution.

Putting It Together 203

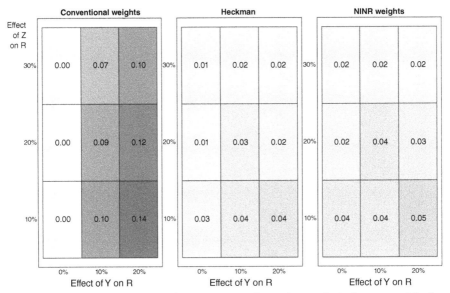

FIGURE 11.3 Comparing error for conventional weights and Heckman models for direct pathway and non-normal errors

11.2 DIAGNOSING NONIGNORABLE NONRESPONSE

One clear pattern in the simulations is that conventional weighting does better when nonresponse is ignorable. This suggests a two-stage approach in which we first assess whether nonresponse is ignorable. If it is, we can weight and be done with things. If we see evidence of nonignorability, then we will need to work harder.

Our goal in this section is to discuss options for testing whether response is ignorable. We begin with the bivariate version of the nonparametric test discussed in Section 10.4, a test that mirrors the tilted fish intuition of Figure 8.3. This test is essentially a difference of means test comparing Y among respondents with $Z = 0$ and $Z = 1$. It is attractive because it does not require any parametric assumptions and is easy to implement. It also seems intuitive that the randomness of Z will allow us to implement this test without other controls.

However, as we discussed in Section 10.4, we need to control for X even though Z is randomly assigned. While Z and X will be uncorrelated in expectation in the entire population, these variables can be correlated in the observed sample if they both affect the probability of response. Hence, our second diagnostic test will be a difference in means for Y across the $Z = 0$ and $Z = 1$ groups, controlling for X. This test works if we observe all X that affect response and Y.

A more robust approach involves testing for nonignorable nonresponse by assessing the statistical significance of key parameters in the models. For

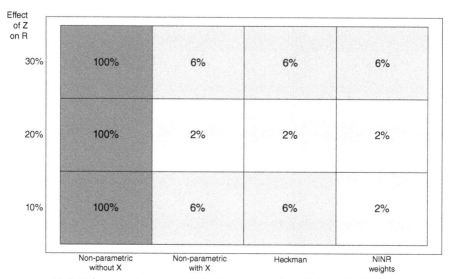

FIGURE 11.4 False positive rates (rejection rates of null hypothesis that error is ignorable when error is ignorable; should be 5 percent)

the Heckman model, a statistically significant ρ parameter implies nonignorable nonresponse. In the NINR weighting model, a statistically significant γ_Y parameter implies nonignorable nonresponse.

For these tests to be useful, they should not reject the null hypothesis of ignorable nonresponse when the null is true. Figure 11.4 shows how several tests do in this regard by displaying the rejection rates of the null hypothesis for the simulations summarized in Figure 11.3 in which $\gamma_Y = 0$. Given standard statistical practice, we do not want to reject the null more than 5 percent of the time for these scenarios; this is the so-called false-positive rate also known as the type I error rate. For each of four possible tests and three levels of γ_Z, we show the percent of times the model incorrectly suggests nonresponse is nonignorable. We highlight good results in lighter shades and poor results in a darker shade.

The nonparametric test without X rejects the null almost every time. If we didn't know any better and used this test naively, we would be seeing nonignorable nonresponse even when it did not exist. The nonparametric test in which we control for X does great, getting the correct answer around 95 percent of the time when response is actually ignorable. The Heckman model and NINR weight model do well, with similar performance as the nonparametric test with X.

Several implications follow from the discussion and simulations. First, the bivariate nonparametric test is bad. Second, even the nonparametric test with covariates is a bit risky. It works well if we do in fact observe the covariates that affect response and outcome, but we can seldom be sure that is the case.

Putting It Together 205

Third, the more involved models such as Heckman and NINR weights are worth the extra effort because they know how to say no. That is, they seldom suggest in the simulations that response is nonignorable when it is ignorable. And this is important because when response is ignorable we would rather use conventional weighting.

11.3 DECISION TREE FOR SELECTION MODELS

We've covered a lot of ground, and it is time to provide a holistic picture of good practices with regard to nonignorable nonresponse. Before getting into details of how to select an appropriate model, we should first assess whether it is worth worrying about nonignorable nonresponse. There are likely cases in which theory and experience suggest that testing for nonignorable nonresponse may not be worth the effort. In the glory days of random sampling, for example, nonignorable nonresponse bias was likely minor given the relatively high response rates and the fact that cultural variables such as social trust were not strongly correlated with political views even as they may have affected people's willingness to respond (David Shor, quoted in Matthews 2020).

These days, it is harder to dismiss nonignorable nonresponse without evidence. Section 5.3 showed how low response rates magnify the effects of nonignorable nonresponse. Response rates could hardly be lower than they are now, so we need to be attentive. And as David Shor emphasizes, the cultural moment is one in which populist-type sentiment in many countries may be stronger among those less likely to engage with pollsters. Such concerns may also carry over to polls about any sensitive topic and other areas such as consumer feedback where experiences may directly affect willingness to respond.

How we assess – and potentially, account for – nonignorable nonresponse will depend on our data. Figure 11.5 maps options given data availability. The first data question is whether one has a response instrument or not. If one does not, one can use the bounding techniques discussed in Chapter 7.

Given a response instrument, the next question is whether the instrument is observational or randomized. Chapter 10 extolled the virtues of randomized response instruments, but sometimes they are not available. In this case, the question is whether the instrument is available only for those who answered the polls or for nonrespondents as well. If we only observed Z for respondents (as, e.g., we use political interest to predict interest in response but do not observe political interest for nonrespondents), we can use a maximum likelihood approach like Peress (2010). This opens up a vast and mostly untapped range of analyses, many of which embody common sense beliefs about who is more likely to respond to polls. However, the Peress approach requires that Z have more than two categories and, if the instrument is observational, suffers from the limits associated with such instruments.

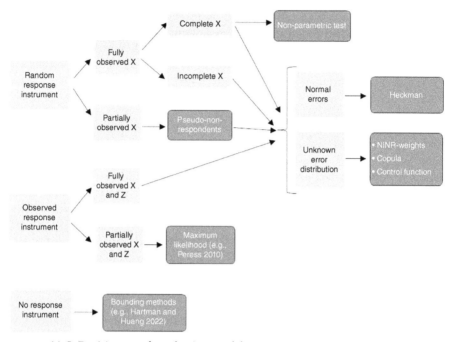

FIGURE 11.5 Decision tree for selection models

With observational response instruments, the full suite of selection models is available if one observes Z and X for respondents and nonrespondents. Chapter 10 showed the risks here. One is that conditional on X, Z may not explain enough difference in R to allow the selection models to perform well. We have seen several times that selection models become unreliable without a strong instrument. Another risk is that Z is not actually a pure response instrument and should be included in the outcome equation as well. In this case, the risk is that the models may attribute differential values of Y to response when they in fact are attributable to direct effects of Z on Y.

One can avoid these challenges if Z is randomized as described in Chapter 10. If X is fully observed, by which we mean that we measure all the covariates that affect both R and Y, we can implement a simple nonparametric test for nonignorability. Since we know that this assumption is a strong assumption, this corner of the decision tree is largely cautionary, highlighting the fact that the nonparametric test can be misleading if we do not observe the complete set of variables that affect both R and Y. Concerns about the completeness of X are not particularly compelling, however, because even when X is incomplete a full suite of selection models is still appropriate. In other words, selection models will work when we have a good response instrument even when – or, more pointedly, *especially* when – there are unobserved variables that affect R and Y.

Putting It Together 207

When we only observe X for the respondents, having a randomized response instrument opens up the door to using pseudo-nonrespondents to enable implementation of the suite of selection models. The reason is that the randomization of Z allows us to calculate the proportions of the nonrespondent pool who had combinations of X and Z, as long as the proportions of X are known in the population, as is common for weighting variables. And these models are appropriate even when there are unobserved variables that affect R and Y or when Y directly affects R.

As the figure makes clear, there are many paths to the suite of selection models. Within that suite, a major decision is about parametric form. Assuming errors are bivariate normal is a relatively strong but convenient assumption that allows us to use the Heckman model. In our results and in others, the Heckman model generally performs well when there is a strong instrument even when the errors in the data generation process are not normal. The Heckman model becomes unreliable when the response instrument is weak, however. The other selection models are designed to deal with broader range of models. Their costs are complexity – the NINR weight model does not always converge, and the copula models include obscure statistical distributions. And control function models do not produce estimates of the population averages, which are often of interest.

After working through the decision tree to an appropriate model, the final decision is whether to go back to conventional weighting. If we find no evidence that nonresponse is nonignorable, conventional weighting is better and we should happily – and confidently – stick to that approach.

11.4 RISKS IN SELECTION MODELS

Selection models have many virtues when we are faced with a polling environment in which nonresponse is plausibly nonignorable. They are not without risks however. The three major sources of problems are poor instruments, complicated functional forms, and researcher degrees of freedom.

The first risk is that the response instrument Z may not be up to the demands of selection models. Recall that a response instrument satisfies two conditions: (1) Z has independent effect on R, and (2) Z has no independent effect on Y.

If the first condition fails, Z does not explain R and selection models will perform poorly. In fact, not only do we want Z to affect R, we want the effect to be large because Section 11.1 showed that the improvement of selection models over weighting models may be modest if the effect of Z on R is small. Sometimes the selection models will fail to converge.

It is easy to diagnose whether Z explain R because we can simply estimate response models and assess the independent effect of Z on R. Section 10.5 showed that we can even do this when nonrespondent data are not observed as long as Z is randomized. If our instrument has a small effect on R, then we know that selection models may have high root mean-squared error and perhaps we need to stick to a more speculative bounding approach as discussed in Chapter 7.

A more nettlesome possibility is that Z *does* explain Y. Researchers reasonably worry that observational response instruments have some effect on Y. Section 10.2 showed how selection models can go astray when this is the case. Selection models are not always worse than weighting models, but they are prone to seeing nonignorable nonresponse even when it is not there and hence hard to trust for observational Z.

The other major source of problems for selection models is functional form: The models we discussed allow for many joint distributions of the errors across the response and outcome equations, but do not cover all possibilities. For example, it is possible that the relationship between R and Y may be non-monotonic. In the tilted fish model, nonignorable nonresponse arises because the eager responders have higher values of Y. The model can, of course, handle the case in which the eager responders have lower values of Y equally well. However, the selection models fail if there is a nonmonotonic relationship such as might occur, for example, if the most eager respondents and the least eager respondents have high values of Y and the middle-level respondents have low values of Y. If response instrument is localized to raising response rates from 5 percent to 15 percent, we may see a lower average Y among the $Z = 1$ respondents and the selection model would essentially extrapolate lower values of Y to all nonrespondents. If in fact, the people least inclined to respond had high values of Y, this effort would be leading us away from the truth.

There are three defenses against such a possibility. First, it is useful to have covariates such that our tests of whether Z affect R will span information about people at various levels of response interest. If we control for education, for example, the coefficient on Z may not be statistically significant if Z has opposite signed effects among high response interest college graduates and low response interest noncollege graduates. One could also subset the analysis by group if nonmonotonicity is a concern. Second, if possible, one could create a randomized treatment variable that has multiple levels. For example, Z could have three categories reflecting low, middle, and high response treatments. Doing so will span more of the response interest and Y space. Third, if one is still concerned about nonmonotonicity one can note this as a threat to validity in the analysis and, ideally, sketch out a plausible scenario that could induce such nonmonotonicity. Nonmonotonicity can arise, of course, even if we can't articulate a such scenario, but a pragmatist would worry less about a scenario that we can't imagine.

Another functional form complication is that the nonignorability of non-response could be heterogenous across groups. Perhaps in some subgroups, interest in response is related to Y while this is not the case in other groups. We will see multiple examples of this in Chapter 12. For example, response interest is associated with higher support for former President Trump among

Putting It Together 209

Republicans and *lower* support for Trump among Democrats. If our interest is estimating support for Trump among the whole population, this may not be terribly problematic because on average there will be no major difference in Y based on Z, leading to an indication of no nonignorability, which is fine because the overly pro-Trump Republicans will essentially be balanced out by the overly anti-Trump Democrats. If our interest is in estimating support for Trump among Republicans or among Democrats, however, we will need to estimate separate models (or separate nonignorability coefficients) by party, subgroups in which the relationship between response interest and Y is monotonic.

A pragmatic approach to the possibility of heterogeneity is relatively straightforward. For subgroups that we suspect have distinctive patterns of nonignorability, we can simply assess them separately. If the nonignorability is in fact distinctive, then we can keep them separate in the analysis and pool them back into the final estimate in proportion to their group size. If we see no signs of distinctive patterns of nonignorability, we can include the subgroups in the full analysis without separate selection modeling. The literature has not, to my knowledge, developed a more systematic search process in this context. Tools developed in other contexts such as the search for heterogenous treatment effects may be useful.

A third challenge for selection models is researcher degrees of freedom. This is a fancy way of noting that there are a lot of choices to be made when using selection models: Which variables to include, which parametric form to model, which subgroups to analyze separately. Any time there are choices, the risk is that an analyst will be tempted, consciously or not, to choose the options that yield some preferred results. This concern is certainly not unique to selection models. Chapter 3 documented many choices involved in weighting, for example.

Defenses against this risk are the same as in other contexts and largely revolve around transparency. First, the analyst should explain major decisions and, if possible, show if results change for different choices. If results depend on the specification choices, then the analyst needs to justify the choices they make. Second, the more that researchers can provide data and code, the easier it will be for others to probe the analysis to see if the results are robust. Third, a researcher can preregister their analysis, noting the tools they will use and, if relevant, the hypotheses they will text. This makes it harder to chip away at a data set with more specifications until the desired results emerge. Preregistration does not prohibit exploration. An analyst should feel free to explore the data, but any results found from this process should be identified as such so that readers can discount them appropriately. For truly interesting results identified in this way, the analyst should redo the survey, preregistering techniques and expectations related to such findings.

11.5 CONCLUSION

The goal of Part III of this book has been to develop a toolkit for dealing with nonignorable nonresponse. Because we have covered a lot of ground, this chapter distilled the discussion into guidance for which models are most appropriate for which contexts.

Three themes stand out. First, selection models work across multiple sources of nonignorable nonresponse. They work when Y directly affects response propensity. They work when there are unobserved variables that affect response and outcome. Conventional weighting models fail in both circumstances.

Second, for all their benefits, we shouldn't use these tools if we do not need them. That is, weighting and related models are fine – great even – when nonresponse is ignorable. Hence, before applying selection models we should ascertain whether we need them. If we are not able to find evidence of nonignorable nonresponse, we should happily stick with conventional weighting. It turns out, however, that the best way to know if we need a selection model involves estimating a selection model.

Third, selection models demand a lot of the data. Without a good response instrument, selection models tend to flail even if they are based on the same parametric assumptions that generated the data. This means the price of entry to selection models is a good instrument. In general, the best response instrument will be a randomized response instrument that will have more independent explanatory power than an observational response instrument, which boosts statistical power and also enables us to know a lot about the nonrespondent pool even when we not directly hear from them. If we simply cannot generate or find a good instrument, we may need to fall back on the bounding strategies discussed in Chapter 7.

There are two important products of these discussions. First was a flowchart that can guide us toward appropriate models depending on the types of data at hand and our beliefs about the data-generating process. Second was a discussion of threats to the validity of selection models. Extrapolating from a sample to a population is hard, especially when nonresponse directly relates to the content of opinions. Selection models work well across a vast range of scenarios, but the range is incomplete. In particular, selection models need good instruments, but even with good instruments may be unable to deal with nonmonotonicities in the relationship between response and outcome outside the range of what we observe.

In Part IV, we turn to applications in which the logic and tools covered so far help us learn about the populations in ways that are more robust to the possibility of nonignorable nonresponse. Chapter 12 presents political polling examples, and Chapter 13 looks at examples related to public health.

PART IV

APPLICATIONS

12

Nonignorable Nonresponse in Political Surveys

> It turns out that people who answer surveys are really weird.
>
> David Shor in Matthews (2020)

We've seen so far that many polls deal with nonresponse and nonrandom samples with the old weighting two-step: Weight ... and pray. Part III of this book suggests that we can and should do more. A long-standing – and rapidly evolving – literature by survey researchers, epidemiologists, economists, and others provides tools that test directly for nonignorable nonresponse. Chapter 9 showed that modern selection models accommodate a broad range of parametric and nonparametric approaches to estimation. Chapter 10 showed how randomized response instruments provide the data needed to make these models work.

While they did not use our terminology, Nate Cohn at the *New York Times* and his partners at Siena College provide an example of how to assess whether nonignorable nonresponse is a problem (Cohn 2022b). Recall that Wisconsin has been both pivotal in national elections and very hard to poll. In 2020, virtually every poll indicated a comfortable Biden lead. The *Washington Post*/ABC News poll even suggested Biden would win by 16 percentage points, when in fact Biden only won Wisconsin by less than one percent.

The Cohn/Siena team sent mailers to households in Wisconsin before the 2022 midterm election with $5 bills plus a promise of $20 for completed surveys. At the same time, they conducted a traditional random contact phone survey. The money did its job: The response rate was 30 percent for those offered cash, compared to only 1.6 percent for the phone survey. Translated into the terminology of this book, the mail survey was the high response treatment and the phone survey was the low response treatment. Differences across these conditions would indicate nonignorable nonresponse; no differences would indicate ignorable nonresponse.

The Cohn/Siena team found that the results were the same across treatment types for Senate and gubernatorial races. In other words, nonresponse appeared ignorable because response propensity was unrelated to survey answers. This was evidence that weighting was likely fine, evidence that was borne out in the election. The *New York Times* surveys showed that the Senate race was very close and that Democrat Tony Evers led by 4 percentage points in the Governor's race. On election day, the Senate race was decided by 1 percent and Evers won by 3.4 percent. The cool thing about the survey experiment is that it provided evidence *before* the election that the Wisconsin polls in 2022 would defy recent history and actually be useful.

The *New York Times*/Siena experiment showed signs of nonignorable nonresponse on other questions. People answering the low response phone surveys were 16 percentage points more likely to follow political news, 12 percentage points less likely to say they were political moderates, 7 percentage points more likely to have been born in Wisconsin, and 4 percentage points more likely to have supported Trump in 2020. For these questions, the evidence suggested that a complete analysis would require the tools described in Part III.

This chapter illustrates in more detail how we can use randomized response treatments to assess possible nonresponse bias. We present results from a survey design that has been implemented multiple times. We'll focus on a survey from 2019, showing how the results indicated that nonignorable nonresponse may have deflated Trump support in the Midwest and among Democrats even as nonignorable nonresponse inflated Trump support among Republicans. We will also see signs that Democrats who responded to the poll were more liberal on race than Democrats who did not respond, a pattern that was particularly strong among White Democrats and absent among non-White Democrats.

This chapter proceeds as follows. Section 1 describes a survey design with a randomized response instrument. Section 2 discusses nonignorable nonresponse bias for turnout questions. Section 3 looks at presidential support, revealing regional and partisan differences in nonignorable nonresponse. Section 4 looks at race, focusing on partisan and racial differences in nonignorable nonresponse. Section 5 assesses nonignorable nonresponse on climate, taxes, and tariffs.

12.1 DESIGNING A SURVEY WITH A RESPONSE INSTRUMENT

Chapters 9 and 10 showed that while parametric flexibility is great, good data may be even better when battling nonresponse. Specifically, if we have a response instrument that affects response propensity without directly affecting opinion, the suite of models available will have the information they need to diagnose and potentially offset potential nonignorable nonresponse.

Nonignorable Nonresponse in Political Surveys 215

Here, we describe a survey design that provided both a randomized response instrument and a continuum of resistance response variable. We use these variables to identify whether the propensity to respond was related to the content of response in our sample. The advantage of this approach is that is simple within existing polling infrastructure and provides data that enable multiple approaches to estimation. This is definitely not the only way to proceed. The *New York Times* example we discussed above is another, and there are many other ways to create a randomized response instrument.

The design has been implemented multiple times.[1] To keep things simple, we focus here on a survey that was fielded from January 18 to February 11, 2019, by Ipsos using their KnowledgePanel of survey respondents. Ipsos recruits panel members by using address-based sampling methods, a probability-based sampling methodology. As is standard for their KnowledgePanel surveys, Ipsos provided households without internet with a web-enabled device and free internet service.

The goal of the research design is to produce high and low propensity survey respondents. In our framework, high propensity survey respondents are people who respond when they've been randomly assigned to a survey protocol with a relatively low response rate. Low propensity respondents are people who respond when they have been assigned to a survey protocol with a relatively high response rate. With such data, we can explore whether the "fish" is tilted as in Figure 8.3 by using selection models to assess whether the high propensity response group has distinctive opinions, controlling for the variables used in weighting.

We do this with the survey design illustrated in Figure 12.1. In the first step, Ipsos contacted a probability sample of 3,500 people from their probability sampled panel. As a poll of an internet panel, the response was higher than a typical probability sample, with 2,218 people responding and 1,355 people not answering. Roughly 50 percent of respondents were assigned to the treatment group.

Among the people willing to respond, we assigned 1,112 individuals to a control protocol in which we asked political questions described below as is standard in political polls.[2] We also assigned 1,106 individuals to a more distinctive treatment protocol. We first asked them whether they would like to answer questions about politics, sports, or movies via the question displayed in Figure 12.2. In this treatment group, 35.7 percent chose politics, 39.2 percent chose health, 23.8 percent chose sports, and 1.3 percent did not answer. The 393 respondents who chose politics were asked the same questions as the control group. The 713 individuals who chose a nonpolitical topic were given a

---

[1] I discuss two other examples in the online appendix.
[2] The figure shows an example for a question in which everyone in the control group responded. A small number of these individuals did not respond. The number varied by question, but was usually around 10. These individuals were included in the nonresponse group.

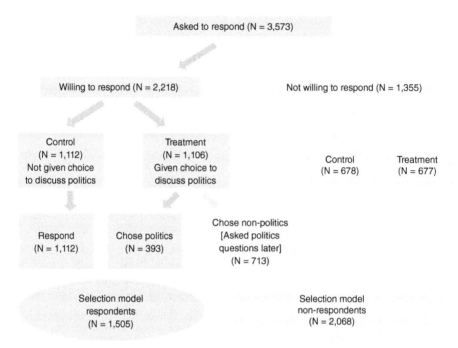

FIGURE 12.1 Survey design with randomized response instrument

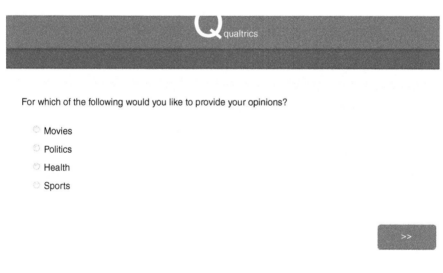

FIGURE 12.2 Opt-in question

Nonignorable Nonresponse in Political Surveys 217

series of questions on their selected topic.[3] Later, these individuals were asked the political questions, providing an additional source of information that we will come back to below.

The treatment in this survey design lowered response rates. Hence, the people who responded in the treatment condition are the high propensity response types. They were eager to discuss politics even though they did not have to. In terms of the tilted fish figure (Figure 8.3), the treated group corresponds to the top panels. The control protocol in this survey design is the high response rate condition, meaning that people in this group who responded had lower response propensity on average than those who responded in the treatment condition. People in the control group may not have been as eager to discuss politics, but went along. The control group corresponds to the lower panels in the tilted fish figure.

We use selection models to ascertain whether the propensity to respond predicted response, conditional on covariates. We estimate response equations based on the entire sample of 3,573 individuals who Ipsos contacted, 1,505 of whom responded. Because this is a panel, Ipsos was able to provide data for the nonrespondents, including demographic information and party identification.[4] The treatment status of non-respondents can be imputed as described in Section 10.5. We will mostly report Heckman selection models. Evidence for nonignorable nonresponse is typically larger when we use copula models. Copula models are harder to explain; there is also a risk of over-fitting because the standard approach to using copulas is to estimate multiple copula models and choose the one with the best fit. For our purposes, Heckman models provide a fixed reference point that is relatively easy to understand, even as we encourage analysts to use multiple selection models to best appreciate the robustness of their findings.

When estimating the selection models, we do not use the survey answers of the 713 people in the treatment group who did not choose politics. However, we implement complementary analyses using their answers. Specifically, using a sample of only the 1,106 respondents in the treatment group we compare the survey answers of those who did and did not choose politics. This choice is an example of a continuum of response variable as such as described in Section 9.4. If nonresponse is nonignorable, we should see no differences between those who do and do not want to talk about politics once we control for covariates. If we do see differences across these two groups, we have evidence that nonresponse is nonignorable. Importantly, this analysis uses different information than selection models because the survey respondents of people who did not choose politics did not make their way into the selection models. This chapter largely focuses on selection models in order to keep things

---

[3] Individuals who selected sports were asked to rate Bryce Harper, Serena Williams, Tom Brady, and LeBron James. Individuals who selected health were asked a question about frequency of exercise.

[4] We include partisan leaners with partisans.

218   *Part IV: Applications*

simple, but in two instances will show the difference of means tests, which are
quite intuitive and produce very similar patterns as in the selection models.[5]

12.2 TURNOUT

We begin by analyzing turnout. Turnout is an important phenomenon. Political pollsters need to know who will turn out in order to anticipate results and perhaps target campaign activities. Political scientists study turnout in order to understand if and how political participation affects democratic representation.

Turnout is also a good starting point because we have strong beliefs about what we should find. Theoretically, it seems likely that the kind of people who participate in the democratic process will be more willing to respond to polls, both because they are more interested in the topic and because they have the background knowledge that makes them comfortable with both interactions. Empirically, one of the most consistent findings in survey research has been that the turnout rates implied by polls exceed actual turnout. While it is possible that people simply lie when answering this question, research based on validated response consistently shows that conditional on covariates, people who answer polls are more likely to have voted (Peress 2010; Jackman and Spahn 2019). We should expect that, therefore, that our toolkit should identify nonignorable nonresponse on turnout questions.

Before discussing selection models, we present a model-free, intuitive analysis in the spirit of Figure 8.3, the tilted fish figure. Is it the case that people who have a high propensity to respond are more likely to say they will vote than people with a low propensity to respond? In our survey design, the 393 treated respondents are high propensity responders because they responded even when they had an option of not responding. The 1,112 respondents in the control group have lower propensity to respond on average because they responded in a context in which response was more common. The 713 people who chose not to respond are also a low propensity response group; their propensity to respond is presumably lower than the average in the control group because the control group includes people who would and would not have chosen politics, while the treated nonresponders consist only of those who chose not to respond.

The survey question we analyzed was "How likely is it that you will vote in the 2020 election?" with answers on a five-point scale ranging from "absolutely certain" to "I will not vote." To keep things simple, we create a

---

[5] Comparing those who did and did not choose to answer political questions is not the hypothesis test described (and critiqued) in Section 10.4. Chapter 10 test looks for differences across the randomized treatment and control groups. The continuum of resistance test assesses differences based on revealed interest in responding. The continuum of resistance test is not feasible in all survey designs. For example, the *New York Times*/Siena poll described earlier does not have survey responses from people in the treated group who chose not to respond.

Nonignorable Nonresponse in Political Surveys 219

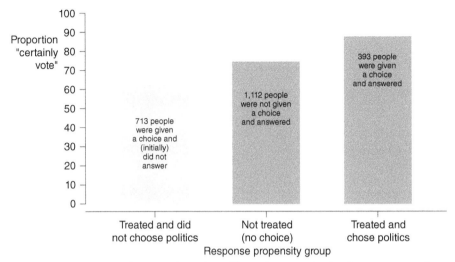

FIGURE 12.3 Estimated proportion who will say they are absolutely or very certain to turn out, by response group. Lines indicate 95 percent confidence intervals

dichotomous variable indicating whether someone was in the top two categories of likelihood of voting; the patterns are stronger if we analyze the dependent variable with all the possible response categories.

The y-axis in Figure 12.3 shows the estimated proportion of respondents who were very or absolutely certain they would vote. On the x-axis, we order groups from the lowest to highest response propensity types. On the far right are people who chose to respond to political questions: 88 percent of them said they would definitely vote. In the middle are the people in the control group: 72 percent of them said they would vote. On the left are the people who did not choose political questions: 63 percent of them said they would vote. In other words, as response propensity went up, people were more likely to say they would turn out, consistent with the idea that response propensity and survey answers were related. This pattern persists even if we control for the covariates discussed below.

The selection models we presented in Part III provide a more formal way to assess nonignorable nonresponse. These models allow us to infer the extent of nonignorable nonresponse-based information in two columns on the right of Figure 12.3 (the nontreated and the treated and chosen politics groups).

Table 12.1 shows the results for a Heckman model of turnout. We show results for a maximum likelihood model; the results for the two-stage model are similar. The response equation is a probit model using all 3,573 observations. The treatment variable is our randomized response instrument. It exerts a large and statistically significant effect with a very high z-statistic. Using the properties of the probit function, we can translate the estimated coefficient of 1.13 into an estimate that people in the treatment group were 38.7 percentage

220   *Part IV: Applications*

TABLE 12.1 *Heckman selection model of turnout*

Variable	Response		Turnout	
	Coefficient	z-statistic	Coefficient	z-statistic
Treatment	−1.13	−23.82	−	−
Female	−0.24	−5.20	0.01	0.13
Black	−0.34	−4.19	0.16	1.27
Hispanic	−0.18	−2.63	0.05	0.46
High school graduate	0.10	1.02	0.08	0.51
Some college	0.09	0.87	0.33	2.13
College graduate	0.26	2.46	0.55	3.34
Graduate school	0.25	2.20	0.53	2.99
Income	0.02	3.65	0.04	4.94
Age	0.02	12.12	0.02	10.32
Intercept	−0.69	−5.51	0.01	0.13
$\hat{\rho}$	−	−	0.49	5.71
Observations	3,573		1,501	

points less likely to respond. Such a large effect is reassuring because, as we saw in Chapter 11, having a strong response instrument is essential for selection models to work well. The other variables in the response equation work in unsurprising ways. Women, African-Americans, and Hispanic were less likely to respond. Graduates of college and graduate school and higher income and older people were more likely to respond. This first-stage selection model is essentially the same for all Heckman models reported below.

The turnout columns in Table 12.1 shows coefficients and z-statistics for the second-stage outcome equation in which the dependent variable was whether an individual said they were absolutely or very certain to vote. As with the response equation, the coefficients should be interpreted as probit coefficients. The key parameter is $\hat{\rho}$, which is 0.49 with a large z-statistic indicating clear statistical significance. This result provides evidence of nonignorable nonresponse; in other words, response propensity is positively correlated with survey responses about turnout.[6]

When there is nonignorable nonresponse, the opinions of respondents differ from the opinions of the population because responses are more likely to come from those people most eager to respond, people are the positive estimate of $\hat{\rho}$ suggests are more likely to say they are certain to vote. In other words, the people who responded to the poll are more likely to say they would vote than the people who did not respond. The Heckman model corrects for this response

---

[6] A reminder: The ρ here is $\rho_{R^*,Y}$, which reflects the correlation between the latent responsiveness variable and outcome. It is different than (albeit related to) $\rho_{R,Y}$, which is used in the Meng equation and reflects the correlation of the 0/1 response variable and Y.

Nonignorable Nonresponse in Political Surveys

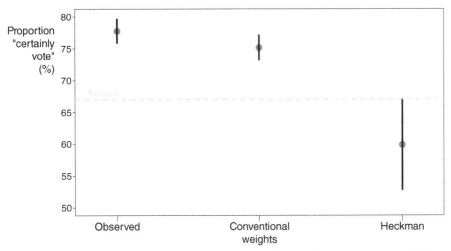

FIGURE 12.4 Estimated proportion who say they will certainly vote, by method. Lines indicate 95 percent confidence intervals

bias and therefore produces a lower estimate of turnout intentions than one would produce from an average (weighted or not) of survey responses.

Figure 12.4 illustrates the magnitude of this effect by showing the estimated proportion who people say they will certainly turn out by estimation method. The estimate from the observed sample is 78 percent; this estimate simply treats the observed sample as a random sample. The estimate based on conventional weights uses the weights provided by Ipsos. Because the respondent sample overrepresented demographic groups that were more likely to say they would vote, estimated turnout falls to 75 percent when weighting. The Heckman estimate of 60 percent is produced by generating fitted values of turnout using the entire sample of 3,573 using the coefficients in Table 12.1.[7]

Given that this survey was more than a year before an election and prospective, we cannot know what the "correct" answer is. One possible reference is the actual turnout in 2020, which was 67 percent, as indicated with a gray line. Given that some people who said they would possibly vote or were unlikely to vote would vote as well, it seems reasonable that the proportion of people who are certain to vote should not be much higher than the actual turnout.

12.3 TRUMP APPROVAL

Presidential approval is a highly salient political topic, useful for anticipating upcoming elections and for understanding how the public responds to actions,

---

[7] Because the initial Ipsos sample is a random sample of the population, the fitted values will estimate the population including those who did not respond. It is also possible to post-stratify by using Census data to describe the proportion of people in the population in the various cells implied by the coefficients and extrapolating from Heckman coefficients.

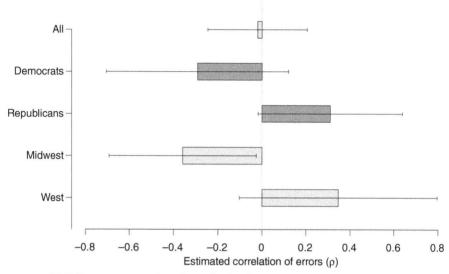

FIGURE 12.5 Trump approval, estimated ρ by data source

policies, and personalities of presidents. The 2019 survey asked respondents whether they approved or disapproved the way Donald Trump was handling his job as President, with answer options on a four-point scale ranging from "strongly disapprove" to "strongly approve."

Figure 12.5 shows the estimated correlation coefficients estimated for a series of Heckman selection models using the randomized response instrument as described above. At the top is the $\hat{\rho}$ estimated from the complete sample. It is close to zero. So as of 2019 in the sample produced by Ipsos, there was no evidence that Trump's 40 percent approval rating observed in the sample (which fell to 38 percent when weighted) was biased by nonignorable nonresponse.

As discussed in Section 11.4, nonignorable nonresponse can be heterogeneous as response propensity could be associated with high values of Y for some groups and low values of Y for others. In politics, this is very common as nonignorable nonresponse bias often goes in opposite directions for Democrats and Republicans. Figure 12.5 shows that this pattern holds here: For Democrats, high propensity to respond was associated with lower evaluations of Trump, while the opposite was true for Republicans. For each party, the effects are statistically significant.[8]

When discussing subgroups, it is useful to reflect on the challenge of identifying subgroups for analysis. A reasonable concern is that if one looks at enough subgroups, one will eventually find something. This is known as the

---

[8] We use the previously reported party affiliation in the Ipsos panel. The nonignorable nonresponse evidence was stronger if we use the contemporaneously reported party affiliation from the 2019 survey. In Section 12.5 of this chapter, we analyze feeling thermometer evaluations of President Trump and Vice President Mike Pence, former President Barack Obama and former House Speaker Nancy Pelosi.

multiple comparison problem in statistics. As consumers of survey results, how can we be confident that we are not consuming the fruits of an exhaustive – and possibly unreported – search?

First, these results have been replicated multiple times. The partisan differences like we see for Trump approval occurred in multiple surveys implemented with this design. The first time we saw this pattern it was based on a theory of how the world worked, but was nonetheless speculative. Hence, caution was appropriate. However, going into the second survey and beyond, we built in a specific expectation with regard to this pattern and every time observed it.

More generally, then, researchers should address multiple comparison concerns with repeated measurement. Findings from an initial survey that were not explicitly articulated before analysis should interpret warily. Subgroup patterns for subsequent surveys should be articulated ahead of time, similar to the way that academic researchers often preregister their expectations for experiments in order to lower the risk that spurious findings will be taken as meaningful.

Second, the proper interpretation of subgroup analysis depends on the purpose of the survey. If the goal is causal inference, then making multiple comparisons clearly risks spurious inference and additional surveys are absolutely needed before one should believe an initially unanticipated group difference. However, surveys are sometimes descriptive: They want to describe levels of support for the president or a policy, for example. In that case, finding strong evidence of nonignorable nonresponse may not necessarily mean that survey responses from a given subgroup will always be biased by nonignorable nonresponse. But it does mean that a particular subgroup in that particular survey is a bit wonky: For some reason, the high response propensity people were different than the low response propensity people and hence we should be cautious about using that data descriptively, regardless of whether the pattern was anticipated.

Future research may be able to provide more systematic identification of nonspurious group differences, perhaps in the way that the literature on heterogenous causal effects has matured. While tracking down every possible difference may become unproductive, it is plausible that there are additional variations in nonignorable nonresponse that are large enough to materially affect our conclusions.

Another potential source of subgroup variation is regional. The underestimates of Trump support in the Midwest in 2016 are seared into the minds of everyone who watched that election. Less widely recognized, but also large in magnitude, were overestimates of Trump strength in the West. In the bottom two rows of Figure 12.5, we limited the sample to respondents in the Midwest and West, respectively. There was statistically significant evidence of a negative ρ in the Midwest, meaning that the people responding were more negative toward Trump than the nonrespondents. In other words, in 2019 at least there were signs that Trump support was understated in polls, raising a warning that

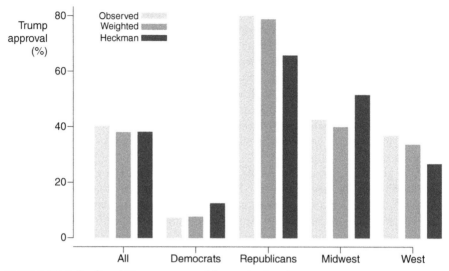

FIGURE 12.6 Predicted Trump approval by method and group

pollsters should have probed their results in that region further before giving the nod to Biden. For the West, $\hat{\rho}$ was positive but not statistically significant. Estimates of ρ for the Northeast and South were small and not statistically significant.

Figure 12.6 illustrates the implications of using selection models by showing estimated proportion of the population who approved of Trump by estimation method. Since averages of a four-point scale are a bit unintuitive, we present results for a model in which the dependent variable is a dummy variable indicating whether or not the respondent approves (strongly or not) of Trump. For the entire sample, the observed, weighted, and selection model estimates are close to each other, as typically happens when $\hat{\rho}$ is close to zero. For Democrats, however, the estimated approval rate rises from 7 percent in the observed sample to 12 percent in the Heckman model. For Republicans, the estimated approval falls from 80 to 66 percent. Notice how polarization is starker in the observed/weighted results than in the selection models: The difference in approval rates between the parties is 73 percent in the observed sample and 54 percent in the estimates corrected for nonignorable nonresponse.

The estimates by region also depend on the model. In the Midwest, the observed support for Trump was 43 percent. Approval fell to 40 percent when the data were weighted. Given the negative $\hat{\rho}$, the Heckman selection model gave a *higher* estimate of Trump support, all the way to 51 percent.[9] The

---

[9] Note that the Heckman model also incorporates weighting logic because its estimate is based on fitted values for the entire population including the nonrespondents who were more likely

Nonignorable Nonresponse in Political Surveys 225

estimates for the Midwest illustrate what is at stake when deciding whether to account for nonignorable nonresponse. If we believe the weighted data, Trump was floundering in the Midwest with a 40 percent approval rating. If we believe the selection model, Trump was actually doing pretty well in the Midwest with a 51 percent approval rating.

The columns on the right of Figure 12.5 show that accounting for nonignorable nonresponse suggested Trump was doing worse in the West that the observed and weighted data suggested. In the observed responses in the West, Trump approval was 37 percent. Trump approval in the West fell to 34 percent in the weighted data and fell even further to 27 percent in the selection model because the model estimated Trump approvers were more likely to respond. The effects for the West are more tentative, however, because the $\hat{\rho}$ estimate was not statistically significant.

12.4 ATTITUDES ABOUT RACE

Attitudes that are socially and politically sensitive are ripe for nonignorable nonresponse because people with socially disfavored views may be less eager to talk about them with a pollster. One of the most sensitive topics in American politics has been race. In this section, we assess whether nonignorable nonresponse may have led survey responses to paint a misleading picture.

We use a racial conservatism index to measure people's views about race. This index aggregates a battery of questions that have been widely used by other survey researchers. For each statement, respondents responded on a strongly agree to strongly disagree scale.

- A history of slavery and discrimination makes it difficult for Black people to work their way out of the lower class.
- If Black people would only try harder, they could be as well off as White people.
- Over the past few years, Black people have gotten less than they deserve.
- Black athletes should not take a knee during the national anthem.

The answers are scaled so that higher values indicate more conservative views and then aggregated into a single scale, as is common in polling about race.

The panel on the left of Figure 12.7 shows estimated $\hat{\rho}$ parameters for several groups. The top row shows that there was statistically significant negative correlation of response propensity and racial conservativism when using the

to be women, non-White and have lower education. (The net effect of weighting is to lower Trump support in this case, but it is hard to anticipate in this case because while women and African-Americans and Hispanics were less likely to support Trump, people with lower levels of education were more likely to support Trump.) Hence, we can think of the selection estimates as including one part that lowers the Trump support due to demographic characteristics of nonrespondents and another part that increases Trump support due to countering nonignorable nonresponse.

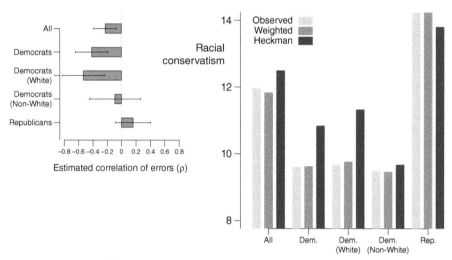

FIGURE 12.7 Racial conservatism: Estimated ρ and predicted mean, by group and model

entire sample. In other words, the selection model suggests that people with more conservative views on race were less likely to respond. This means that the population estimates for the whole population will vary depending on model. Using the observed or weighted survey data to estimate racial conservatism in the population produces an estimate around 12. Using the selection model, estimated racial conservatism rises to 12.5, which is the equivalent of an average move of one half a category on the four-point scale on one question.

The effects differ across subgroups. We begin by looking at Democrats. The increasing liberalism of Democrats on race in recent years has drawn a lot of attention. How much are liberal views found in surveys due to attitude change and how much are they due to self-censorship? While this single survey cannot assess trends over time, the data from it provide clear indication of that Democrats with relatively conservative views on race were less likely to respond. The second row of the left panel of Figure 12.7 shows that $\hat{\rho}$ was quite negative among Democrats, indicating that high response propensity Democrats were less racially conservative. The right panel of the figure shows that when we correct for nonignorable nonresponse bias, Democrats in the full population were roughly one point higher on the racial conservatism score than Democrats in the observed sample. This difference corresponds roughly to moving one step to the right on one of the race questions in the index.

We also divided Democrats by race in order to see if nonignorable nonresponse was the same among White and non-White Democrats. The third row of the left panel of Figure 12.7 shows that $\hat{\rho}$ was more negative among White Democrats. The fourth row of the left panel of Figure 12.7 shows that $\hat{\rho}$ was

Nonignorable Nonresponse in Political Surveys 227

essentially zero among non-White Democrats. In other words, nonignorable nonresponse on race was concentrated among White Democrats.

The bottom row of the left panel of Figure 12.7 shows that racial conservatism among Republicans exhibited a different pattern. More racially conservative Republicans were *more* likely to respond, although the effect was not statistically significant at conventional levels (p = 0.09, one-tailed). This means that the selection model estimate of racial conservatism of Republican was lower than the level observed in the sample.

12.5 POLICY PREFERENCES

The survey also asked respondents about their views on several policy questions on a five-point scale ranging from "strongly disapprove" to "strongly approve" including the following items:[10]

- *Global warming*: Views on "efforts to prevent future damage from global warming," scaled with higher values indicating support for more efforts to counter global warming.
- *Pro-tax cut*: Views on "the tax cut from December 2017," scaled with higher values indicating support for the tax cuts.
- *Pro-tariff*: Views on "increases on tariffs on goods imported into the US," scaled with higher values indicating support for tariffs.

For ease of interpretation, we analyze a dummy variable that equals one for respondents who selected the somewhat or strongly approve options; the results are similar if we use the ordered dependent variable.

The results are consistent across variables and models: There are limited signs of nonignorable nonresponse in the general population, but there are strong signs of nonignorable nonresponse within each party. We first discuss selection models and then turn to a comparison of those who did and did not choose to discuss politics, a comparison based on substantially different data, but which nonetheless reveals similar patterns.

SELECTION MODELS Figure 12.8 shows results from selection models for the global warming question. The top line of the panel on the left shows that the $\hat{\rho}$ parameter is very close to zero when the entire sample is used. However, as we have seen before, this masks party-level heterogeneity. The second bar in the left panel shows nonignorable nonresponse inflated support among Democrats, as the $\hat{\rho}$ parameter was positive with p = 0.08 (two-tailed). The third bar in the left panel shows nonignorable nonresponse deflated support among Republicans, as the $\hat{\rho}$ parameter was negative with p = 0.04 (two-tailed).

---

[10] The policy questions had wording experiments built into them. We control for treatment status for those experiments, but the results were similar whether we included this variable or not.

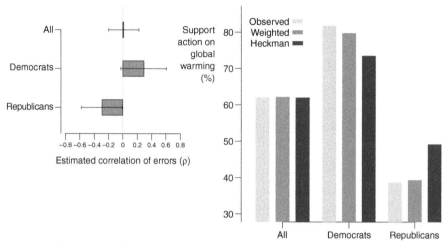

FIGURE 12.8 Support for action on global warming: Estimated ρ and predicted mean by group and model

The panel on the right of Figure 12.8 shows how model choice affects predicted values. When analyzing the whole data set, the observed, weighted, and selection model predictions are essentially unchanged. When analyzing Democrats, selection models produce lower levels of predicted support for efforts to fight global warming than the observed and weighted models because the selection model undoes the effects of positive response bias among Democrats. When analyzing Republicans, selection models produce higher levels of predicted support for efforts to fight global warming because the selection model undoes the effects of negative response bias among Republicans.

Figure 12.9 shows results for the tax cut question. The top line of the panel on the left shows that the $\hat{\rho}$ parameter is positive (p = 0.09, two-tailed) suggesting that support for the tax cut was overstated in the raw survey data. As before, there was party-level heterogeneity. The second bar in the left panel shows nonignorable nonresponse deflated support among Democrats but was not statistically significant by any reasonable standard. The third bar in the left panel shows that among Republicans, however, there were high levels of nonignorable nonresponse as the $\hat{\rho}$ parameter was large, positive, and statistically significant (p = 0.00, two-tailed).

The panel on the right of Figure 12.9 translates the models into predicted values. Among the entire population, support for tax cuts goes from 36 in the raw survey data to 33 percent in the weighted data and 28 percent in the data corrected for nonignorable nonresponse. Democratic support went up modestly across these models. The action was concentrated among Republicans, however. In the observed data, 66 percent of Republicans supported the tax cuts. Weighting pushed predicted support down a bit to 63 percent.

Nonignorable Nonresponse in Political Surveys

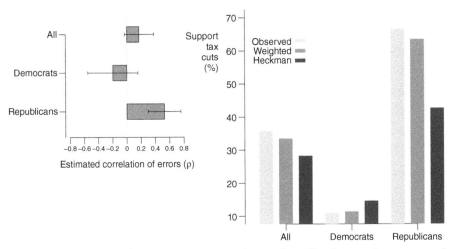

FIGURE 12.9 Support for tax cuts: Estimated ρ and predicted mean by group and model

Using a selection model to correct for nonignorable nonresponse reduced predicted support much more, down to 43 percent among Republicans, painting a substantially different picture than in the raw survey data.

The tax cut results suggest that nonignorable nonresponse inflated observed support for tax cuts. But the analysis of race of the same sample in Figure 12.7 suggested nonignorable nonresponse deflated conservative racial views. This seems odd: That nonresponse biases push in a conservative direction on taxes and a liberal direction on races. The partisan analysis clarifies what is going on. Democrats respondents were more liberal on race, so much so that they pulled the entire observed sample to the left on race. Meanwhile, Republican respondents were more conservative on taxes, so much so that they pulled the entire sample to the right on taxes. This highlights how question-dependent selection models can be, with results going in different directions depending on the topic.

Figure 12.10 shows results for the tariff question. The results are similar to the tax cut results, as the overall sample showed an inflation of support, which was concentrated among Republicans. The top line of the panel on the left shows that the $\hat{\rho}$ parameter is positive, although not statistically significant (p = 0.18, two-tailed). The second bar in the left panel shows nonignorable nonresponse deflated support among Democrats but was not statistically significant by any reasonable standard. The third bar in the left panel shows that among Republicans, however, there were high levels of nonignorable nonresponse as the $\hat{\rho}$ parameter was large, positive, and statistically significant (p = 0.00, two-tailed). The panel on the right of Figure 12.10 translates model results into predictions, showing how support for tariffs among Republicans is much lower when correcting for nonignorable nonresponse.

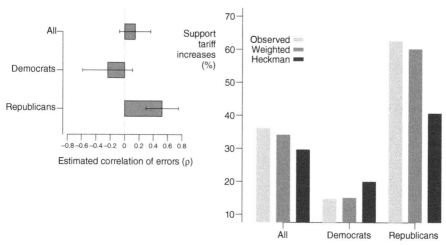

FIGURE 12.10 Support for tariffs: Estimated ρ and predicted mean by group and model

CONTINUUM OF RESPONSE MODELS Figure 12.1 shows that the treatment group included 393 people who chose to answer questions about politics and 713 people who chose to discuss something else. In a quirk of this survey design, we were able to later ask the politics questions of the 713 individuals who initially declined to discuss politics, giving us a sample of responses from people who were less interested in discussing politics. Such data allow us to implement a continuum of response analysis in which we measure response interest by whether or not an individual chose to discuss politics. In an ignorable nonresponse world, the people most and least interested in answering will have the same average values of Y once we control for covariates. In a nonignorable nonresponse world, these groups will have different political opinions.

The key point to keep in mind when viewing these results is that they are based on *different* data than the selection models, but yield the same results. The selection models used the political opinions of the 1,505 people who either were given no choice or chose to discuss politics as depicted in Figure 12.1. We included the covariates and treatment status of these 713 individuals in the first-stage response equation, but did not include anything data on them in the second-stage outcome models. Here, we winnowed down the data to the 1,106 people given a choice and are comparing the 393 people who chose politics to the 713 who did not. While data on the political views of the 393 people who chose politics were part of the selection models, this is a fresh use of the opinions of the 713 people who did not choose politics.

Figure 12.11 shows results from a continuum of response analysis of feeling thermometers toward prominent politicians in which we compare those who did and did not choose politics for Democrats and Republicans separately. The

Nonignorable Nonresponse in Political Surveys

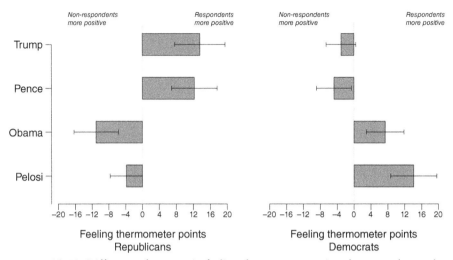

FIGURE 12.11 Differences by party in feeling thermometer ratings between those who chose political questions and those who did not, 2019 survey. Lines indicate 95 percent confidence intervals

lines indicate 95 percent confidence intervals. We controlled for age, gender, education, income, race, and Hispanic ethnicity.

The panel on the left shows that the Republicans who chose to discuss politics were 14 points warmer toward Trump, 13 points warmer toward Pence, 11 points cooler toward Obama, and 4 points cooler toward Pelosi. In other words, the eager respondents had more partisan views. The panel on the right shows that the Democrats who chose to discuss politics went the other way. They were 3 and 5 points cooler toward Trump and Pence and 7 and 14 points warmer toward Obama and Pelosi. The differences were smaller and not statistically significant for some of the models such as the one for Republican evaluations of Pelosi. That does not mean that Republicans viewed Pelosi favorably. They did not. It signifies only that the Republicans who did and did not choose to discuss politics had similar views about her, controlling for demographics.

Figure 12.12 shows results from a continuum of response analysis of other questions. In order to make the comparisons across questions roughly comparable, we have standardized them. As before, we compare those who did and did not choose politics for Democrats and Republicans separately. The lines indicate 95 percent confidence intervals. We controlled for age, gender, education, income, race, and Hispanic ethnicity.

Turnout is at the top of the figures for each party. For Republicans and Democrats, the people who chose politics were substantially more likely to answer positively about their likelihood of voting. Notably, the differences go in the same direction and are of similar magnitude for both parties. Whether

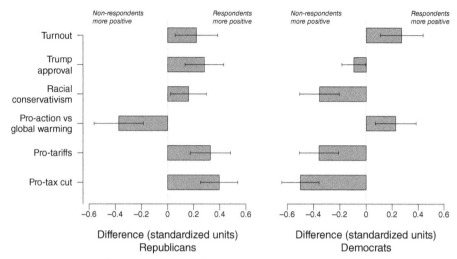

FIGURE 12.12 Differences among all respondents in answers to political questions between those who chose political questions and those who did not, 2019 survey, by response group. Lines indicate 95 percent confidence intervals

people are Democrats or Republicans, choosing to discuss politics, was associated with being more willing to say they would vote. The parties do not agree in this way on any of the other questions.

For the rest of the questions, the Republicans who chose politics expressed more conventionally conservative or pro-Trump opinions on approval of Trump, race, climate, tariffs, or taxes.[11] Meanwhile, Democrats who chose politics expressed more conventionally liberal opinions on all these questions.

12.6 CONCLUSION

This book argues that we should fight nonignorable nonresponse bias. This chapter shows how. I summarized results from a single survey, but the patterns were similar in other surveys that used a similar design.

The findings are interesting on several fronts. For turnout, selection models always find signs of nonignorable nonresponse. This is reassuring – if we're ever going to see nonignorable nonresponse, turnout is where we'll see it. It is also useful as the selection models put us on a path toward more accurate assessment of turnout and its associations.

On support for politicians, we saw an example in which there were no signs of nonignorable nonresponse in the general population. This was not always the case for all politicians across all surveys, but was common. When

---

[11] Tariffs do not map easily onto traditional left-right or partisan divisions (Bailey 2001). In 2019, the tariffs were backed by Trump and appear to have therefore appealed to the Republicans more willing to discuss politics.

Nonignorable Nonresponse in Political Surveys 233

support was analyzed by party, however, it was almost universally the case that there were partisan differences. Democrats eager to talk about politics loved Democratic politicians and reviled Republican politicians. Republicans did the opposite: They adored Republican politicians and loathed Democratic politicians. Polls – even after weighting – appear prone to mislead about within party support and, therefore, to exaggerate cross-party differences.

Selection models also prove useful when analyzing attitudes and policy preferences. On a sensitive topic such as race, our poll showed strong signs that people with more racially conservative views were less likely to respond. This effect was concentrated among Democrats and White Democrats in particular, suggesting that we should be cautious about raw or weighted survey data about Democratic views on race.

On other policies, the pattern was similar to that seen in support for politicians. Among the general population, we saw occasional evidence of nonignorable nonresponse. Among partisan subgroups, however, we always found partisan differences in nonignorable nonresponse. As with questions about political leaders, one consequence was that differences across parties appeared larger in observed and weighted data than they did when that data were corrected for nonignorable nonresponse.

There are, of course, limits to what we have found. First, this is one, but only one, way to design a survey with a randomized response instrument. The *New York Times*/Siena team offered another, and there are countless other possible permutations. Which approach is best will depend on the resources and interests of the survey designer.

Second, the specific estimates of population levels depend on parametric form. We have focused on Heckman selection models in this chapter, but could also estimate copula and NINR weights (see Bailey 2023). The literature has yet to definitely land on an optimal way of choosing among competing models. For now, I recommend creating randomized response instruments and running selection models for questions and subgroups where nonignorable nonresponse is a credible possibility. If there is no sign of nonignorable nonresponse, the analyst should stick with weights, with their confidence bolstered by having using data to justify the assumption of ignorable nonresponse needed for weighting to work. If there are signs of nonignorable nonresponse – and we saw many such signs in this and other surveys – then the analysis should at a minimum highlight the possibility that the weighted data are wrong. Analysts can also use multiple surveys and multiple methods to identify a range of plausible outcomes consistent with selection model output.

Even as the results in this chapter should not be taken as a comprehensive account of what is possible when modeling nonignorable nonresponse, they provide several key lessons.

1. Nonignorable nonresponse is a chronic, not acute, problem. It can arise on any survey and on any question and potentially within subsamples.

There will never be a single parameter or model that fixes data across all surveys and questions. The fight must be fought question-to-question, survey-to-survey. While we may wish for an easier answer, surely it is the only realistic one given that just as opinions vary over time, so too does people's willingness to engage with pollsters.

2. While the scale of the fight is daunting, it is not overwhelming. Once we have response-related variables, there is a range of diagnostics available to us and they tend to lead to similar conclusions for any given question and subsample. Serious polling teams should build diagnostics and, if necessary, correctives for nonignorable nonresponse into their workflow. While model choice is important, the fundamental decision is to create a randomized response instrument.

3. People who want to talk about politics are indeed weird as David Shor noted in the epigraph for this chapter. Not surprisingly, survey respondents tend to be more partisan and ideological. Survey respondents may also be more likely to show up at political rallies, volunteer for campaigns, post on Facebook, and otherwise engage in political life. The good news is that these biases often offset each other when extreme Democrats balance extreme Republicans. The bad news is that surveys as currently analyzed are prone to exaggerating partisan differences (see Cavari and Freedman 2018, 2023). Political differences across parties are, no doubt, serious and may be growing. We should not let our polls make matters worse.

13

Nonignorable Nonresponse in Public Health

> We need smart coronavirus testing, not just more testing.
> Mostashari and Emanuel (2020)

There are many fields where nonresponse looms large. Economists use polls to gauge employment, income, expectations, and other quantities important to the functioning of the economy. What if the most or least well-off are most likely to respond? Many businesses live and die based on marketing data from consumers. What if they hear disproportionately from consumers who are most or least pleased with their products and ideas? Sociologists' surveys often include sensitive topics; what if only the least embarrassed respond? Data scientists seek to generalize observed behavior on social media to broader populations. What if having distinctively strong opinions is what leads people to be active on social media? In all of these efforts, it is clear that analysts must take seriously the possibility that the quantity of interest may directly or indirectly affect the probability that individuals make it into their data.

This chapter focuses on population health, an area where nonignorable nonresponse is particularly relevant. For many conditions, the decision to get tested or the willingness to allow a test is deeply wrapped up in the likelihood of having the condition. During Covid, for example, people who thought they might have been exposed to the virus were almost certainly more likely to get tested. For tuberculosis, doctors guide patients with high-risk profiles to get tested (Burger and McLaren 2017). Is it possible to estimate population-level prevalence given such targeted testing?

In Chapter 12, we discussed the *New York Times'* Wisconsin survey experiment in which some people were paid to respond and others were not. The people offered money responded at much higher rates. If their responses were similar to the responses of the people who did not get paid, we would have evidence that response is ignorable. And, indeed, that was the case for the questions about the 2022 midterm election. That was not the case for

236   *Part IV: Applications*

all questions, though. There were, for example, differences across response treatments with regard to Covid vaccinations. The people who responded to the nonpayment protocol were 6 percentage points more likely to have had three or more shots and 8 percentage points less likely to have two or fewer shots, suggesting that response propensity could be correlated with vaccination behavior. If that's the case, of course, simply weighting the observed survey responses from a conventional survey would likely overstate vaccination uptake, something consistent with the Bradley et al. (2021) findings reported in Chapter 1.

Nonignorable nonresponse complicated our ability to understand the Covid outbreak. Two measures of prevalence data were widely available at the regional level during the pandemic: The total number of people testing positive and the positivity rates of those being tested. The usefulness of both pieces of information depends on the testing environment. For example, what do we make of reported case numbers in a region? Surely extrapolation to the population hinges on how widespread testing is and the extent to which sick people are more likely to get tested. Or, what are we make of changes in positivity rates? Is it because of a change in testing or prevalence or – most likely – both?

The ideal way to assess prevalence is, of course, randomized testing. As with public opinion polling, this is easier said than done. People do not always accept an invitation to test, perhaps balking at devoting time to show up for a potentially unpleasant test that could yield results that could prove inconvenient or worse. And the costs to researchers are much higher than polling given the need for physical samples, making it harder to implement at granular geographies or over time. Hence, disease testing, even disease testing that is part of a randomized process, is deeply vulnerable to the now all-too-familiar problems associated nonignorable nonresponse.

This chapter uses the tools presented in this book to characterize the problem and explore potential tools for producing meaningful community-level measures of disease prevalence. Section 1 discusses the challenge of estimating public health variables in terms of a nonignorable missing data problem. Section 2 explores how first-stage instruments can improve the efficiency and accuracy of efforts to assess prevalence. Section 3 presents a framework for comparing Covid positivity rates across regions even when testing rates differ.

13.1 POPULATION-LEVEL HEALTH AS A NONRESPONSE PROBLEM

We begin with a two-stage model in which the propensity to be tested is

$$R_i^* = \gamma_0 + \gamma_1 X_i + \tau_i$$

where γ_1 is $1xk$ parameter vector, X_i is a $kx1$ vector of covariates, and τ_i is a mean-zero random variable. We observe i's test results if $R_i^* > 0$.

Nonignorable Nonresponse in Public Health 237

The outcome of interest, Y_i, is whether person i has the coronavirus. $Y_i = 1$ if $Y_i^* > 0$ where

$$Y_i^* = \beta_0 + \beta_1 X_i + \epsilon_i$$

Prevalence is a function of the β parameters. In most of our illustrations, we'll assume that the errors are bivariate normally distributed with the correlation of ϵ_i and τ_i equal to ρ. Any analysis of data would, of course, explore the parametric and semi-parametric landscape using the tools described in Chapter 9.

There are two sources of nonresponse. First is ignorable nonresponse. If we believe that nonresponse can be fully explained by measured demographics such as age, gender, and education, we can use the tools described in Chapter 3 to fully offset nonresponse problem. Chapter 5 discussed a 2020 California study of Covid antibody seroprevalence that used weights to account for nonresponse (Bendavid et al. 2020). Researchers recruited participants with targeted Facebook ads. The 3,330 people who were tested were demographically unrepresentative of the county. For example, 8 percent of the sample was Hispanic, lower than the 26 percent of the county population. The unadjusted prevalence was 1.5 percent; the weighted prevalence was 2.8 percent.

For such a weighting approach to be valid, the nonresponse needed to be ignorable. That is, conditional on covariates, the distribution of disease in the sample is the same as in the population. Many commenters on the California study noted that the sample may have differed from the underlying population not only in terms of observable characteristics such as age, ethnicity, and zip code, but also in terms of unobserved characteristics such as health status.

Hence, many efforts to assess population-level health characteristics focus on the second, more insidious version of nonresponse that occurs when nonresponse is related to the outcome the test is trying to measure (Marden et al. 2018; Sun, Liu, Miao, Wirth, Robins, and Tchetgen Tchetgen 2018; Wang, Shao, and Kim 2014; Miao, Ding, and Geng, 2016). For most Covid testing, we suspect those tested are more likely to be sick, even after controlling for demographics; this is true for tuberculosis as well (Burger and McLaren 2017). For some diseases such as HIV, it is possible those tested are less likely to be sick (Marra et al. 2017; McGovern, Canning, and Bärnighausen 2018).

As discussed in Section 8.2, nonignorable nonresponse creates a statistical identification problem. Figure 13.1 shows the relationship between prevalence and observed positive test results when 10 percent of the population is tested and the errors are assumed to follow a bivariate normal distribution with various levels of ρ, the correlation in errors in the two equations.

The line at the top of Figure 13.1 shows the relationship between actual and observed test results when the propensity to get tested is strongly related to the propensity to be sick ($\rho = 0.9$). Point A indicates that for this level of ρ, the test results will be positive 60 percent of the time when the prevalence in the general population is 8 percent. When there is no relationship between

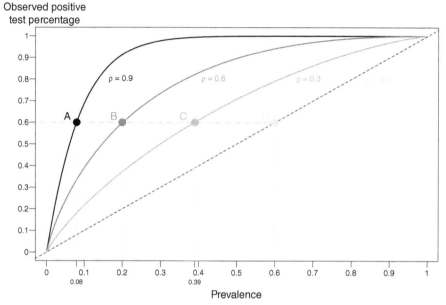

FIGURE 13.1 Relationship between prevalence and test results for various levels of ρ

getting tested and being sick ($\rho = 0$), a 60 percent positive test rate is simply associated with a 60 percent prevalence (point D). In other words, points A, B, C, and D all explain the observed outcome of 60 percent positive tests equally well: A prevalence of 8 percent with a ρ of 0.9 (point A) explains the data as well as a prevalence of 60 percent with a ρ of 0.0 (point D).

As testing rates change, the mapping of results back to prevalence becomes more complex and depends on ρ. Figure 13.2 illustrates how testing rates and identification problems interact. In the top panel, expected rates of positive tests (out of those being tested) are plotted as a function of prevalence for two testing regimes for $\rho = 0.7$, an environment in which sick people are much more likely to be tested. The dark line on the top is for a low testing regime in which only 1 percent of the population is tested. As one would expect, when tests are rare and sick people are more likely to get tested, the positive test rate is quite high. Point A indicates prevalence is 2 percent when the expected positive rate is 40 percent and 1 percent of the population for $\rho = 0.7$.

The lighter colored line in the top panel of the figure plots the positive test rate for a regime in which testing is vastly expanded (to 20 percent of the population). While the positive test rate is still much higher than the prevalence, it is lower than when 1 percent was being tested as many more people are being tested. Point B in the top panel of the figure indicates that prevalence is 5 percent when the expected positive rate is 20 percent and 20 percent of the population is tested.

Nonignorable Nonresponse in Public Health

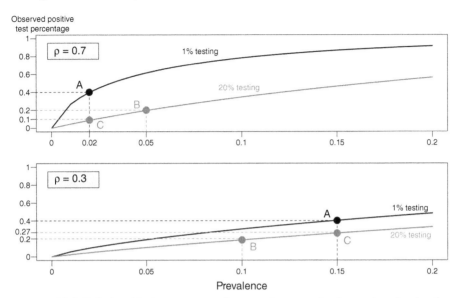

FIGURE 13.2 Relationship between prevalence and test results for various levels of ρ and testing rates

In the scenario depicted in the top panel of the figure, it is actually bad news to observe the positive test rate falling from 40 percent to 20 percent when we increase the testing percent from 1 to 20 percent. That is, going from point A to point B suggests that prevalence has gone from 2 percent to 5 percent, even as the positive test rate has fallen markedly. In order to infer the prevalence is the same or falling, the increase in testing would need to produce a positive rate lower than that indicated by point C, which is about 10 percent. In other words, when the sick are much more likely to be tested, increasing testing needs to lead to a dramatic fall in positive test rates in order to suggest a fall in prevalence.

The lower panel of the figure shows a similar plot but for a situation in which the relationship between testing and being sick is much lower ($\rho = 0.3$). In this bottom panel, point A indicates that the expected positive rate is 40 percent when prevalence is 15 percent, 1 percent of the population is tested, and $\rho = 0.3$. Compared to the top panel, there is a weaker relationship between being sick and testing and a given positive test rate is associated with a higher prevalence. Point B indicates that the expected positive rate is 20 percent when prevalence is 10 percent and 20 percent of the population is tested. In the limit, when $\rho = 0$ the positive test rate is, in expectation, the prevalence.

In the scenario depicted in the bottom panel of Figure 13.2, a drop from 40 percent positive rate to a 20 percent positive rate is good news. That is, going from point A to point suggests prevalence has fallen from 15 percent to

10 percent. When $\rho = 0.3$, any drop below the point indicated by point C (27 percent positive rate) is consistent with a fall in prevalence.

These scenarios make it clear that the mapping from observed positivity rates to community prevalence is a complex function of testing rates and the relationship between the likelihood of being sick and choosing to test. The problems are not necessarily insurmountable, however. If we were able to estimate ρ (or an analogous parameter for a different parametric model), we could use information such as that shown in Figure 13.1 to map observable test percentages back to prevalence in light of testing rates. That is, if we know which curve to look at, positivity rates will map back to specific prevalence rates.

13.2 FIRST-STAGE INSTRUMENTS FOR RANDOMIZED TESTING WITH NONRESPONSE

In the spirit of "design trumps analysis," the best way to know ρ is to design the data collection so that it must be zero. This is done, of course, via randomized testing, which ensures that $\rho = 0$ in expectation (Mostashari and Emanuel 2020). Early in the pandemic, Iceland randomly identified 6,782 Icelanders between the ages of 20 and 70 to be tested (Gudbjartsson et al. 2020). Many other regions also considered or implemented such programs.

There are two major challenges with randomized testing. The first is that not everyone chosen to be tested will submit to a test. In the Iceland study, only 33.7 percent of those randomly chosen to be tested were tested (Gudbjartsson et al. 2020). The risk is clear: If only the sickest third of randomly targeted people in the Iceland study were tested, the observed test results would vastly overestimate prevalence.[1] The second challenge is cost. Prevalence surveillance requires labs, personnel, and marketing. And if the goal is to monitor changes over time and across regions, this infrastructure will have to be large-scale and ongoing.

A second approach to dealing with nonignorable nonresponse is to analyze the data using minimal assumptions, as is done via the bounds approach discussed in Chapter 7. While the generality of bounds makes them attractive, they often are not useful practically. Bounds analysis for high-impact regions in April 2020 bounded infection rates between 0 and 50 percent for Illinois and New York and between 0 and 64 percent for Italy (Manski and Molinari 2020).

A third approach to dealing with nonignorable nonresponse is to use first-stage instruments. Nonignorable nonresponse models generally require that we must have at least one variable that explains whether people get tested and does not explain whether they test positive. Recent epidemiological research has shown that prevalence can be estimated with data short of a full-scale randomization (Sun, Liu, Miao, Wirth, Robins, and Tchetgen Tchetgen 2018;

---

[1] Contact tracing also suffers from nonresponse (Siegel, Abdelmalek, and Bhatt 2020).

Nonignorable Nonresponse in Public Health 241

Wang, Shao and Kim 2014; Miao, Ding and Geng, 2016). Specifically, if we have data that predict testing propensity but not health status, prevalence is statistically identifiable under a broad range of assumptions.

Broadly speaking, first-stage instruments allow us to estimate ρ, which in turn allows to home in on the correct prevalence. The existence of a first-stage instrument implies that there are high and low probability of being tested groups. If $\rho > 0$, the low probability group will have a higher probability of testing positive. The high testing probability group will include not only the types who would have gotten tested if they had been in the low probability group, but also a group of people who would not have gotten tested in the low probability group. If $\rho > 0$, these people will have lower probability of testing positive because they have a lower propensity of being tested.

A metaphor may be helpful. Imagine a hospital with two doors. Two hundred people show up in order of how sick they are, with the sickest people showing up first. They line up at these two doors, with the choice of doors being completely random. The first 20 people at door A are tested, and the first 80 people at door B are tested. If the proportion who are sick from these two groups is the same, the eagerness of getting tested is not related to being sick, which suggests $\rho = 0$. If people at door A test positively at a higher rate, we have evidence that eagerness to get tested is related to testing positive. The specific difference in proportions of positive tests at the two doors will be a function of ρ.

The key step in that metaphor is the randomized assignment of patients to the high-test or low-test door. A variable, T_i, measuring assignment therefore belongs in the response equation but has no direct effect on Y. For example, one could identify a random sample of people to be tested (as done in Iceland) and then also randomly divide these people into a group that is contacted once and a group that is contacted multiple times. Being in the multiple contact group will not directly affect the likelihood of being sick but will likely increase participation, an expectation that is easily tested empirically.

This approach is particularly useful for a large-scale randomized sample approach when nontrivial noncompliance is expected. To illustrate the estimation process, I simulate data and then use the model discussed earlier to estimate prevalence for three hypothetical states. We assume each state has identified a random sample of 3,000 people for testing. We also assume a strong relationship between the testing and outcome equations ($\rho = 0.7$).

Table 13.1 describes the states. Importantly, states 1 and 2 implement a first-stage randomization protocol such that 20 percent of those selected initially are subject to more extensive outreach that increases their probability of consenting to being tested by 20 percentage points. State 3 does no such randomization.

Figure 13.3 shows the results based on 50 simulations for each state using maximum likelihood via the optim function in R. The bars in the panel on the left show the observed positive rates among those tested, and the black lines

TABLE 13.1 *Characteristics of states in simulation*

State	Prevalence	Baseline response rate	Testing approach
State 1	10 percent	50 percent	First-stage instrument
State 2	20 percent	30 percent	First-stage instrument
State 3	30 percent	30 percent	No randomization

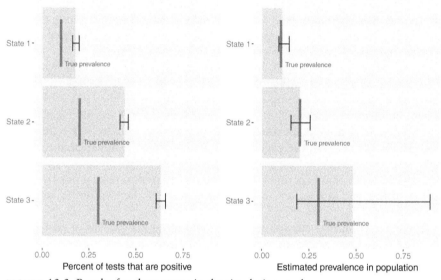

FIGURE 13.3 Results for three states in the simulation study

show the 95th percentile range across the simulations. The thick gray lines at 0.1, 0.2, and 0.3 in the states 1, 2, and 3, respectively, show the prevalence in the states. For every state, the percent of tests that are positive is clearly higher than the true prevalence indicated with the thick gray line. This panel illustrates the well-known fact that positive test rates will run higher than prevalence when sick people are more likely to be tested.

The panel on the right of Figure 13.3 shows the more important point that prevalence can be estimated from data when we have a first-stage instrument. The bars are the estimated prevalence results using a Heckman model and the first-stage instrument when available. The prevalence estimates for states 1 and 2 are, on average, quite accurate. In state 1, the average prevalence estimate across the simulations is 10.7 percent, which is close to the true prevalence. In state 2, the average prevalence estimate across the simulations is essentially equal to the true prevalence.

Not only are the average estimates accurate, but they are also precise. The prevalence estimates range from 9 percent to 14 percent for state 1 and from

Nonignorable Nonresponse in Public Health 243

15 percent to 25 percent for state 2. Increasing the sample size, the size of the treatment group or the magnitude of the effect of the randomization on the probability of being tested will increase accuracy.

State 3, the state with no first-stage instrument, presents a very different story in the panel on the right of Figure 13.3. The average estimate of prevalence for state 3 is 48 percent, far from the true value of 30 percent. The confidence interval ranges from 18 percent to 89 percent. The poor estimate for state 3 occurs because, as illustrated in Figure 13.1, the observed test results can be explained by many different combinations of ρ and prevalence when there is no variable that affects the decision to test, but not the results of the test. Note that this is the case even though we have in some sense made it easier for us to estimate the correct prevalence in state 3 because our parametric model matches the parametric model used to generate the data.

Adding a first-stage instrument to randomized testing is a low-cost approach to addressing inevitable nonresponse in randomized testing. However, it is likely that most locales will not have the resources to conduct randomized testing once, let alone across multiple time periods. It is likely that sampling people who have already shown up at a given location is likely to be more feasible and sustainable. For example, the Centers for Disease Control and Prevention created a system to test 325,000 people in 25 metropolitan areas at blood donation centers (Janes 2020). Similarly, the state of New York tested 15,000 people at grocery stores and community centers in April (Cuomo 2020).

As we have seen so far, we cannot translate the positivity rates from such testing into prevalence measures. We could lower our ambitions and take the changes in positivity rates as a sign of accelerating or abating prevalence, but even that requires an assumption that ρ is constant over time. If, however, we can estimate ρ over time, we can normalize the estimates to make them comparable over time and useful for estimating community prevalence.

The key to being able to extract useful information from localized nonrandom testing would be to for testing authorities to pick a random subset of the population to encourage to visit the testing site. Perhaps this would simply be a text message, email, phone call, or letter. As long as there would be an identifiable group for whom the probability of visiting the testing site was higher for reasons unrelated to their propensity to be sick. With such information, prevalence and change over time would be potentially identifiable even when the people being tested are not a representative sample of the full population.

Table 13.2 summarizes approaches to dealing with this problem. Weighting is likely biased due to nonignorable nonresponse. Randomized testing reduces nonignorable nonresponse bias, but may not eliminate it if there is less than perfect compliance. Randomized first-stage instruments can build in the data to diagnose and adjust for the nonresponse and can be extended to localized nonrandom testing as well. The challenges of such an approach include the fact that a complete analysis would need to explore a range of functional

244   *Part IV: Applications*

TABLE 13.2 *Summary of approaches to nonresponse*

Approach	Advantages	Disadvantages
Weighting	Simple given census data	Requires sick people who are no more/less likely to get tested
Randomized testing	Produces unbiased estimates	Expensive. Potentially biased if not everyone responds
First-stage instrument	Produces unbiased estimates	Can be model dependent. Not widely understood

forms, with either copulas or semi-parametric models. In addition, the logic of response instruments has yet to be broadly recognized (Bailey 2020).

13.3 ADJUSTING PREVALENCE FOR TESTING RATES

One of the challenges in the Covid era is that it has been difficult to compare testing data across regions when both prevalence and testing vary across regions. If it is true that sick people are more likely to get tested, we're likely to observe high positivity rates when testing is limited. As a region expands testing, the people getting tested may continue to be unrepresentative of the entire population, but will nonetheless pull in more healthy people into the testing pool and positivity rates may decline even if prevalence is unchanged or even increasing.

This means that it is hard to compare testing data across states. Figure 13.4 shows positivity rates and testing rates in US stages at a given point in time. Four states are shaded in gray. The positivity rates in Louisiana and Kansas are similar. Should we infer that Covid prevalence is similar as well? Is Arizona really as extreme an outlier as it appears? And can we say anything about a state like Minnesota that is in the middle of a cluster of states with similar testing and positivity rates?

These issues arise in many contexts. Mostashari and Emanuel (2020) noted that "based simply on the number of positive cases, young adults would appear to be at highest risk of covid-19 in South Korea. But is that due to higher testing rates among this age group? We don't know." In India, differences in testing rates across states are even larger than in the United States. (Khaitan and Bharadwa 2020). In addition, there are substantial differences in testing rates and positivity by gender, with men testing at almost twice the rates of women. Among those tested, women have a higher positivity rate. Does that mean that incidence is higher among women?

The nonignorable nonresponse toolkit can also help us calibrate the observed positivity rates across the contexts in light of the differences in testing rates. We will present a simple version of this approach, one in which we

Nonignorable Nonresponse in Public Health 245

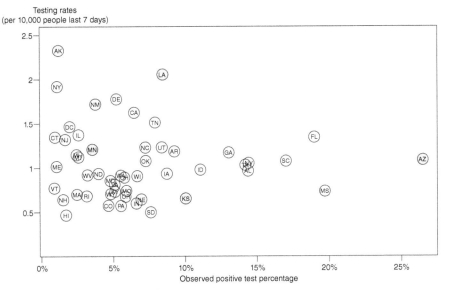

FIGURE 13.4 Testing rates and positivity

normalize testing data for a given ρ. A complete approach would be to estimate ρ or equivalent parameters across states and then back out prevalence. Given that first-stage response instruments have not been created, we do not have the infrastructure to estimate ρ. However, we can at least calibrate for hypothesized reasonable values of this parameter.

The core challenge is that any given state's test results can be consistent with almost any level of prevalence in the state. To see this, consider the case of Arizona in late July 2020, a time when around 1 percent of the people were tested in a week and, of those tested, a remarkable 25 percent tested positive. How can we translate this information into an estimate of prevalence in the broader Arizona population?

Figure 13.5 illustrates the issue by presenting prevalence as a function of ρ which indicates how strong the relationship between being sick and getting tested is. When ρ equals zero, there is no relationship between health status and getting sick and, as noted above, we can reasonably estimate that 25 of people in Arizona are sick. As ρ gets higher, the population tested becomes systematically more likely to be sick and we should, therefore, lower our prevalence estimate relative to the $\rho = 0$ case. In the extreme, as noted above, our prevalence estimate becomes very low. (For completeness, Figure 13.5 also shows estimated prevalence for negative values of ρ, cases in which sick people are *less* likely to get tested. While not impossible, this seems unlikely. But logically, it's useful to see that if ρ were negative, prevalence is *higher* than the 25 percent positivity rate observed.)

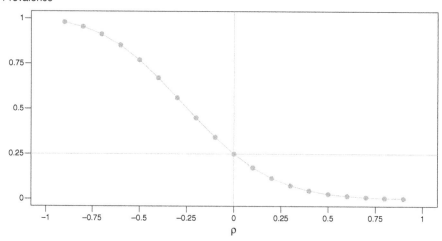

FIGURE 13.5 Prevalence as a function of ρ for Arizona

Knowing the value of ρ allows us to translate test results combined with testing percent into a prevalence estimate. We can then estimate the expected number of cases a state would produce for any given level of testing. We can then set the testing level to be the same for all states and thereby compare their prevalence estimates, net of differences in actual testing proportions.

We do this by creating equivalence lines that show how the combinations of testing rates and positivity rates reflect similar levels of prevalence. Figure 13.6 illustrates an example in which there is a strong relationship between the probability of being sick and getting tested ($\rho = 0.75$). More generally, these lines will depend on ρ and the parametric model connecting response and outcomes. A quick rule of thumb is the higher ρ is, the flatter the equivalence lines become. The lower the ρ is, the more vertical the lines become. In the limit, the lines are vertical when ρ, which is the case when sampling is truly random and the positivity rates can be directly compared.

We focus first on Arizona on the right in Figure 13.6. The line through the state indicates what the observed positivity rate would be as Arizona changed its testing. Higher testing would lead to a lower positivity rate; less testing would lead to higher positivity rates. Whatever the level of testing, it is clear that Arizona was in dire straits.

Next, look at Louisiana, highlighted and toward the top of the figure. The state's positivity rate was near that of Kansas, but Louisiana tested at a higher rate. The line indicates that if Louisiana tested at the same rate as Kansas they would have had a higher positivity rate. Specifically, the gray horizontal line in the figure indicates that if Louisiana lowered its testing rate to Kansas's testing rate, Louisiana would have had a positivity rate of about 17 percent, much higher than Kansas's positivity rate of about 10 percent. In other words,

Nonignorable Nonresponse in Public Health 247

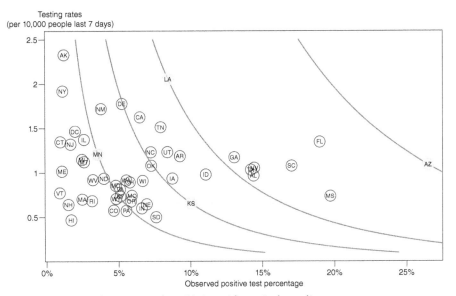

FIGURE 13.6 Testing rates and positivity with equivalence lines

accounting for differences in testing, Covid prevalence was higher in Louisiana than in Kansas even though both states had similar positivity rates. We can also see that once we normalize positivity rates for testing rates, Kansas was quite similar to Oklahoma and Delaware, as these two states were on Kansas's equivalence line.

Finally, look at Minnesota. The state's 4 percent positive tests and testing rate of 1.2 per 10,000 put it in the middle of a cluster of states. South Dakota's 6 percent positive test percentage was higher, but it tested many fewer people (0.5 per 10,000), putting it near the equivalence line for Minnesota. In other words, despite a substantially higher positivity rate, the low rate of testing in South Dakota meant that the prevalence was quite similar as in Minnesota.

This exercise is both constructive and cautionary. On the constructive side, we have compared positivity rates given a set of plausible assumptions. At a minimum, we can use something like this to make positivity rates more comparable than what we currently are able to do. The exercise is cautionary as well, however. Comparing positivity rates requires a model and some information that can be hard to come by. Most obviously, we need an estimate of ρ or its equivalent for another parametric model. This parameter will likely vary by state and over time.

So even as we appreciate the tentative nature of these estimates, we can at least conceptually map out how adjusting for testing rates could affect our understanding of the progression of the disease. This is particularly relevant

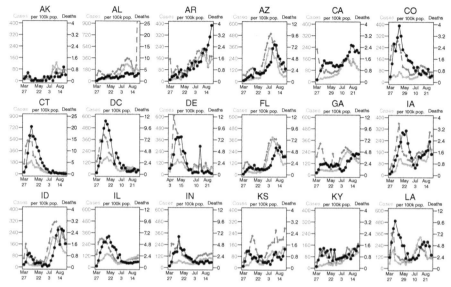

FIGURE 13.7 Cases, adjusted cases, and deaths by state, part 1

when looking over time as testing capacity was extremely limited early in the pandemic meaning that it would be ill advised to directly compare prevalence based on either per capita positive cases or positivity rates over time.

Figures 13.7 through 13.9 show the caseloads, deaths, and adjusted caseloads for each state. All measures are reported per 100,000 in people. Deaths are denoted with a darked line with the values on the right side of the figures; reported caseloads are solid gray lines and adjusted caseloads dashed gray lines based on the logic presented in this section.

The value of ρ used in the adjusted case load calculated was selected to maximize the predictive power of the model with regard to future deaths. Specifically, the above model was used to estimate prevalence for a series of values of ρ. Then, these values were converted to the predicted number of observed cases in the case that the given state tested 2 percent of its population in a given week. This produces adjusted caseloads per 100,000 people per week for each state for each value of ρ, the lagged values of which were then used to predict death rates per 100,000 people per week. The value of ρ that produced the highest fit was 0.4. This should be taken as a plausible value rather than a fully defensible estimate (which would require first-stage instruments, as discussed in Section 13.2).

The data for most states are scaled from 0 to 400 for the case variables and from 0 to 4 for deaths. However, some state measures exceed these limits for one or both. New York and New Jersey are on a scale of 0 to 900 for cases and 0 to 25 for deaths, for example. Some data reported by states are

Nonignorable Nonresponse in Public Health 249

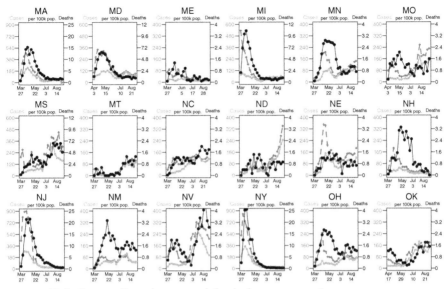

FIGURE 13.8 Cases, adjusted cases, and deaths by state, part 2

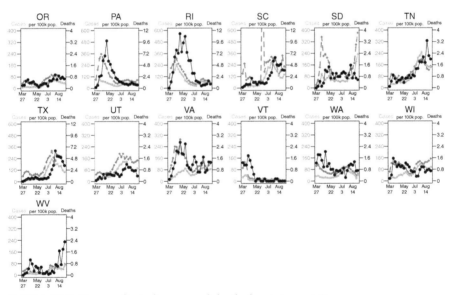

FIGURE 13.9 Cases, adjusted cases, and deaths by state, part 3

clearly anomalous. For example, Colorado reported *negative* 200 deaths on one day in May. Louisiana reported *minus* 2,999 negative results on a single day in April. New Jersey added 1,854 cases in a single day when they started

250   *Part IV: Applications*

including probable cases. These observations have been excluded and show up as either gaps in the lines or data that starts later than week 1.

Even accepting the imprecise adjustments, we see that adjusting caseloads for testing rates casts the evolution of the disease in a starkly different light. Consider Colorado in Figure 13.7. The actual cases depicted by the solid gray line show modest variation, variation that seems unrelated to the death rates depicted with the dark line. The dashed gray line adjusts for testing rates. Early in the pandemic when testing was limited, the caseloads are adjusted up; later in the pandemic when testing was more common, there adjustments are smaller. Notice how the adjusted case load depicted by the dashed gray line anticipates the spike death rates, something not clear with the actual case load data. Something similar is apparent in other states such as Connecticut, Delaware, Iowa, Illinois, Indiana, and others.

Although these adjusted measures seem to better predict death rates for some states, they should be taken as a test of concept rather than firm estimates. The value of ρ used, while reasonable, is estimated via a calibration that is not particularly precise. The space of parametric models has not been thoroughly explored, and the value of ρ or equivalent parameter likely varies across states and time.

13.4 CONCLUSION

Nonignorable nonresponse can cause bias in many contexts. This chapter applies the concepts and tools for dealing with nonignorable nonresponse developed in this book to public health, with a particular focus on Covid. The point is not only to show that nonignorable nonresponse plays an important role in public health, but more generally to show how the ideas developed in this book can travel from politics to other realms.

For Covid, a challenge is that it is difficult to generalize about disease prevalence when those who are sick are more likely to get tested and different regions test at different rates. Weighting requires assumptions that are unreasonable in the disease testing context. Randomized testing is expensive and inevitably suffers from nonresponse.

The nonignorable nonresponse approach offers a path toward improving data collection. Specifically, response instruments enable estimation of prevalence even when nonresponse is nonignorable. The statistical properties of first-stage instruments have received increasing attention as discussed in the literature reviewed here. But first-stage instruments are also relatively simple tools for policymakers. Typically, one identifies a sample of interest and randomly picks a subset who are recruited more heavily. This is easy to add on to any large-scale randomization effort and can also be incorporated into location-based testing. First-stage randomizations do not solve all testing challenges. The sensitivity and specificity of testing technology need to be accounted for, as do the practical challenges of implementing any testing

Nonignorable Nonresponse in Public Health 251

approach. Nonetheless, they offer a path for distilling real information from any real-world testing regime that will likely suffer from nonresponse, much of which may be nonignorable.

One of the frustrating aspects of the Covid pandemic was that information was *available*, but not *informative*. Many states and countries reported how many people tested positive and the percent of tests that were positive. But such information did not directly inform us about community prevalence. If we model the testing process as a nonignorable nonresponse problem, however, we can convert such information into community prevalence estimates. Fully doing this would require randomized testing and randomized response instruments, but even with the data we have and some estimates about the nonignorability of testing can convert test results into community prevalence. Until full protocols to estimate full selection models are implemented, these results can provide a conceptual framework for putting the results into context.

14

Conclusion

> The future is really messy.
>
> Bob Groves, in Habermann, Kennedy, and Lahiri (2017)

It is important to get surveys right. Surveys help us anticipate, validate, and understand political, social, and economic life. Right now, they have been getting things wrong often enough that distrust of them is widespread.

It is difficult to get surveys right. Technical and social changes have unmoored survey research from the elegance of random sampling theory. Response rates are low. Probability-based polling is becoming untenable. Nonignorable nonresponse is more likely to arise and more likely to cause damage in the modern context.

Hard as the problem may be, it is not impossible. While no unambiguously definitive solution is at hand, new models, new data, and simply new commitment to dealing with the problem can help us better counter nonignorable nonresponse. Sometimes the signs of nonignorable nonresponse have been hiding in plain sight, such as the drop-off in support for Biden in 2020 among people uninterested in politics. Other times well-designed surveys force nonignorable nonresponse to leave a trace, as happens when we use randomized response instruments.

The direction forward is clear, even if the path is not. The time for assuming away problems is past. We should begin with a paradigm that reflects all the ways that polling can go wrong and then identify, model, and measure all the sources of bias, not just the ones that are easy to fix. Much work remains to be done, though, as these new models and data sources will require much evaluation and development theoretically, empirically, and practically. The payoff will be that survey researchers will be able to remain true to their aspirations of using information about a small number of people to understand the realities about many people, even as it gets harder and hear from anyone, let alone the random samples that our previous theory relied on.

References

Achen, Chris. 1986. *The Statistical Analysis of Quasi-Experiments*. University of California Press.

Ackerman, Eli. 2016. A Closer Look at Our 2016 Election Coverage. luc.id/blog/a-closer-look-at-our-2016-election-coverage

Agiesta, Jennifer. 2021. How Pollsters Are Trying to Fix Election Polls after 2020. *cnn.com* July 19. www.cnn.com/2021/07/19/politics/polling-error-2020-report/index.html

American National Election Studies. 2002. Data Quality. Available at electionstudies.org/data-quality.

Ansolabehere, Stephen and Douglas Rivers. 2013. Cooperative Survey Research. *Annual Review of Political Science* 16: 307–329.

Ansolabehere, Stephen and Brian F. Schaffner. 2014. Does Survey Mode Still Matter? Findings from a 2010 Multi-Mode Comparison. *Political Analysis* 22(3): 285–303.

Bailey, Michael A., Daniel J. Hopkins, and Todd Rogers. 2016. Unresponsive and Unpersuaded: The Unintended Consequences of a Voter Persuasion Effort. *Political Behavior* 38(3): 713–746.

Bailey, Michael A. 2001. Ideal Point Estimation with a Small Number of Votes: A Random Effects Approach. *Political Analysis* 9(3): 192–210.

Bailey, Michael A. 2020. Normalizing Covid Positivity Rates across States. Manuscript, Georgetown University.

Bailey, Michael A. 2021. *Real Stats: Using Econometrics for Political Science and Public Policy*. Oxford University Press.

Bailey, Michael A. 2023. Doubly Robust Estimation of Non-ignorable Non-response Models of Political Survey Data [Paper Presentation.] Summer meeting of the Society for Political Methodology at Stanford University, Stanford, CA.

Baker, James A, III. 2020. Good Grief, the Pollsters Got It Wrong. *Wall Street Journal*, November 10. www.wsj.com/articles/good-grief-the-pollsters-got-it-wrong-11605049069

Baker, Reg, Stephen J. Blumberg, J. Michael Brick, Mick P. Couper, Melanie Courtright, J. Michael Dennis, Don Dillman, Martin R. Frankel, Philip Garland, Robert M. Groves, Courtney Kennedy, Jon Krosnick, and Paul J. Javrakas. 2010. AAPOR Report on Online Panels. *Public Opinion Quarterly* 74(4): 711–781.

Bartels, Larry M. 2000. Panel Effects in the American National Election Studies. *Political Analysis* 8(1): 1–20.

254 References

Behaghel, Luc, Bruno Crepon, Marc Gurgand and Tomas Le Barbanchon. 2015. Please Call Again: Correcting Non-Response Bias in Treatment Effect Models. *The Review of Economics and Statistics* 97(5): 1070–1080.

Bendavid, Eran, Bianca Mulaney, Neeraj Sood, Soleil Shah, Emilia Ling, Rebecca Bromley-Dulfano, Cara Lai, Zoe Weissberg, Rodrigo Saavedra, James Tedrow, Dona Tversky, Andrew Bogan, Thomas Kupiec, Daniel Eichner, Ribhav Gupta, John Ioannidis, and Jay Bhattacharya. 2020. *COVID-19 Antibody Seroprevalence in Santa Clara County, California*. Cold Spring Harbor Laboratory Press.

Bera, Anil K., Carlos M. Jarque, and Lung-Fei Lee. 1984. Testing the Normality Assumption in Limited Dependent Variable Models. *International Economic Review* 25(3): 563–578.

Berinsky, Adam J. 2004. *Silent Voices: Public Opinion and Political Participation in America*. Princeton University Press.

Berinsky, Adam J. 2006. American Public Opinion in the 1930s and 1940s: The Analysis of Quota-Controlled Sample Survey Data. *Public Opinion Quarterly* 70(4): 499–529.

Bethlehem, Jelke G. 2002. Weighting Nonresponse Adjustments Based on Auxiliary Information. In Groves, Robert M., Don A. Dillman, John L. Eltinge, Roderick J. A. Little, eds. *Survey Nonresponse*. New York: Wiley Series in Probability and Statistics: 275–288.

Bethlehem, Joel. 2009. The Rise of Survey Sampling. *Statistics Netherlands*. Discussion paper 09015.

Bialik, Carl. 2016. Why the Polls Missed Bernie Sanders's Michigan Upset. *fivethirtyeight.com* March 9. https://fivethirtyeight.com/features/why-the-polls-missed-bernie-sanders-michigan-upset/

Biemer, Paul P. 2010. Total Survey Error: Design, Implementation, and Evaluation. *Public Opinion Quarterly* 74(5): 817–848.

Blumenthal, Mark M. 2005. Toward an Open-Source Methodology: What We Can Learn from the Blogosphere. *Public Opinion Quarterly* 69: 655–669.

Bollinger, Christopher and Barry Hirsch. 2013. Is Earnings Nonresponse Ignorable? *The Review of Economics and Statistics* 95(2): 407–416.

Bradburn, Norman M. 1992. Presidential Address: A Response to the Nonresponse Problem. *Public Opinion Quarterly* 56(3): 391–397.

Bradley, Valerie C., Shiro Kuriwaki, Michael Isakov, Dino Sejdinovic, Xiao-Li Meng, and Seth Flaxman. 2021. Unrepresentative Big Surveys Significantly Overestimated US Vaccine Uptake. *Nature* 600: 695–700.

Brehm, John. 1993. *The Phantom Respondents: Opinion Surveys and Political Representation*. University of Michigan Press.

Bryson, Maurice C. 1976. The Literary Digest Poll: Making of a Statistical Myth. *The American Statistician* 30(4): 184–185.

Burden, Barry C. 2000. Voter Turnout and the National Election Studies. *Political Analysis* 8(4): 389–398.

Burger, Rulof P. and Zoë M. McLaren. 2017. An Econometric Method for Estimating Population Parameters from Non-random Samples: An Application to Clinical Case Finding. *Health Economics* 26(9): 1110–1122.

Bushway, Shawn, Brian D. Johnson, and Lee Ann Slocum. 2007. Is the Magic Still There? The Use of the Heckman Two-Step Correction for Selection Bias in Criminology. *Journal of Quantitative Criminology* 23: 151–178.

References 255

Callegaro, Mario and Charles Disogra. 2008. Computing Response Metrics for Online Panels. *The Public Opinion Quarterly* 72(5): 1008–1032.

Cantor, David, Bonnie Fisher, Susan Chibnall, Shauna Harps, Reanne Townsend, Gail Thomas, Hyunshik Lee, Vanessa Kranz, and Randy Herbison. 2020. Report on the AAU Campus Climate Survey on Sexual Assault and Misconduct. Prepared for: The Association of American Universities by Westat Revised January 17.

Caughey, Devin, Adam Berinsky, Sara Chatfield, Erin Hartman, Eric Schickler, and Jasjeet Sekhon. 2020. *Target Estimation and Calibration Weighting for Unrepresentative Survey Samples.* Cambridge University Press.

Cavari, Amnon and Guy Freedman. 2018. Polarized Mass or Polarized Few? Assessing the Parallel Rise of Survey Nonresponse and Measures of Polarization. *Journal of Politics* 80(2): 719–725.

Cavari, Amnon and Guy Freedman. 2023. Survey Nonresponse and Mass Polarization: The Consequences of Declining Contact and Cooperation Rates. *American Political Science Review* 117(1): 332–339.

Cha, Ariana Eunjung. 2020. Five Years after an Abortion, Most Women Say They Made The Right Decision. *Washinton Post* January 12.

Chen, Baojiang, Pengfei Li, and Jing Qin. 2018. Generalization of Heckman Selection Model to Nonignorable Nonresponse Using Call-back Information. *Statistica Sinica* 28(4): 1761–1785.

Civic Science. 2016. Beware the Professional Survey Panelist! civicscience.com/wp-content/uploads/2016/03/CivicScience-Survey-Panelist-Webinar-March-2016-with-recording.pdf

Clinton, Joshua D. 2021. Presentation at the Massive Data Institute, Georgetown University. February 25.

Clinton, Joshua D. Jennifer Agiesta, Megan Brenan, Camille Burge, Marjorie Connelly, Ariel Edwards-Levy, Bernard Fraga, Emily Guskin, D. Sunshine Hillygus, Chris Jackson, Jeff Jones, Scott Keeter, Kabir Khanna, John Lapinski, Lydia Saad, Daron Shaw, Andrew Smith, David Wilson, and Christopher Wlezien. 2021. *Task Force on 2020 Pre-Election Polling: An Evaluation of the 2020 General Election Polls.* American Association for Public Opinion Research.

Clinton, Joshua D., John S. Lapinski, and Marc J. Trussler. 2022. Reluctant Republicans, Eager Democrats? Partisan Nonresponse and the Accuracy of 2020 Presidential Pre-election Telephone Polls. *Public Opinion Quarterly*, forthcoming.

Cohn, Nate. 2016a. We Gave Four Good Pollsters the Same Raw Data. They Had Four Different Results. *New York Times*, September 20. www.nytimes.com/interactive/2016/09/20/upshot/the-error-the-polling-world-rarely-talks-about.html

Cohn, Nate. 2016b. How One 19-Year-Old Illinois Man Is Distorting National Polling Averages. *New York Times*, October 12. www.nytimes.com/2016/10/13/upshot/how-one-19-year-old-illinois-man-is-distorting-national-polling-averages.html

Cohn, Nate. 2018a. Live from the Battleground Districts: Polls of the Key Races for House Control. *New York Times*, September 6. www.nytimes.com/2018/09/06/upshot/midterms-2018-polls-live.html

Cohn, Nate. 2018b. Our Polling Methodology: Underneath the Hood of the Upshot/Siena Survey, September 6. www.nytimes.com/2018/09/06/upshot/live-poll-method.html

Cohn, Nate. 2022a. Who in the World Is Still Answering Pollsters' Phone Calls? *New York Times*, October 12. www.nytimes.com/2022/10/12/upshot/midterms-polling-phone-calls.html

Cohn, Nate. 2022b. Will One Small Shift Fix the Polls in 2022? *New York Times*, November 7. www.nytimes.com/2022/11/02/upshot/polls-2022-midterms-fix.html

College Polling. 2021. About Us. https://emersoncollegepolling.com/about/

Comer, Pattrick. 2017. Sampling in the Digital Age. April 25. comerpatrick .medium.com/sampling-in-the-digital-age

Concha, Joe. 2020. Frank Luntz: Polling Profession 'Done' after Election Misses. *The Hill*, November 4. https://thehill.com/homenews/media/524478-frank-luntz-polling-profession-done-after-election-misses-devastating-to-my/

Converse, Jean M. 2009. *Survey Research in the United States: Roots and Emergence 1890–1960*. Transaction Publishers.

Cooperative Congressional Election Study. 2014. Sample Design. Accessed at projects.iq.harvard.edu/cces/book/sample-design on January 23, 2017.

Copas, J. B. and H. G. Li. 1997. Inference for Non-Random Samples. *Journal of the Royal Statistical Society. Series B (Methodological)*. 59(1): 55–95.

Coppock, Alexander, Alan S. Gerber, Donald P. Green, and Holger Kern. 2017. Combining Double Sampling and Bounds to Address Nonignorable Missing Outcomes in Randomized Experiments. *Political Analysis* 25(2): 188–206.

Cornesse, Carina, Annelies G. Blom, David Dutwin, Jon A. Krosnick, Edith D. De Leeuw, St Ephane Legleye, Josh Pasek, Darren Pennay, Benjamin Phillips, Joseph W. Sakshaug, Bella Struminskaya, and Alexander Wenz. 2020. A Review of Conceptual Approaches and Empirical Evidence on Probability and Nonprobability Sample Survey Research. *Journal of Survey Statistics and Methodology* 8: 4–36.

Cox, Daniel. 2020. Could Social Alienation Among Some Trump Supporters Help Explain Why Polls Underestimated Trump Again? FiveThirtyEight.com November 20.

Cramer, Katherine J. 2016. *The Politics of Resentment: Rural Consciousness in Wisconsin and the Rise of Scott Walker*. University of Chicago Press.

Cuomo, Andrew. 2020. Amid Ongoing COVID-19 Pandemic, Governor Cuomo Announces Results of Completed Antibody Testing Study of 15,000 People Showing 12.3 Percent of Population Has COVID-19 Antibodies. www.governor .ny.gov/news/amid-ongoing-covid-19-pandemic-governor-cuomo-announces-results-completed-antibody-testing (May 2).

Das, Mitali, Whitney K. Newey, and Francis Vella. 2003. Nonparametric Estimation of Sample Selection Models. *The Review of Economic Studies* 70(1): 33–58.

Dorofeev, Sergey and Peter Grant. 2006. *Statistics for Real-Life Sample Surveys*. Cambridge University Press.

DiNardo, John, Justin McCrary, and Lisa Sanbonmatsu. 2006. Constructive Proposals for Dealing with Attrition: An Empirical Example. Manuscript, University of Michigan.

Dutwin, David and Paul J. Lavrakas. 2016. Trends in Telephone Outcomes, 2008–2015. *Survey Practice* 9(2). www.surveypractice.org/article/2808-trends-in-telephone-outcomes-2008-2015

Dutwin, David and Trent D. Buskirk. 2017. Apples to Oranges or Gala vs. Golden Delicious? Comparing Data Quality of Nonprobability Internet Samples to Low Response Rate Probability Samples. *Public Opinion Quarterly* 81(Special Issue): 213–249.

References 257

Enns, Peter and Jake Rothschild. 2020. Revisiting the 'Gold Standard' of Polling: New Methods Outperformed Traditional Ones in 2020. Medium.com, March 18. https://medium.com/3streams/revisiting-the-gold-standard-of-polling-new-methods-outperformed-traditional-ones-in-2020-451650a9ba5b

Enns, Peter K., Jonathon P. Schuldt, Julius Lagodny, and Alexander Rauter. 2016. Why the Polls Missed in 2016? Was it Shy Trump Supporters after All? *Washington Post: MonkeyCage* (December 13). www.washingtonpost.com/news/monkey-cage/wp/2016/12/13/why-the-polls-missed-in-2016-was-it-shy-trump-supporters-after-all/

Erikson, Robert S. and Kent L. Tedin. 2001. *American Public Opinion*, 6th ed. Longman Publishers.

ESOMAR World Research. 2014. Guidelines for Online Sample Quality: Consultation Draft. April. https://grbn.org/wp-content/uploads/2016/12/Online_Sample_Quality_Guideline.pdf

Fortune Magazine. 1948. The Fortune Survey. (October).

Franco, Annie, Neil Malhotra, Gabor Simonovits, and L.J. Zigerell. 2017. Developing Standards for Post-Stratification Weighting in Population-Based Survey Experiments. *Journal of Experimental Political Science.* 4(2): 161–172

Fricker, Scott and Roger Tourangeau. 2010. Examining the Relationship Between Non-response Propensity and Data Quality in Two National Household Surveys, *Public Opinion Quarterly.* 74(5): 934–955.

Fry Anna, Thomas J. Littlejohns, Cathie Sudlow, Nicola Doherty, Ligia Adamska, Tim Sprosen, Rory Collins, and Naomi E. Allen. 2017. Comparison of Sociodemographic and Health-Related Characteristics of UK Biobank Participants with Those of the General Population. *American Journal of Epidemiology* 186(9): 1026–1034.

Galimard, Jacques-Emmanuel, Sylvie Chevret, Emmanuel Curis, and Matthieu Resche-Rigon. 2018. Heckman Imputation Models for Binary or Continuous MNAR Outcomes and MAR Predictors. *BMC Medical Research Methodology.* 18:90.

Gelman, Andrew. 2007. Struggles with Survey Weighting and Regression Modeling. *Statistical Science* 22(2): 153–164.

Gelman, Andrew, Sharad Goel, Douglas Rivers, and David Rothschild. 2014. The Mythical Swing Voter. Manuscript, Columbia University, Stanford University and Microsoft.

Gittelman, Steven H., Randall K. Thomas, Paul J. Lavrakas, and Victor Lange. 2015. Quota Controls in Survey Research: A Test of Accuracy and Intersource Reliability in Online Samples. *Journal of Advertising Research* 55(4): 368–379.

Goldstein, Ken. 2016. The Bloomberg Politics Poll Decoder – Post-Election Edition. bloomberg.com. www.bloomberg.com/politics/graphics/2016-poll-decoder/

Gomes, Manuel, Rosalba Radice, Jose Camarena Brenes, and Giampiero Marra. 2019. Copula Selection Models for Non-Gaussian Outcomes that are Missing Not at Random. *Statistics in Medicine.* 38(3): 480–496.

Graham, David A. 2020. The Polling Crisis Is a Catastrophe for American Democracy. *The Atlantic* November 4. www.theatlantic.com/ideas/archive/2020/11/polling-catastrophe/616986/

Greene, William H. 2003. *Econometric Analysis* (5th edition). Prentice Hall.

Groves, Robert M. 2004. *Survey Errors and Survey Costs.* Wiley.

Groves, Robert M., Floyd J. Fowler Jr., Mick P. Couper, James M. Lepkowski, Eleanor Singer, and Roger Tourangeau. 2009. *Survey Methodology*, 2nd ed. Wiley-Interscience.

Groves, Robert M., Mick P. Couper, Stanley Presser, Eleanor Singer, Roger Tourangeau, Giorgina Piani Acosta, and Lindsay Nelson. 2006. Experiments in Producing Nonresponse Bias. *Public Opinion Quarterly* 70(5): 720–736.

Groves, Robert M. and Emilia Peytcheva. 2008. The Impact of Nonresponse Rates on Nonresponse Bias: A Meta-Analysis. *Public Opinion Quarterly* 72(2): 167–189.

Groves, Robert M. and Lars Lyberg. 2010. Total Survey Error: Past, Present and Future. *Public Opinion Quarterly* 74(5): 849–879.

Groves, Robert M. 2011. Three Eras of Survey Research. *Public Opinion Quarterly*, 75(5): 861–871.

Grynbaum, Michael M. 2019. How to Cover 2020: Assume Nothing and Beware of Twitter. *New York Times*, April 16. www.nytimes.com/2019/04/16/business/media/2020-campaign-journalism-advice.html

Gudbjartsson, Daniel F., Agnar Helgason and Hakon Jonsson, Olafur T Magnusson, Pall Melsted, Gudmundur L Norddahl, Jona Saemundsdottir, Asgeir Sigurdsson, Patrick Sulem, Arna B Agustsdottir, Berglind Eiriksdottir, Run Fridriksdottir, Elisabet E Gardarsdottir, Gudmundur Georgsson, Olafia S Gretarsdottir, Kjartan R Gudmundsson, Thora R Gunnarsdottir, Arnaldur Gylfason, Hilma Holm, Brynjar O Jensson, Aslaug Jonasdottir, Frosti Jonsson, Kamilla S Josefsdottir, Thordur Kristjansson, Droplaug N Magnusdottir, Louise le Roux, Gudrun Sigmundsdottir, Gardar Sveinbjornsson, Kristin E Sveinsdottir, Maney Sveinsdottir, Emil A Thorarensen, Bjarni Thorbjornsson, Arthur Love, Gisli Masson, Ingileif Jonsdottir, Alma Moller, Thorolfur Gudnason, Karl G Kristinsson, Unnur Thorsteinsdottir, and Kari Stefansson. 2020. Spread of SARS-CoV-2 in the Icelandic Population. *medRxiv*

Gutsche, Tania L., Arie Kapteyn, Erik Meijer, and Bas Weerman. 2014. The RAND Continuous 2012 Presidential Election Poll. *Public Opinion Quarterly* 78, Special Issue: 233–254.

Habermann, Hermann, Courtney Kennedy, and Partha Lahiri. 2017. A Conversation with Robert Groves. *Statistical Science* 32(1): 128–137.

Hanretty, Chris. 2016. Here's Why Pollsters and Pundits Got BrexitWrong. *Monkey Cage Blog* June 24. www.washingtonpost.com/news/monkey-cage/wp/2016/06/24/heres-why-pollstersand-pundits-got-brexit-wrong/

Hargittai, Eszter. 2020. Potential Biases in Big Data: Omitted Voices on Social Media. *Social Science Computer Review* 38(1): 10–24.

Hartman, Erin and Melody Huang. 2023. Sensitivity Analysis for Survey Weights. *Political Analysis* (forthcoming).

Hartman, Erin, Chad Hazlett, and Ciara Sterbenz. 2021. Kpop: A Kernel Balancing Approach for Reducing Specification Assumptions in Survey Weighting. *arXiv preprint* arXiv:2107.08075.

Heckman, James J. 1979. Sample Selection Bias as a Specification Error. *Econometrica* 47(1): 153–161.

Hill, Anthony, Julian Roberts, Paul Ewings, and David Gunnell. 1997. Non-response Bias in a Lifestyle Survey. *Journal of Public Health Medicine* 19(2): 203–207.

Hillygus, D. Sunshine, Natalie Jackson, and McKenzie Young. 2014. Professional Respondents in Non-Probability Online Panels. In *Online Panel Research: A Data Quality Perspective*, edited by Mario Callegaro, Reg Baker, Jelke Bethlehem, Anja Göritz, Jon A. Krosnick, and Paul J. Lavrakas, 219–237. John Wiley & Sons, Ltd.

Huff, Connor, and Dustin Tingley. 2015. "Who are These People?" Evaluating the Demographic Characteristics and Political Preferences of MTurk Survey Respondents'. *Research & Politics* 2(3): 1–12.

References 259

Igo, Sarah E. 2007. *The Averaged American: Surveys, Citizens and the Making of a Mass Public.* Harvard University Press.

Isakov, Michael and Shiro Kuriwaki. 2020. Toward Principled Unskewing: Viewing 2020 Election Polls Through a Corrective Lens from 2016. *Harvard Data Science Review* 2(4). https://doi.org/10.1162/99608f92.86a46f38

Jackman, Simon. 2017. House Effects, Back By Popular Demand. huffpost.com. Updated December 6. www.huffpost.com/entry/house-effects-by-back-by_b_2007907

Jackman, Simon and Bradley Spahn. 2019. Why Does the American National Election Study Overestimate Voter Turnout? *Political Analysis* 27: 193–207.

Jacobson, Gary C. 2022. Explaining the Shortfall of Trump Voters in the 2020 Pre- and Post-Election Surveys. Manuscript, University of California, San Diego.

Janes, Chelsea. 2020. How Many People are Infected with the Coronavirus? *Washington Post* (May 20). www.washingtonpost.com/health/how-many-people-are-infected -with-the-coronavirus-a-major-study-will-attempt-to-provide-an-answer/2020/05/20 /a1c867f4-9a2b-11ea-a282-386f56d579e6_story.html

Jennings, W. and Christopher Wlezien. 2018. Election Polling Errors across Time and Space. *Nature Human Behavior.* 2(4): 276–283.

Johnson, Timothy P., Diane O'Rourke, Jane Burris, and Linda Owens. 2002. Culture and Survey Nonresponse. In Groves, Robert M., Don A. Dillman, John L. Eltinge, and Roderick J.A. Little, ed. *Survey Nonresponse.* John Wiley & Sons.

Katz, Daniel. 1944. The Polls and the 1944 Election. *Public Opinion Quarterly* 8(4): 468–482.

Kennedy, Courtney and Hannah Hartig. 2019. Response Rates in Telephone Surveys Have Resumed Their Decline. Available at www.pewresearch.org/fact-tank/ 2019/02/27/response-rates-in-telephone-surveys-have-resumed-their-decline/

Kennedy, Courtney, Mark Blumenthal, Scott Clement, Joshua Clinton, Claire Durand, Charles Franklin, Kyley McGeeney, Lee Miringoff, Kristen Olson, Doug Rivers, Lydia Saad, G. Evans Witt, and Christopher Wlezien. 2018. An Evaluation of the 2016 Election Polls in the United States: AAPOR Task Force Report. *Public Opinion Quarterly* 82(1): 1–33.

Kennedy, Courtney, Andrew Mercer, Scott Keeter, Nick Hatley, Kyley McGeeney, and Alejandra Gimenez. 2016. Evaluating Online Nonprobability Surveys. Pew Research Center. May 2. www.pewresearch.org/methods/2016/05/02/evaluating-online-nonprobability-surveys/

Kennedy, Courtney, Jesse L. Lopez, Scott Keeter, Arnold Lau, Nick Hatley, and Nick Bertoni. 2021. Confronting 2016 and 2020 Polling Limitations. Pew Research Center. April 8. www.pewresearch.org/methods/2021/04/08/ confronting-2016-and-2020-polling-limitations/

Kennedy, Courtney, Andrew Mercer, Nick Hatley, and Arnold Lau. 2022. Does Public Opinion Polling about Issues Still Work? Pew Research Center. September 21. www.pewresearch.org/short-reads/2022/09/21/does-public-opinion-polling-about-issues-still-work/

Khaitan, Shreya and Surbhi Bharadwaj. 2020. Study On COVID-19 Testing Data Calls For Random Testing, Improved Data Quality. *IndiaSpend.com* (June 2). www.indiaspend.com/study-on-covid-19-testing-data-calls-for-random-testing-impr oved-data-quality/

Kimball, Spencer. 2019. Presidential Statewide Polling – A Substandard Performance: A Proposal and Application for Evaluating Preelection Poll Accuracy. *American Behavioral Scientist* 63(7): 768–788.

Kish, Leslie. 1965. *Survey sampling*. New York: John Wiley and Sons.

Kotak, Aditya and Don A. Moore. 2020. Public Election Polls Are 95% Confident but Only 60% Accurate. PsyArXiv. October 20.

Kreuter, Frauke and Stanley Presser, and Roger Tourangeau. 2008. Social Desirability Bias in CATI, IVR, and Web Surveys The Effects of Mode and Question Sensitivity. *Public Opinion Quarterly* 72: 847–865.

Kuhn, Thomas S. 1970. *The Structure of Scientific Revolutions*. University of Chicago. Press.

Leonhardt, David. 2020. 'A Black Eye': Why Political Polling Missed the Mark. Again. *New York Times*, November 12. www.nytimes.com/2020/11/12/us/politics/election-polls-trump-biden.html

Leonardi, Anthony. 2020. Nearly One-third of Black Voters will Vote for Trump, Rasmussen report finds. *Washington Examiner* October 29. www.washingtonexaminer.com/news/nearly-one-third-of-black-voters-will-vote-for-trump-rasmussen-report-finds

Lin, I-Fen and Nora Cate Schaffer. 1995. Using Survey Participants to Estimate the Impact of Nonparticipation. *Public Opinion Quarterly* 59(2): 236–258.

Little, Roderick J. A. and Mei-Miau Wu. 1991. Models for Contingency Tables With Known Margins When Target and Sampled Populations Differ. *Journal of the American Statistical Association* 86(413): 87–95.

Little, Roderick J. and Sonya Vartivarian. 2005. Does Weighting for Nonresponse Increase the Variance of Survey Means? *Survey Methodology* 31(2): 161–168.

Liu, Ruixuan and Zhengfei Yu. 2022. Sample Selection Models with Monotone Control Functions. *Journal of Econometrics* 226(2): 321–342.

Lohr, Sharon L. 1999. *Sampling: Design and Analysis*. New York: Duxbury Press.

Lorch, Scott A., Michael Baiocchi, Corinne S. Ahlberg, and Dylan E. Small. 2012. The Differential Impact of Delivery Hospital on the Outcomes of Premature Infants. *Pediatrics* 130: 270–278.

Lusinchi, Dominic. 2012. 'President' Landon and the 1936 Literary Digest Poll: Were Automobile and Telephone Owners to Blame? *Social Science History* 36(1): 23–54.

MacInnis, Bo, Jon A. Krosnick, Annabell S. Ho, and Mu-Jung Cho. 2018. The Accuracy of Measurements with Probability and Nonprobability Survey Samples: Replication and Extension. *Public Opinion Quarterly* 82(4): 707–744.

Malhotra, Neil, and Jon A. Krosnick. 2007. The Effect of Survey Mode and Sampling on Inferences about Political Attitudes and Behavior: Comparing the 2000 and 2004 ANES to Internet Surveys with Nonprobability Samples. *Political Analysis* 15(3): 286–323.

Manski, Charles F. 1989. Anatomy of the Selection Problem. *The Journal of Human Resources* 24(3): 343–360.

Manski, Charles F. 1990. Nonparametric Bounds on Treatment Effects. *The American Economic Review* 80(2): 319–323.

Manski, Charles F. and Francesca Molinari. 2020. Estimating the COVID-19 Infection Rate: Anatomy of an Inference Problem. Manuscript, Northwestern University.

Marden, Jessica R., Linbo Wang, Eric J. Tchetgen Tchetgen, Stefan Walter, M. Maria Glymour, and Kathleen E. Wirth. 2018. Implementation of Instrumental Variable Bounds for Data Missing Not at Random. *Epidemiology* 29(3): 364–368.

Marra, Giampiero and Rosalba Radice. 2017. GJRM: Generalised Joint Regression Modelling [computer program]. R package.

References 261

Marra, Giampiero, Rosable Radice, Till Bärnighausen, Simon N. Wood, and Mark E. McGovern. 2017. A Simultaneous Equation Approach to Estimating HIV Prevalence with Nonignorable Missing Responses. *Journal of the American Statistical Association* 112(518): 484–496.

Mason, Robert, Virginia Lesser, and Michael W. Traugott. 2002. Effect of Item Nonresponse on Nonresponse Error and Inference. In Groves et al, ed. *Survey Nonresponse*. Wiley, 149–162.

Matthews, Dylan. 2020. One Pollster's Explanation for Why the Polls Got it Wrong. *Vox.com* November 10. www.vox.com/policy-and-politics/2020/11/10/21551766/election-polls-results-wrong-david-shor

McGeeney, Kyley. 2016. Pew Research Center will call 75 percent cellphones for surveys in 2016. January 5. www.pewresearch.org/short-reads/2016/01/05/pew-research-center-will-call-75-cellphones-for-surveys-in-2016/

McGovern, Mark, David Canning, and Till Bärnighausen. 2018. Accounting for Non-Response Bias Using Participation Incentives and Survey Design. CHaRMS Working Papers 18-02, Centre for Health Research at the Management School (CHaRMS).

Mellon, Jonathan and Christopher Prosser. 2017. Twitter and Facebook are Not Representative of the General Population: Political Attitudes and Demographics of British Social Media Users. *Research & Politics* 4(3). https://doi.org/10.1177/2053168017720008

Meng, Xiao-Li. 2018. Statistical Paradises and Paradoxes in Big Data (1): Law of Large Populations, Big Data Paradox, and the 2016 Presidential Election. *The Annals of Applied Statistics* 12(2): 685–726.

Meng, Xiao-Li. 2021. Data Defect Index: A Unified Quality Metric for Probabilistic Sample and Non-Probabilistic Sample. Presentation. Harvard University.

Mercer, Andrew. 2016. 5 Key Things to Know about the Margin of Error in Election Polls. Pew Research Center. www.pewresearch.org/fact-tank/2016/09/08/understandingthe-margin-of-error-in-election-polls/.

Mercer, Andrew. 2020. Decomposing Selection Bias in Nonprobability Surveys. Pew Research Center. www.websm.org/db/12/18634/Web%20Survey%20Bibliography/Decomposing_Selection_Effects_in_Nonprobability_Samples_/

Mercer, Andrew W., Arnold Lau, and Courtney Kennedy. 2018. For Weighting Online Opt-In Samples, What Matters Most? Pew Research Center. pewresearch.org. January 26.

Mercer, Andrew W., Frauke Kreuter, Scott Keeter, and Elizabeth Stuart. 2017. Theory and Practice in Nonprobability Surveys: Parallels between Causal Inference and Survey Inference. *Public Opinion Quarterly* 81 Special Issue: 250–279.

Miao, Wang, Peng Ding, and Zhi Geng. 2016. Identifiability of Normal and Normal Mixture Models with Nonignorable Missing Data. *Journal of the American Statistical Association* 111(516): 1673–1683.

Miao, Wang, Peng Ding, and Zhi Geng. 2017. Identifiability of Normal and Normal Mixture Models with Nonignorable Missing Data. *Journal of the American Statistical Association.* 111(516): 1673–1683.

Mishel, Lawrence and Jori Kandra. 2020. Wages for the top 1% Skyrocketed 160% since 1979 while the Share of Wages for the Bottom 90% Shrunk. *Economic Policy Institute*, December 1. www.epi.org/blog/wages-for-the-top-1-skyrocketed-160-since-1979-while-the-share-of-wages-for-the-bottom-90-shrunk-time-to-remake-wage-pattern-with-economic-policies-that-generate-robust-wage-growth-for-vast-majority/

Moffett, Matt. 2016. The "Spiral of Silence": How Pollsters got the Colombia-FARC Peace Deal Vote so Wrong. *Vox.com* October 6. www.vox.com/world/2016/10/6/13175608/polls-colombia-farc-peace-deal-vote-wrong

Moore, David. W. 1995. *The Superpollsters: How they Measure and Manipulate Public Opinion in America*. New York: Four Walls and Eight Windows.

Morris, G. Elliot. 2022a. *Strength in Numbers: How Polls Work and Why We Need Them*. W.W. Norton and Company.

Morris, G. Elliot. 2022b. The (Good) Pollsters Got the Midterms Right. *Politics by the Numbers* gelliottmorris.substack.com. (November 11). https://gelliottmorris.substack.com/p/the-pollsters-got-the-midterms-right

Mostashari, Farzad and Ezekiel J. Emanuel. 2020. We Need Smart Coronavirus Testing, Not Just More Testing. *StatNews.com*. (March 24). www.statnews.com/2020/03/24/we-need-smart-coronavirus-testing-not-just-more-testing/

Mosteller, Frederick, Herbert Hyman, Philip J. McCarthy, Eli S. Marks, and David B. Truman. 1949. *The Pre-Election Polls of 1948: Report to the Committee on Analysis of Pre-Election Polls and Forecasts*. New York: Social Science Research Council.

Mutz, Diana C. 2011. *Population-Based Survey Experiments*. Princeton University Press.

Panagopoulos, Costas. 2021. Polls and Elections Accuracy and Bias in the 2020 U.S. General Election Polls. *Presidential Studies Quarterly* 51(1): 214–227.

Pasek, Josh. 2010. ANES Weighting Algorithm: A Description. Manuscript, Stanford University. web.stanford.edu/group/iriss/cgi-bin/anesrake/resources/Raking Description.pdf

Pasek, Josh. 2018. anesrake. R Package at cran.r-project.org.

Peress, Michael. 2010. Correcting for Survey Nonresponse Using Variable Response Propensity. *Journal of the American Statistical Association* 105(492): 1418–1430.

Peterson, Sandra, Norilsa Toribio, James Farber, and David Hornick. 2021. Nonresponse Bias Report for the 2020 Household Pulse Survey Version 1.0 (March 24). U.S. Census Bureau.

Peytchev, Andy. 2013. Consequences of Survey Nonresponse. *Annals of the American Academy of Political and Social Science*, 645 (1): 88–111.

Pew Research Center. 2012. Assessing the Representativeness of Public Opinion Surveys. www.people-press.org (May 15).

Puhani, Patrick. 2000. The Heckman Correction for Sample Selection and Its Critique. *Journal of Economic Surveys* 14(1): 53–68.

Rasmussen Reports. 2016. Rasmussen Reports Calls It Right. www.rasmussenreports.com (December 6). www.rasmussenreports.com/public_content/politics/elections/election_2016/rasmussen_reports_calls_it_right

Robinson, Claude E. 1932. *Straw Votes*. New York: Columbia University Press.

Rogers, Lindsay. 1949. *The Pollsters: Public Opinion, Politic and Democratic Leadership*. Alfred A. Knopf.

Rubin, Donald B. 2008. For Objective Causal Inference, Design Trumps Analysis. *Annals of Applied Statistics* 2(3): 808–840.

Sartori, Anne. 2003. An Estimator for Some Binary-Outcome Selection Models without Exclusion Restrictions. *Political Analysis* 11: 111–138.

Schoenmueller, Verena, Oded Netzer, and Florian Stahl. 2020. The Polarity of Online Reviews: Prevalence, Drivers and Implications. *Journal of Marketing Research* 57(5): 853–877.

References 263

Sheffield, Matthew. 2018. Survey: A Majority of Americans Don't Believe Polls are Accurate. *The Hill.* December 27. https://thehill.com/hilltv/ what-americas-thinking/423023-a-majority-of-americans-are-skeptical-that-public-opinion-polls/

Shepard, Steven. 2016. How Could the Polling Be So Wrong? *Politico,* November 9, 2016.

Shirani-Mehr, Houshmand, David Rothschild, Sharad Goel, and Andrew Gelman. 2018. Disentangling Bias and Variance in Election Polls. *Journal of the American Statistical Association* 113 (522): 607–614.

Siddique, Juned and Thomas R. Belin. 2008. Using an Approximate Bayesian Bootstrap to Multiply Impute Nonignorable Missing Data. *Computational Statistics & Data Analysis* 53(2): 405–415.

Siegel, Benjamin, Mark Abdelmalek, and Jay Bhatt. 2020. Coronavirus Contact Tracers' Nemeses: People who Don't Answer their Phones. *abcnews.go.com* (May 15). https://abcnews.go.com/Health/coronavirus-contact-tracers-nemeses-people-answer-phones/story.

Silver, Nate. 2016. Pollsters Probably Didn't Talk To Enough White Voters Without College Degrees. FiveThirtyEight.com. *fivethirtyeight.com* December 1. https://fivethirtyeight.com/features/pollsters-probably-didnt-talk-to-enough-white-voters-without-college-degrees/

Silver, Nate. 2021a. The Death Of Polling Is Greatly Exaggerated. *fivethirtyeight.com* (March 25). https://fivethirtyeight.com/features/the-death-of-polling-is-greatly-exaggerated/

Silver, Nate. 2021b. FiveThirtyEight's Pollster Ratings. *fivethirtyeight.com,* March 25.

Silver, Nate. 2017. Are the U.K. Polls Skewed? *fivethirtyeight.com* (June 3). https://fivethirtyeight.com/features/are-the-u-k-polls-skewed/

Silver, Nate. 2018. The Polls Are All Right. *fivethirtyeight.com* (May 30). https://fivethirtyeight.com/features/the-polls-are-all-right/

Singer, Eleanor and Cong Ye. 2013. The Use and Effects of Incentives in Surveys. *The Annals of the American Academy of Political and Social Science* 645(1): 112–141.

Sohlberg, Jacob, Mikael Gilljam, and Johan Martinsson. 2017. Determinants of Polling Accuracy: The Effect of Opt-in Internet Surveys. *Journal of Elections, Public Opinion and Parties* 27: 433–447.

Solon, Gary, Steven J. Haider, and Jeffrey Wooldridge. 2015. What are We Weighting For? *Journal of Human Resources* 50(2): 301–316.

Squire, Peverill. 1988. Why the 1936 Literary Digest Poll Failed. *Public Opinion Quarterly* 52(1): 125–133.

Stemberg, Joseph. 2020. The Polls Are Dead, Long Live Politics. *Wall Street Journal* (November 19). www.wsj.com/articles/the-polls-are-dead-long-live-politics-11605809242

Stolzenberg, Ross M. and Daniel A. Relles. 1997. Tools for Intuition about Sample Selection Bias and Its Correction. *American Sociological Review* 62: 494–507.

Sturgis, Patrick, Jouni Kuha, Nick Baker, Mario Callegaro, Stephen Fisher, Jane Green, Will Jennings, Benjamin E. Lauderdale, and Patten Smith. 2018. An Assessment of the Causes of the Errors in the 2015 UK General Election Opinion Polls. *Journal of the Royal Statistical Society: Series A (Statistics in Society)* 181: 757–781.

Sun, BaoLuo, Lan Liu, Wang Miao, Kathleen Wirth, James Robins, and Eric J. Tchetgen Tchetgen. 2018. Semiparametric Estimation with Data Missing Not at Random Using an Instrumental Variable. *Statistica Sinica* 28: 1965–1983.

Tourangeau, Roger, Robert M. Groves, and Cleo D. Redline. 2010. Sensitive Topics and Reluctant Respondents: Demonstrating a Link between Nonresponse Bias and Measurement Error. *Public Opinion Quarterly* 74: 413–432.

Tourangeau, Roger and Thomas J. Plewes, ed. 2013. *Nonresponse in Social Science Surveys: A Research Agenda*. National Research Council, National Academies Press.

Tourangeau, Roger and Tom W. Smith. 1996. Asking Sensitive Questions: The Impact of Data Collection Mode, Question Format, and Question Context. *Public Opinion Quarterly*. 60(2): 275–304.

Tourangeau, Roger, Darby Miller Steiger, and David Wilson. 2002. Self Administered Questions by Telephone: Evaluating Interactive Voice Response. *Public Opinion Quarterly* 66: 256–266.

Trafalgar Group. 2021. Polling Methodology. www.thetrafalgargroup.org/polling-met hodology

Traugott, Michael W. 1987. The Importance of Persistence in Respondent Selection for Preelection Surveys. *Public Opinion Quarterly* 51(1): 48–57.

Urbatsch, Robert. 2018. Gun-shy: Refusal to Answer. Questions about Firearm Ownership. *The Social Science Journal* 56(2): 189–195.

Valliant, Richard, Jill A. Dever, and Frauke Kreuter. 2013. *Practical Tools for Designing and Weighting Survey Samples*. Springer.

Vella, Francis. 1998. Estimating Models with Sample Selection Bias: A Survey. *Journal of Human Resources* 23(1): 127–169.

Voigt, Lynda F., Thomas D. Koepsell, and Janet R. Daling. 2003. Characteristics of Telephone Survey Respondents According to Willingness to Participate. *American Journal of Epidemiology* 157(1): 66–73.

Wallace-Wells, Benjamin. 2022. Why Republican Insiders Think the G.O.P. Is Poised for a Blowout: The Consensus among Pollsters and Consultants is this Tuesday's Election Will be a "Bloodbath" for the Democratic Party. *New Yorker* (November 4). www.newyorker.com/news/the-political-scene/why-republican-insiders-think-the-gop-is-poised-for-a-blowout

Wang, Sheng, Jun Shao, and Jae Kwang Kim. 2014. An Instrumental Variable Approach for Identification and Estimation with Nonignorable Nonresponse. *Statistica Sinica* 24(3): 1097–1116.

Wang, Wei, David Rothschild, Sharad Goel, Andrew Gelman. 2015. Forecasting Elections with Non-representative Polls. *International Journal of Forecasting* 31: 980–991.

Washington Post. 2020. Post-ABC polls: Biden Leads Trump Narrowly in Michigan, Significantly in Wisconsin. www.washingtonpost.com (October 28).

Weinschenk, Aaron C. and Christopher T. Dawes. 2019. The Effect of Education on Political Knowledge: Evidence from Monozygotic Twins. *American Politics Research* 47(3): 530–548.

Weisberg, Herbert F. 2009. *The Total Survey Error Approach: A Guide to the New Science of Survey Research*. University of Chicago Press.

Weisberg, Herbert F. and Jon A. Krosnick. 1996. *An Introduction to Survey Research, Polling, and Data Analysis*. Sage.

West, Brady T. and Annelies G. Blom. 2017. Explaining Interviewer Effects: A Research Synthesis. *Journal of Survey Statistics and Methodology* 5(2): 175–211.

Wilcox-Archuleta, Bryan. 2019. Survey Sampling with Voter Files: Improving on Affordable Survey Options for Public Opinion Researchers. Manuscript, Michigan State University.

References

Winship, Christopher and Robert D. Mare. 1992. Models for Sample Selection Bias. *Annual Review of Sociology* 18: 327–350.

Wooldridge, Jeffrey M. 2002. *Econometric Analysis of Cross Section and Panel Data.* Cambridge, Massachusetts: The MIT Press.

Wooldridge, Jeffrey M. 2007. Inverse Probability Weighted Estimation for General Missing Data Problems. *Journal of Econometrics* 141: 1281–1301.

Yeager, David S., Jon A. Krosnick, LinChiat Chang, Harold S. Javitz, Matthew S. Levendusky, Alberto Simpser and Rui Wang. 2011. Comparing the Accuracy of RDD Telephone Surveys and Internet Surveys Conducted with Probability and Non-Probability Samples. *The Public Opinion Quarterly* 75(4): 709–747.

Yglesias, Matthew. 2022. Pre-registering Some Takes on the Midterms. *Slow Boring.com* (October 20). www.slowboring.com/p/pre-registering-some-takes-on-the

YouGov. 2014. Sampling and Weighting Methodology for the February 2014 Texas Statewide Study. www.yougov.com. https://static.texastribune.org/media/documents/utttpoll-201402-methodology.pdf

Index

address based sampling (ABS), 79
Agiesta, Jennifer, 12
Amazon, 151
American Association for Public Opinion Research (AAPOR), xx, 45, 95
American Community Survey, 56, 89
Arceneaux, Kevin, xx
Arend, Tony, xx

Baker, James, 7
Berinsky, Adam, xix, 31, 62, 66, 86, 120
Biden, Joseph, 3, 15, 22, 44, 48, 55, 70, 103, 213, 224, 252
big data paradox, 19
Bolsonaro, Jair, 3
bounds, 137, 180, 240
Bradley, Valerie, xix, 13, 123, 127, 131
Brexit, 3
Brown, Nadia, xx
Busch, Marc, xx

Cancian, Maria, xx
Cardon, Dominique, xx
Caughey, Devin, xix, 67
Cavari, Amnon, xix, 234
Central Limit Theorem, 34
Clinton, Hillary, 3, 26, 43, 47, 102, 120
Clinton, Josh, xix, 71, 80, 82, 85, 96
Cohn, Nate, 4, 18, 47, 61, 71, 79, 213
Cointet, Jean-Philippe, xx
Collins, Susan, 44
Congressional elections, 6, 44
continuum of resistance, 178, 231
contour plots, 152, 168
control functions, 172
convenience polling, 85, 127, 187
Converse, Jean, 25, 29, 34
copulas, 167, 185, 217

Covid, 7, 13, 20, 69, 82, 104, 189, 235, 237, 244
Crossley, Archibald, 29

decision tree, 205
Des Moines Register, 70
Dewey, Thomas, 31

effective sample size, 124
Eissa, Nada, xx
Evers, Tony, 214

Facebook, 13, 104, 127
finite population correction, 39
Fischer, Johannes, xix
Fortune magazine, 23
Freedman, Guy, xix, 234
functional form, 160, 184

Gallup, 27, 28, 32, 40
Gelman, Andrew, 47, 74, 76, 84, 91, 103
Gill, Jeff, xix
GJRM package, 169
global warming attitudes, 227
Goldstein, Ken, xix, 12, 101, 152, 168
Gormley, Bill, xx
grade point average, 109
Grand Auto Theft, 78
Groves, Robert, xix, 12, 47, 49, 82, 119, 130, 252
Guardado, Jenny, xx
gun ownership, 10, 106

Habyarimana, James, xx
Hartman, Erin, xix, 14, 137, 140
Hassan, Maggie, 97
Heckman model, 151, 155, 160, 176, 185, 192, 203, 217

268 _Index_

Hillygus, Sunshine, xix, 91
HIV, 170
Hopkins, Dan, xvii, xix
house effects, 96
Huang, Melody, 140
Huddy, Leonie, xix, 15

Iceland, 240
instruments, observational, 188
instruments, randomized, 191, 193, 214, 240
interactive voice response (IVR) polls, 80, 84, 95
Inverse Mills Ratio, 154, 162, 192
Ipsos, 13, 80, 97, 215, 221, 245
item nonresponse, 49

Jackman, Simon, 16, 101
Jackson, Natalie, xix, 91
Jacobson, Gary, xix, 48
job training, 105

Kellstedt, Paul, xix
Kennedy, Courtney, 7, 33, 42–44, 61, 67, 69, 73, 79–82, 85, 87
Kinsey Reports, 106
Klasnja, Marko, xx
Kuhn, Thomas, 24
Kuriwaki, Shiro, xix, 21, 103

Ladd, Jon, xix
Landon, Alf, 23, 26
Leonhardt, David, 77
Linzer, Drew, xix
Literary Digest, 23, 24, 46, 120, 123
Lohr, Sharon, 10, 12, 34, 38, 39, 48, 61, 131
Los Angeles Times, 61
Lucid, 56, 67, 74
Ludema, Rod, xx
Lula de Silva, Luiz, 3
Luntz, Frank, 3

Manski, Charles, 137, 138, 240
margin of error, 39, 73
marketing, 11, 151
maximum likelihood estimation, 155, 167, 180
McLaren, Zoe, 181
McNamara, Kate, xx
mean squared error, 124, 187, 190, 199
Mechanical Turk, 86, 94
Meng, Xiao-Li, xviii, xix, 5, 13, 19, 21, 114, 121, 129, 131, 134

Mercer, Andrew, xix, 7, 61, 67, 91, 119
Morris, G. Elliot, 4

National Basketball Association, 107
New York Times, 4, 8, 18, 47, 81, 97, 213
NINR-weights, 175
Nixon, Richard, 6
Noel, Hans, xx
nonresponse, ignorable, 9, 26, 49, 113, 150
nonresponse, nonignorable, 10, 17, 26, 45, 50, 113, 115, 129, 150, 174, 193, 203
nonresponse, rates, 4, 41, 130

Obama, Barack, xvii, 77, 103, 231

panel conditioning, 92
Pasek, Josh, xix, 49
Pelosi, Nancy, 231
Pence, Michael, 231
Peress, Michael, xix, 16, 178
Pew Research, 15, 79, 83, 97, 103
Peytchev, Andy, 11, 47, 82, 119
Peytchev, Emilia, 42, 119, 130
professional survey panelists, 91
public health, 11, 103, 181, 236

Quinn, Dennis, xx
quota sampling, 28, 88

racial attitudes, 225
Ramaciotti Morales, Pedro, xx
random contact, 19, 127
random digit dialing (RDD), 79
Redford, Robert, 198
Reed, Doug, xx
registration based sampling (RBS), 79
response propensity, 113, 145, 168, 199, 236
Richardson, Mark, xx
Rivers, Doug, xix, 72, 85, 91, 103
Robinson, Jonathan, xix
Rogers, Todd, xvii
Rom, Mark, xx
Romney, Mitt, 77, 103
Roosevelt, Franklin, 23, 24, 30
Roper, Elmo, 29, 31
Rubin, Donald, 183
Rudra, Nita, xx

sampling frame, 84
Schoenmueller, Verena, 11, 92, 151
Schwenzfeier, Meg, xix
Scott, Jamil, xx

Index

selection model, risks, 207
Selzer, Ann, 70, 106
Shambaugh, George, xx
Shor, David, 45, 205, 213, 234
Silver, Nate, 4, 22, 44, 56, 96
South Africa, 171, 181
Spahn, Bradley, 16
standardized tests, 109
Stoto, Michael, xx
stratified sampling, 48
Sun, Liu, Miao, Wirth, Robins and Tchetgen
    Tchetgen, 174
Swaziland, 171
Swers, Michele, xx

tariff attitudes, 225
tax cut attitudes, 225
Thurmond, Strom, 31
Tillis, Thom, 44
tilted fish, 113, 117, 127, 149, 168, 172, 203,
    208, 215, 217
Tobin, Jen, xx
Truman, Harry, 31
Trump, Donald, 3, 8, 15, 22, 44, 47, 61, 69,
    102, 119, 221, 231
tuberculosis, 181
turnout, 18, 181, 218, 231
Twitter, 106

unit nonresponse, 49
United Kingdom, 56, 95

Vanderbilt University, 79
variance, 37, 73, 118, 162

Vella, Frank, xx, 173
Voeten, Erik, xx
Vreeland, Jim, xx

Wallace, Henry, 31
Wallace-Wells, Benjamin, 7
Walter, Amy, 20
Washington Post, 43, 70, 97, 213
Wasserman, David, 45
Weaver, Kent, xx
weighted least squares, 75
weighting, 12, 16, 30, 47, 48, 51, 61,
    67, 73, 79, 82, 90, 95, 102, 104,
    111, 141, 153, 155, 159, 161, 165,
    175, 177, 180, 185, 191, 194, 199,
    201, 207, 210, 213, 214, 224, 228,
    233, 237, 243
weighting, cell weighting, 51
weighting, for non-ignorable nonresponse,
    174, 190, 203
weighting, raking, 61
weighting, variable selection, 67, 95
Weymouth, Steve, xx
Whitten, Guy, xix
Wilcox, Clyde, xx
Wlezien, Christopher, 4, 22

Xbox, 77, 103

Yglesias, Matthew, 6
YouGov, 72, 75, 88, 97

Zambia, 171
Zimbabwe, 171

www.ingramcontent.com/pod-product-compliance
Ingram Content Group UK Ltd.
Pitfield, Milton Keynes, MK11 3LW, UK
UKHW030358171224
452390UK00025B/423